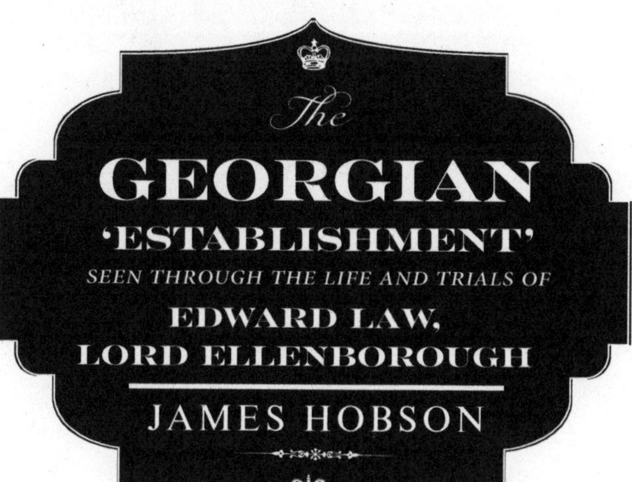

The GEORGIAN 'ESTABLISHMENT'

SEEN THROUGH THE LIFE AND TRIALS OF

EDWARD LAW, LORD ELLENBOROUGH

JAMES HOBSON

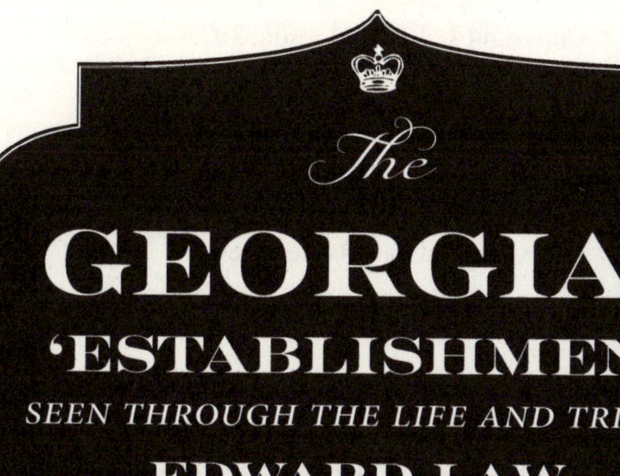

The GEORGIAN 'ESTABLISHMENT'

SEEN THROUGH THE LIFE AND TRIALS OF

EDWARD LAW, LORD ELLENBOROUGH

JAMES HOBSON

AN IMPRINT OF PEN & SWORD BOOKS LTD.
YORKSHIRE – PHILADELPHIA

First published in Great Britain in 2025 by
PEN AND SWORD HISTORY
An imprint of
Pen & Sword Books Ltd
Yorkshire – Philadelphia

ISBN 978 1 39905 404 1

A CIP catalogue record for this book is available from the British Library.

Typeset in Times New Roman 11/14.5 by
SJmagic DESIGN SERVICES, India.
Printed and bound in the UK by CPI Group (UK) Ltd.

The Publisher's authorised representative in the EU for product safety is Authorised Rep Compliance Ltd., Ground Floor, 71 Lower Baggot Street, Dublin D02 P593, Ireland.
www.arccompliance.com

For a complete list of Pen & Sword titles please contact:
PEN & SWORD BOOKS LIMITED
George House, Units 12 & 13, Beevor Street, Off Pontefract Road,
Barnsley, South Yorkshire, S71 1HN, England
E-mail: enquiries@pen-and-sword.co.uk
Website: www.pen-and-sword.co.uk

or

PEN AND SWORD BOOKS
1950 Lawrence Rd, Havertown, PA 19083, USA
E-mail: uspen-and-sword@casematepublishers.com
Website: www.penandswordbooks.com

Contents

Introduction

This book is a biography of one man and a review of the Georgian ruling class in the period 1770–1820. It covers their institutions, their mentality, their modus operandi, and how they maintained their position as the ruling establishment. The story of Georgian Britain's top ten thousand is told through one of its members, Edward Law (1750–1818). He was typical of the establishment in most ways, but also untypical, as he was far, far more reactionary than most. He is not a character who garners much sympathy in the twenty-first century, and in the late Georgian period he was hated by the powerless and poor. In turn, his disdain for them turned to contempt if they dared to challenge the authority of the state and the established church in any way. Law lived in an age when the ruling classes neither needed nor wanted to be popular, and he went one step further and was openly contemptuous of the notion. Popularity was dangerous, as was political, legal, or social innovation. Leniency in any area of society was a mistake, and the views and opinions of most people were worthless. As a lawyer and later a politician, he was involved in all of the contentious issues of the time.

This book is an attempt to do two things, one general and one particular, but it is mostly about the particular – the life of Edward Law. Firstly, because Law deserves a modern biography, but mainly because he and his family can be observed operating in all sections of the establishment, triumphing as he progressed through each, telling us as much about him as it does about the context he operated within. We visit the established church, the public schools, the inns of court, the only universities in England, the law courts, the Houses of Commons and Lords, and the royal family. Our subject supported all of these institutions with a ferocity that surprised even the most fervent proponents of the status quo.

As a biography, it is incomplete. The evidence is at times too patchy, and at other times, too overwhelming to be processed. There is at least one decade when we can rely only on generalisations; at other times, his every word and facial expression were reported in the newspapers. We know what kind of man he was; indeed, as a judge we know his views in highly self-opinionated detail, and these opinions from Law actually became law.

The title needs some justification. 'Establishment', in the sense of a broadly based ruling-class was not a word that the Georgians would have recognised. The phrase was first used in 1955 by the journalist Henry Fairlie:

> By the 'Establishment' I do not mean only the centres of official power – though they are certainly part of it – but rather the whole matrix of official and social relations within which power is exercised. The exercise of power in Britain (more specifically, in England) cannot be understood unless it is recognised that it is exercised socially.

This definition works well for our period two centuries earlier; the establishment is to be found in a lot of places, and political power is maintained through social relations between individuals and groups. That comes as a relief, as this book is intended to be a lot more than a dry constitutional and political history.

So, Law is not an easy man for the modern reader to like. He did not suffer fools at all. He was rude, sarcastic and arrogant, using his considerable intelligence and ability to hurt, harm and intimidate; his terrible but inconsistent temper meant he was feared by lawyers, witnesses and juries. His overbearing manner and great learning enabled him to get his own way in crucial trials, rejecting every concession in the legal system and treating his political enemies very badly.

This book is not a character assassination, although that aim was quite near to my mind when the book was started. It cannot be so for a variety of reasons – the obvious one is the need to avoid anachronism. To paraphrase L.P. Hartley, the past is a different country where they did things differently; the system was rotten, but the rottenness could not be detected by those who had grown up in it and prospered from it. The present is yet another place, where there is a growing tendency to condemn people in the past for not being and thinking like 'us'. To modern sensibilities, he seemed like a reactionary bully with massive prejudices and favourites; the truth is a little more nuanced, as the book will show.

Chapter One

The Curate's House at Buck Crag

The best way to describe the establishment is to locate its bottom rung and work upwards. In Georgian Britain, the bottom of the heap was the grammar school teacher and the church curate, who were often the same person. Edmund Law, grandfather of our subject Edward Law, fulfilled both roles in the village of Staveley-in-Cartmel, Cumberland, a week's stagecoach ride away from the centre of political power.

Edmund was poor, living on a curate's stipend of £20 a year, a miserly amount even by the scandalous treatment of the lower Georgian clergy. In 1752, investigations by Richard Osbaldeston, the Bishop of Carlisle, reported that 32 per cent of the livings in his diocese were worth under £20 per annum. Edmund was the wage-slave workhorse of the Georgian establishment, paid by the vicar to hatch, match and dispatch the locals (which would have included members of my own family on my mother's side, the Bethoms of Ings and Grassgarth), and generally care for their souls, while the legal incumbents resided elsewhere where the livings were more lucrative, or hunted in the local fields as honorary members of the gentry.

Curates were burdened with inequality and jokes were made about their poverty, unless one of them was about to enter a well-to-do family, when the jokes became reproaches. The attitude persisted into the next century. Charles Hayter, the country curate in Jane Austen's *Persuasion* (1811) was a gentle and learned man, just like Edmund Law, but not marriage material for a member of the Musgrove family. One family member, Mary Musgrove, bitched: 'And, pray, who is Charles Hayter? Nothing but a country curate. A most improper match for Miss Musgrove of Uppercross'. Other Austen curates were accused of being 'nobody, quite unconnected, and certainly not a gentleman or a man of property'. Mary's father also despises a naval officer whose father was 'a country curate, without bread to eat'.[1]

Curates were still generally acknowledged to be a respectable and useful part of the national fabric. Most were Oxford or Cambridge graduates, second sons of respectable families cast adrift by the rules of primogeniture. Some could prosper through learning or connections; more accurately, without such advantages, prosperity was impossible.

Edmund Law the curate and teacher showed more application than ambition, spending forty-nine years doing the same jobs. In order for ambition to have any purpose, connections where needed, and Law had none. He had no university education; his family were yeoman farmers with secure tenancies, which was the highest rung of the non-establishment in the Georgian age. His cottage at Buck Crag, which still stands, was on a 570 metre high rocky headland jutting out from a mountain range, five miles from Staveley and a million miles away from the centre of power. It would be nearly another hundred years before fashionable people decided that the Lake District was interesting.

Edmund would have walked to work every day. His income would not allow him a servant, nor the purchase and upkeep of a horse. It has been computed that he must have travelled 2,504 miles by foot every year, and during the time he was curate and schoolmaster he walked 122,696 miles, or a distance nearly equal to five times the circumference of the globe – and this for a pittance, and nobody cared except his poor parishioners. His achievements in life were pedestrian, in both senses of the word.[2] Despite all this, his son was to become a bishop, his grandson a lord and a high court judge, and his great-grandson an earl and Governor-General of India, with many other of his successors achieving high positions in the law, the government and the military, up to the present day.

A local historian from the 1870s tells a story that about the year 1818, when a grandson of our humble curate visited the house at Buck Crag, accompanied by his secretary and a posse of clergymen.[3] He examined every part of the premises, and overwhelmed the then-occupant with questions; the poor tenant, when he had recovered from his amazement exclaimed in the local dialect that 't'bishop inquir't t'dog tail oot a-joint'.[4]

Who was this man who wanted to know the far end of everything? He was certainly one of the descendants of the humble curate's son, also called Edmund Law. It was not our Edward Law; the visit took place in high summer, and Edward was dying in his home in St James's Square, London. It was not Thomas Law, wealthy businessman and investor, as he had moved to the United States in 1793. It could have been Ewan Law, a member of parliament, but the curious visitor was clearly an ecclesiastical figure. The Law family were so accomplished that this does not help much – two of Edmund's grandsons were bishops. George Law was Bishop of Chester in 1818. Another brother, John Law, had been Bishop of Elphin, in Ireland.

John had died in 1810, so it was probably George Law who inspected every room of this yeoman's cottage to glean information about his grandfather; legend has it that he had to scold the young curates who ran off to climb the hills to frolic with the farmer's daughters, so much so that they kept him waiting. Legend also has it that the dignitary pointed to the chair in the inglenook that Edmund sat on after a hard day's work, and said that he 'had to have it'. A 70-year-old chair sounds unlikely today, but this was an age when cutlery and furniture were passed down in wills, so it was quite possible – or else it was a canny transaction by a local who knew that the bishop was transfixed by his own humble beginnings and had now risen high enough to flaunt them.

The rise of the family from farmers to bishops, lords and administrators of the Empire in four generations was remarkable. How did they rise so quickly? They started from a respectable base. The Laws before Edmund had been yeoman farmers, and Buck Crag was a testament to their social status; they were secure in the tenancies, so were never actually poor. The mid-Victorian author of the *Cartmel Chronicles* put the family success down to hard work. Edmund's name cropped up and was celebrated regularly in Cumbrian newspapers during the Victorian craze for self-help. There was truth in it, but some went too far. In 1888, with trade unionists striking and socialists agitating in Trafalgar Square, the *Christian World* dug up the story of the Law family to prove that England was already a paradise for the poor as well as the rich, one which was going to be ruined by strident action in favour of so-called economic and social equality.

Edmund junior, the future bishop and father of Edward Law, was born in the poor curate's house at Buck Crag in 1703. His father was able to arrange a decent education – the local school at Cartmel, the Free Grammar School at Kendal, and then – crucially – to St John's College Cambridge, where he took the option of working very hard rather than fooling about.

He followed his father into the church – there are no manufacturers in this Georgian establishment family, just clerics, lawyers and politicians and aristocratic landowners. Edmund Law junior was given his first job in Greystoke, Cumberland, so achieving in his first step what had taken his father a lifetime.

By 1750, he was rector at Great Salkeld in Cumberland. He collected tithes on behalf of the archdeaconry while living in a substantial house, which still stands in a village that was not much more than a few sandstone houses, an endowed school and the mediaeval church of St. Cuthbert's. Edward was born here on 16 November 1750, either in his father's house or in a carriage (some nineteenth-century reports say that he was born on the road as his mother Mary travelled to nearby Greystoke).

This house was big enough to accommodate many children – of which Edward Law was neither the first nor the most favoured. He was to be the fourth of twelve children born to Edmund's wife, Mary Christian, between 1741 and 1761, of whom three died prematurely. The first son, Edmund, after his father, died aged 17; another son, Christian, died aged 21, and they lost their first daughter, Bridget, less than a week after her birth. This was average misfortune for an eighteenth-century family, but it was above average fecundity. Clergy families were notoriously bigger than average.

The children only stopped coming when Mary died in 1762, aged 39, when Edward Law was 12. She was married for 261 months and was pregnant for at least 108 of those months – that's 42 per cent of the time. Mary Christian was a very pious woman, and the obvious pun on her surname was made constantly by later commentators. Her eulogy noted that her death was 'early rather than untimely', the implication being that the Lord had called his faithful servant unto heaven. She was, it was punned, a Christian in more than name.

The list of vows Mary made on her wedding day has survived. The embossed illustration asks for God's assistance to obey the following rules: never to contradict her husband, unless it was absolutely necessary, and then to do it with good nature; not to fret about small matters; to count her blessings; to be neat and clean; and to rely on providence. These pieties were published in a pamphlet after her early death which was still available as a wedding present for brides in the 1860s. It concludes with a piece of poetry of her own invention:

Thus I would live
Thus would I die
And when this world I leave
To heaven I'd fly

Had she lived longer, she would have had the *Bounty* mutineer Fletcher Christian as her nephew, much to her disappointment. This meant, of course, that Edward Law was his cousin. It was never mentioned during his lifetime and, therefore, never became an embarrassment.

How had Edmund Law senior prospered, considering that his father, Edmund, had been a poor curate and a schoolteacher? The answer was hard work and talent, made more effective by the fact that the establishment would always recruit its lower echelons from the people below. The Georgian ruling class may have been a network of favouritism, nepotism and 'knowing the right people', but it was clearly much more than that. There was social mobility; indeed, any establishment would entropy without it.

Edmund Law was a new talent. He left Cumberland in 1754 to become a master at a Cambridge College and later Bishop of Carlisle. Another given about joining any ruling class is that you had to toe the line to prosper, and once again, with Edmund, the truth was a little more nuanced. His theological views were very much outliers at the time, but that did not stop him from rising through the ranks. Edmund believed in the 'sleep of the soul' – that the immortal part of man was inactive until the day of judgement. This meant that all of the dead would be resurrected at the same time, or, more precisely, at the end of time. He also believed that the clerics of the church should not be tied to the Thirty-Nine Articles of Religion, a view that he made public in a book of 1774; it was anonymous, as he was already a bishop and responsible for the type of strict adherence to doctrine that he was attacking.

How did he prosper? The answer is nepotism, or, more generously, networks and connections. Some bishops did so from the support networks in their own families, but more modest men like Law needed the patronage of others. Law knew the right people and was approved by them. In this case, Law hit the jackpot by being friendly with the Duke of Grafton, who was briefly Prime Minister from October 1768 to January 1770, when he was able to use his influence for Law. Both men wrote books about the moral reformation needed in society, yet neither of them could see the contradiction that was to come. The duke was mired in scandal. Law's great friend had a mistress, Nancy Parsons, but this was not the real problem. She had been a courtesan for other members of the aristocracy and went by other names, but this was not the problem either. Far from being unusual, it was expected and condoned.

Conventional morality was more honoured in the breach than in the observance. Grafton broke social convention when he refused to be secretive about his adultery. It wasn't just an 'open secret' that members of the establishment could pretend they didn't know – it was in the newspapers. Grafton (like Edmund Law) loved making highfalutin statements about moral improvement, but he also (unlike Law) enjoyed drinking, gossiping, and especially field sports – hunting and horsing – and extra-marital relations. Grafton gave offence in an era that was reluctant to receive it. He disobeyed the law that demanded secrecy beyond the charmed circle; he and his mistress visited the opera house together while the queen was present, and she was at the head of his table at his house in Grosvenor Square. The vice could be excused, but not the attitude.

Grafton's wife was also an adulterer, and this provoked the duke to initiate legal proceedings to obtain a very rare parliamentary divorce. Until the recent example of Boris Johnson, he was the only Prime Minister to be divorced while in office; his wife gave birth to her lover's child, and they were divorced by Act of Parliament in March 1769. Divorces were rare, always legislative acts, and therefore confirmed by the establishment and used only in an emergency when 'looking the other way' had failed.

When Grafton recommended Law to a bishopric, none of this would have mattered much to either man. It was said of Edmund that he was always tolerant and even-tempered, interested in theological debate, and very reluctant to fall out with people over religion – which clearly included a Prime Minister who was not even prepared to pay lip service to the seventh commandment. These aspects could be compartmentalised in a way we find difficult, but William Paley – Law's friend and biographer – said that Law regarded his elevation as a satisfactory proof that decent freedom of inquiry was not discouraged in the established church; this was true, but was just a safe way of saying that Grafton and Law shared the same religious latitudinarianism and Whiggery, so it was as much a case of powerful people promoting people who mirrored their own views. Grafton himself was a protégé of the Duke of Newcastle, another Whig grandee, and it was the family's link with politicians rather than any association with brazen adulterers that did the family harm; his son's career was tainted by his, and his father's, Whig connections.

When Edmund became bishop of Carlisle in 1768, it was the smallest (in terms of parishes) and one of the poorest. Its income was no more than £500 a year but it covered only one hundred parishes (the largest, Lincoln, had 1,312). At least the job did not keep him away from home very often. Bishop Nicholson, his predecessor, was seldom kept above two nights from his own bed, which was useful for Edmund, who held a second prestigious post in Cambridge. Law was in a very strong position to ensure that his children did even better, and once again, the first step was schooling.

Chapter Two

An Establishment Education

Georgian childhoods tend to go undocumented, and Edward Law's was no exception. There are no anecdotes from the family, and Law rarely referred to his early life, so the stories about his character do not start to flow until he went to school. We can say with certainty that childhood itself would not have lasted long. There was no cosseting and compromising, and no gradual phasing-in of adult responsibilities. Edward would have been breeched – put in long trousers – at about 5, and from that time would have been treated as much as an adult as was practicably possible. At that the point his childhood ended, with his name reverting to Edward from the childish Ned. After being taught to read and write at home, he was sent to his maternal uncle, the Reverend Humphrey Christian at Docking Hall in Norfolk, to continue his education, toughen him up and, according to one Victorian biographer, modify his Cumbrian twang.[1] The latter aim seems unlikely. A Norfolk accent would have replaced it, and Law's itinerant nurse would have been a Cumbrian who talked to the child a thousand times more than his parents. He retained his accent for the rest of his life, earning him the ridicule of people who could not hurt him in any other way.

Some of his schooling seemed to have been near home, but probably not for very long. In later life, Law was reputed to have said that there was nothing more inconvenient than children who came home for the holidays and this is often cited as an example of his lack of empathy, but it was based on his experience and that of thousands of other Georgian children, and he was presumably of the view that it 'had not done him any harm'. Evidence seems to suggest that he attended two endowed grammar schools, which were the backbone of middle-ranking education in the Georgian period. Law seemed to have attended a modest grammar school about ten miles from his home in Blencow. It provided a reasonably priced classical curriculum; if anything else was required, it would be an extra payment.

Most of his education was in Suffolk at another decent and moderately distinguished school, but one that disappeared in Victorian times so identifying and locating it is not easy. Some sources suggest it was in Bury, Lancashire, because of its nearness to Cumberland, but that would not have been a consideration for people who did not worry about pushing their young offspring out of their home. It is generally believed to be Botesdale Grammar School near Bury St Edmunds. Described by William Townsend, Law's biographer, as 'a school of some repute', it was one of the many endowed grammar schools founded by Protestants who had done well out of the reformation. Its main building at its foundation in 1561 was a chantry chapel, and the buildings survived even after the school closed in 1878. It was a modestly sized school with around sixty pupils, and a curriculum based on Latin grammar which people today may find irrelevant but was useful for the church or law, and definitely good as a class marker for the establishment. The school itself counted Law as one of its prominent alumni, according to Victorian newspaper sources. Unlike his first grammar school, the curriculum here was a little wider than the classics.

So far, this was an education similar to that of his father and grandfather, but the difference was that his father was a bishop and his grandfather was a curate, and bishops have contacts that curates must live without. Edward was not at Botesdale long, possibly less than a year, and then made a giant leap upmarket when he went to Charterhouse School at the age of 11 in January 1761 – the year before his mother died.

Georgian public schools are often conflated with later Victorian ones, which vastly overstates the quality of the former, but Charterhouse was still in a different league from the modest school in Bury. It was of equivalent in status to Winchester, Eton or Harrow. A school of this fame would need a personal recommendation from one of the governors. This came from Thomas Sherlock, Bishop of London, who was closely aligned theologically with Law senior. Prime Minister Grafton, the friend of Edmund Law, was connected to the school and made a governor in 1770. It was not just a case of who you knew – it mattered that the person also agreed with you. Edward Law became a governor in 1803, as did his close friend and political ally Henry Addington, later Lord Sidmouth, who both recommended students to the school. In the summer of his first year, he may well have attended the Charterhouse school play of 1761, which was attended by one archbishop, five bishops, three dukes and the Lord Chancellor. [2]

There is direct evidence of his personality from this point. His biographer Lord Campbell summarizes it well – arrogance and bonhomie, harshness and kindness: 'He was at once moody and good natured, a bluff burly boy ever ready to inflict a blow or perform an exercise for his schoolfellows.'[3]

He seems to have been an excellent friend but a formidable enemy. Whatever the situation, Law developed an intense love and affection for the place and is buried there; his memorial has these heart-felt words of thanks: 'He died 13 December 1818 in the 69th year of his age and in grateful remembrance of the advantages he had derived through life from his Education upon the Foundation of the Charterhouse desired to be buried in this church'[4]

He was Captain of School during his six-year spell, and he regularly said that this was the greatest honour of his life, more than his later professional success; this did not, however, prevent him being dressed in judicial wig and gown on his full size memorial in the founder's vault.

Edward Law matriculated at Peterhouse, Cambridge, in May 1767. This is not an academic achievement in itself but meant (and still means) no more than being formally entered on to the college books. He was 17, an average age for the time. His later friend William Wilberforce matriculated at St. John's at the same age in 1776. His later political enemy, William Pitt, was not quite 14 when he went to Pembroke in 1773. Pitt's father was Prime Minister at the time, but that was not the reason for the early entry. Like in other areas inhabited by the privileged, there were few hard-and-fast rules for them.

Cambridge was a community of a thousand of the most privileged sons of the establishment, never more than a fifteen-minute walk away from each other. It returned two members of parliament at a time when Manchester, Leeds and Birmingham had none, and London had only four. The electorate of 600 graduates also had another vote in the place that they went on to reside, a privilege not abolished until 1948.

Peterhouse was the centre of the Georgian establishment. The smallest and oldest of the Cambridge Colleges (although not having the word 'college' in its name) it is still at the centre of our establishment today, although its members are more diverse (more recent alumni include comedian David Mitchell and politician Michael Portillo). Even today, Law is remembered at Peterhouse. He is one of thirty Eminent Petreans on the college's website.[5]

The most important influence on Law was the Professor of Moral Philosophy and master of his college. This was his own father, Edmund Law. He was installed in 1756 and had sent his eldest child Edmund junior to his own college as well – he died while studying there in 1758, aged 17. Law had recently taken up another post as the fifty-first Bishop of Carlisle as well. That Law senior was an absentee bishop was not perceived as a problem. Edmund would return each July to September to Rose Castle, his palace in Carlisle; the fact that he spent all but two summers there during nineteen years as bishop was regarded as proof that he was doing a good job. In the spirit of nepotism (or family loyalty) another of his sons, John, was an archdeacon there.

What happened at Cambridge? Its main role was to produce Anglican Clergyman (Roman Catholics and Jews were barred from attending), and that fact would not have been far from Law senior's mind when Edward arrived. What was actually studied was more extensive than just Theology, and more fluid: Greek and Roman texts, Natural History, Medicine, Mathematics, Moral Philosophy and Political Philosophy, and the balance and emphasis was a negotiated choice with the tutor.

Apart from learning, the main occupation was dissipation. The exact weighting would be a matter of personal choice. For these young members of the establishment, they would commence their eating, drinking and playing at university and then practise it for a lifetime. Byron reported from Trinity College (1807) that it was a wretched place, 'a villainous chaos of dice and drunkenness, nothing but hazard and burgundy, hunting, mathematics and Newmarket, riot and racing'.[6] There were some caveats: it was better than the dull town he came from; he had money – having just withdrawn £125 from his allowance – and he was busy making love, enemies and verses. Not everybody managed the fame and the poetry, but the dissipation came easily to most. It was the preserve of the rich and idle; it was a manly thing to do – as William Blake said: in order to spend your strength you needed a large supply of it. He was talking about the habit of genius to be dissipated, but it applied to average students as well.

Drink was a major cause of dissipation and a gateway to many others, both for the ruling classes at university and afterwards: 'they drink a great deal here in general, and appear to be very idle', wrote one French visitor to the university. The second part is untrue. They did not 'appear' to be idle – they *were* idle; they were not secretly working and concealing it from their friends. Their teachers were also idle, and the instruction was feeble and unimaginative. Qualifications were achieved simply by time spent – nine terms were enough. Many people did not even bother to graduate, often staying for no more than a year.[7]

This all sounds unjust from our modern perspective, but the situation was completely logical. University was not designed to improve their life chances; they were not at university to advance their careers because the money and connections that had got them to university in the first place guaranteed success afterwards. Not only was work not necessary, but also any vice or peccadillo could be indulged in without shame, comment, or much punishment. In that way, university was a kind of perverse preparation for a privileged adult life. Students like Law would meet people like themselves and avoid interaction with the 'average' citizen who may have the impudence to alarm or contradict them. That was another preparation for the future.

James Woodforde, later an Essex cleric who escaped obscurity by writing a five volume diary of his life, joined New College Oxford in 1759, aged 19. His moderate level of dissipation and fun was similar to Law fifteen years later. He drank a lot, in the pub and in his lodgings, and sometimes on his own. On 6 October, after a mere four days in residence, he and two other students clubbed together and purchased a hogshead of port from a wine merchant in Southampton. So they began their studies with a cache of nearly one hundred bottles each. Port was the middle-ranking drink for relatively poor students like Woodforde; it was another two days before he purchased any paper and ink. On 29 November, he and two friends stayed up until 2 am and consumed six bottles of port between them. [8]

Apart from drinking, there were sports like shooting and cricket, novel diverting events like watching a man ride three horses, and jolly japes like raiding his friends' room when drunk on punch, or being thrown out of his own room naked. He failed to turn up for prayers and struck up a platonic relationship with two sisters. Abetted by two friends, he beat up an apprentice for making rude verses about him, went to criminal trials, got drunk and shouted under the Dean's window, and took part in ridiculous wagers (there is some evidence that Law did this too). One of his friends claimed to be able to drink three bottles of wine in three hours and then correctly write out five Bible verses. Woodforde was chased for bad debts (by the Southampton agent who had sold him the bottles of port). They ate out a lot, and the vacations were extensive – it took two days to get home, and he seemed to have done much of his work there, putting up a tent in his garden where the chances to dissipate were fewer.

William Wilberforce arrived at college in October 1776. On his first day he was introduced to 'as licentious a set of men that could well be conceived'. He noticed their drinking and dissipation, 'and their conversation was even worse than their lives'. He looked for more moderate company and advice about studying. They were incredulous when he tried to do some work: 'Their object seemed to be to make me idle. If I occasionally appeared studious, they would say to me, why in the world should a man of your fortune trouble himself with fagging?'[9]

Wilberforce defied peer pressure, but it was clear to him that the university was not just immoral and non-intellectual – it was amoral and anti-intellectual. William Pitt and Wilberforce were friends at the university, and both seemed to have done more work than average.

Was Edward Law like this at Cambridge? He seemed not to be guilty of full-blown dissipation. It was said by Campbell that the greatest struggle he ever made 'was leaving a pleasant party and retiring to his rooms to read'.[10] This author had the same struggles in the late 1970s as well, but at least, like the author, he did eventually get to his room and do some work. This would have taken some force of personality to go against the ethos, but he was helped by the strong family values, the success of his brothers in the past, and the fact that unlike Wilberforce and Pitt, he was not independently wealthy. He fitted his work around his social life, making connections that would last him a lifetime; that was still happening in the 1970s as well.

So, Law did do some work. William Coxe, who had shot, fished and loitered away his first year at university (this did not stop him becoming an archdeacon) was mightily impressed by Law's work rate as much as his passion. What were Law's interests? He admired Virgil and, more commonly for the educated Englishman, Milton; he loved the classics but was clever enough to make cogent exceptions (like Sophocles) for reasons that would defeat the twenty-first century graduate. He loved history but was contemptuous of a particular history book that was too nice to James II. His hatred and fear of Catholics would last a lifetime, an opinion he would share with most British Protestants. Law seemed to be best at law and classics, but was generally very good at everything. Science and mathematics seemed important to him; later, he was an early convert to economics.

He had no particular interest in theology, and this was about to become significant. He took his BA in 1771 (some aristocrats were allowed to graduate without taking exams, like Pitt, although to be fair, Pitt never enjoyed full health as a youth or for the rest of his life – although the drinking did not help) and was awarded the Third Wrangler, which is the third-best examination score in the whole university. This undeniable triumph was diminished a little with disappointment, as it seems that most people (Law included) expected him to come on top and be the Senior Wrangler. Campbell believed this was due to arrogance; in mathematics Law was beaten by two people who were less talented than him, but tried harder. It's hard to work out how Campbell knew this, but it does ring true.

He never quite made it as a brilliant academic. He obtained a fellowship at the college two years after his BA, but that was his exit from academia rather than the start. His brothers John and George both outshone him by achieving Second Wrangler; Law won some Latin prizes after graduation as well, but his heart was never in it. He spent much of his later life scorning academic achievements, and it later turned out that he was never as good at writing and formal examinations as he was at speeches and arguments. Unlike other successful judges, he was to produce no major law publications. Campbell said that in the last two years of study, he started to read light novels.

Cambridge is our second glance into his personality. His friend William Coxe reported in his own memoirs that:

> As all his views are honest and his intentions are direct, he scorns to disguise his feelings or palliate his sentiments. This disposition has been productive of uneasiness for himself and for his friends, for his open and unsuspecting temper leads him to use a warmth of expression that sometimes assumes the appearance of *fierté*. This has frequently disgusted his acquaintances, but his friends know the goodness of his heart and pardon the foible that arises from the candour and openness of his temper.

Essentially, Law was a great person to know well, but more than a pain if you never made it past acquaintance, as he could be rude, dismissive and arrogant. This was a mirage, said his friends; deep down he was lovely, and it was only his high morals and principles that made him horrible to people. He was, in that foreboding modern phrase, a 'bit of a perfectionist'. There was more: he was always passionate about debate; he could stray into rudeness, but always apologised afterwards; and his understanding friends always forgave him. He never made the slightest effort to be diplomatic, or to be respectful of those who fell below his standards, or to suffer fools gladly. He would be an ideal Georgian high court judge.

Chapter Three

Law Chooses Law

Having paid his three guineas, Edward Law was admitted to Lincoln's Inn on 10 June 1769. He did not need to study law, or indeed anything; his future was assured. He had an ecclesiastical living already set out for him if required; his father wanted all of his sons to take holy orders. This would have been an easy progression, as the loving father would have offered him a comfortable living somewhere within his bishopric. He did the same for his two other clerical sons: John was 'given the living of Warkworth by his father', as the newspapers were happy to say without comment, and then a prebendary stall at Carlisle Cathedral – essentially an undemanding but rewarding administrative post. Law's younger brother started his career as a prebendary of Carlisle Cathedral as well.

Law seemed to have broken away from his father's wishes without causing any family arguments, and his father was probably mollified by a promise to take a clerical route if the law career did not work out. Law opted for the uncertain option when nepotism was the easy one, although it may be observed cynically that nepotism would always be available as a fallback. None of this would have come as a shock or a shame to the casual observer; indeed, shock would have come if he hadn't supported his own sons. As ever and as now, the ruling class had options and could afford to fail, and in a way, he had failed, as his academic career had not been an obvious success. He took modest rooms in the Temple, but was bankrolled by his father and suffered few deprivations. The Inns of Court were similar to the ancient universities, offering accommodation and the chance to learn if that was desired; for Law this was, in theory, another unnecessary step, but it seems clear that he actively chose the law.

It is not surprising that Law junior followed a different path – father never was like son. The father was a liberal bishop, reliant on Whig connections and mostly living in a time when they could help him. Edmund was quiet, diffident, and had a voice that was never raised above its ordinary pitch. Campbell described his father's reluctance to cause pain or have what we would call today, 'difficult conversations'. He was regarded as unworldly and naïve. His desire to avoid temper, confrontation and distress for people was occasionally counted as a weakness for a man of authority.

Edward Law was much more like his mother, Mary Christian, both physically and emotionally: firm, determined and rigid – although in later life Law admitted that he had not inherited his bellowing and intemperate bad temper from either parent. His intimate thoughts about his parents are unknown, but years later, when he was allowed to choose a hereditary title for himself, he chose Ellenborough in Cumberland, a location associated with his mother rather than his father; of course the mother's family was more eminent as well. He was always aware of that.

A lot more is known about Law's life than might be expected because of a remarkable survival. Law was a member of a club, the Honourable Society of the Bears, whose records have survived. Such voluntary associations ran through all parts of the Georgian establishment, few of which were very serious and even fewer were less serious than the Honourable Society of the Bears, who were neither ancient (founded around 1738) nor particularly honourable – unless you believe that gambling, drinking and eating are meritorious.[1]

The surviving minutes show that Law joined by invitation on 26 November 1776. It was exclusive in the sense that it was by invitation only, and not very large. Twenty new gentlemen paid their two guineas in April 1777. His first attendance in January was a meeting of eight; this was enough because most of the time would be spent around the lunch table, starting around 4 pm with the food to allow the evening for the drink and frolics. At his first meeting, three members of the society were elected to grandiose and meaningless titles, with speeches and lots of port. Sir Thomas Tancred was removed from the society because he was now married: 'His strength & valour is now required elsewhere.' This was a club to talk *about* women, not to be in their company.

There were usually four meetings annually to accommodate the legal year. It was an enjoyable, non-improving social event. The society's minutes also covered the bets they made; these personal wagers were regarded as much more interesting and honourable than gambling with cards, and they prided themselves on their audacity, originality and intelligence. Bets were written in a special book, and when there was a resolution, it was recorded in the minutes. Exactly the same procedure took place in the top gentlemen's clubs in London, such as White's and Brook's, which was where these young gentlemen were heading.

Some wagers were based on the law; most were frivolous. On 30 November 1780, there was a convoluted bet that involved Law as Deputy Secretary:

> Mr President, Mr Dundas, Mr Palmer, & Mr Deputy Secretary sitting on the right-hand side of the room, & Mr Attorney General, Mr Treasurer, Mr Recorder, Mr Stokes & Mr Bower sitting on the left, Mr President betted one bottle of Claret with Mr Deputy Sec that one Gentleman on the right, would Enter into the holy Estate of matrimony before any Gent on the left.

Betting on who married first was common: a note in the minutes for five years later showed the result: 'Lost by Mr Dep Sec pd by Mr Law to Comptr Aug 17. 85.'

It was all very serious, in a self-mocking way. In May 1781, the discussion veered (presumably drunkenly) towards the historic names of the Bishops of Worcester. Law bet Mr Recorder Thomson that there had been one by the name of Fleetwood in the last century; at the next meeting (in November), Thomson paid up. Any legal promotions or personal successes of members were toasted in claret; sometimes a gallon of claret was shared among eight people, which would be only the beginning of their drinking.

Some bets were in what we would regard today as poor taste, but are an example of the fact that no topic of conversation was off limits: 'Mr Coke bets Mr Leycester a Gallon of Claret that Lord Mansfield is not alive at the first of January 1787.'

He was. This was not the first time Law would speculate about the arrival of the Grim Reaper at the door of the Lord Chief Justice.

Law continued to dine at the Society of the Bears long after his training had finished: Oxford and Cambridge graduates had to study for a reduced amount of time. In 1787, when Law and another member of the Bears became King's Council, 'gallons of claret' were consumed; Law paid for this himself. He seems to have left the society immediately afterwards, as most members did when they achieved important legal promotions or married.

This light-hearted organisation had a serious purpose. It cemented the connections between members of the elite that would last a lifetime. Many of Law's drinking, eating and womanising companions would become his professional colleagues for life. Simon Le Blanc would be one of his deputies at King's Bench, and they would meet many times, sometimes on the same side and sometimes in opposition – it didn't really matter. Richard Pepper Arden started as a drinking companion of Edward Law but ended up as a fellow common law judge; he was appointed Chief Justice of the Court of Common Pleas in 1801, a year before Law, and generally his career progressed faster than Law because Arden had been a drinking buddy of William Pitt, living on the same staircase. In June 1787 Thomas Plumer and Law were sharing yet another bottle to celebrate Plumer's entry into the honourable and ancient society; a year later, they were making a name for themselves at the impeachment of Warren Hastings. It was not really about drinking the claret.

Law continued to take the path of law and this meant painstaking work, the guarantee of a reasonable income, but with the problem of how to stand out from the crowd – there were many Georgian lawyers. In 1771 he took up what was essentially a high-end legal apprenticeship with George Wood in order to become a special pleader, which sounds like a post for somebody needy and inferior but was not the case at all. Special pleaders drafted statements of cases, gave opinions and prepared papers for various court proceedings. It was vital for two reasons: English law, while not full of justice to modern eyes, was incredibly attached to the rules of procedure. Cases in which the defendant was clearly going down would be abandoned if the wording was incorrect, even the apparently inconsequential detail. Trials tended to be shockingly quick compared to the modern experience and the correct paperwork at the correct time was vital. Special pleading played to Law's strengths: research, detail, knowledge and careful writing. It also swerved his weaknesses – extensive writing and engaging oratory. It was a useful and increasingly common career path for ambitious lawyers.

Someone became a special pleader in the same way as they did everything else in the establishment – by knowing the right person. George Wood was that person; he also taught some of the other up and coming legal celebrities, Charles Abbott, Law's successor at the King's Bench, and his rival Thomas Erskine. It was dreary work. A letter to his friend William Coxe survives from that period. It adds to our knowledge of the man:

> 18 June, 1773 Temple, Friday night. After holding a pen most of the day in the service of my profession, I will use it a few minutes longer in that of friendship. I thank you, my dearest friend, for this and every proof of confidence and affection. Let us cheerfully push our way in our different lines: the path of neither of us is strewed with roses, but they will terminate in happiness and honour. I cannot, however, now and then help sighing when I think how inglorious an apprenticeship we both of us serve to ambition – while you teach a child his rudiments and I drudge at the pen for attorneys. But if knowledge and a respectable situation are to be purchased only on these terms, I, for my part, can readily say '*hac mercede placet.*' Do not commend my industry too soon: application wears for me at present the charm of novelty: upon a longer acquaintance I may grow tired of it.[2]

In an age before the photocopier and typewriter, men were employed writing exact versions of documents, so he is quite exhausted by doing a lot of 'Bob Cratchit' type copying. This is a warm and empathetic letter from an exhausted young man who could understand the feelings of another person in a precarious situation, although his belief that life was an inglorious apprenticeship and their path was not strewn with roses was untrue. They both lived in a charmed circle. Coxe was a fellow at King's at the same time as Law at Peterhouse, and in 1773 Coxe was travelling as a tutor for the children of the nobility while also writing books. He settled down as the vicar of a prosperous Richmond parish. Law accepts the terms, despite his mock complaining – that is the meaning of *hac mercede placet* – because there is better to come for both men. Law's work rate was never in doubt; his father had given him a piece of advice, in Latin *hoc age* – literally 'do this' – with the implication of doing what was right, and working methodically, even when it hurt a little.

Law became a special pleader in 1775, took on pupils himself, and the whole system of localism and nepotism continued. Campbell tells us that the normal fee was 100 guineas per year to be a pupil of Ellenborough; compare this with the £15 prize for the second best Latin prose prize at university. One pupil was William Lowndes, a man with Cumbrian connections. Lowndes was only two years younger than Law; he was at Charterhouse at the same time. In any case, Lowndes was known to the family; Law's father was acquainted with Lowndes's grandfather. After the initial recommendation of the Headmaster of Charterhouse for Lowndes to go to St John's (his own college), Bishop Law had him moved to Peterhouse, where he would have encountered Edward again.

Like Law, Lowndes's family held some ecclesiastical preferments and he would have slipped easily into the church, but he preferred a legal career. When Law himself was called to the bar, Lowndes took many of his clients. In 1787, he joined the Northern Circuit like Law. At this point, Lowndes's own nepotist network gained momentum and he became an ally of William Pitt, via two intermediaries. Lowndes's skill at framing legal instruments meant he had an influential job as Chief Commissioner at the Treasury and drew up the law that introduced Income Tax into Britain for the first time. The trust of Pitt made him rise above Law until the death of Pitt allowed Law to overtake him.[3]

Law was admitted to the Inner Temple in 1782, as he had already graduated *ad eundem gradum* – 'to the same degree' – there was a Latin term for everything, Law had started his career in 1780, when he was called to the bar on the Northern Circuit. Pitt – a man who had done less well than Law at Cambridge, had taken no examinations, had no legal experience, and had not done a five-year slog as a special pleader – was called to the bar in the same year. This was no cause for resentment, for the son of a prime minister and a scion of a more august family, that is the way it went. Indeed, Pitt was only four years away from being Prime Minister himself.

The Northern Circuit was the 'long circuit', not much sought after, but it did produce some good lawyers. Law chose it because he could do no wrong in Appleby and Carlisle. His father's position and mother's family would have been helpful to him, but he had other friends and connections who promoted his career in a way that was not so for most men on the same journey. Tradition has it that his first appearance was not in Cumberland but in York in at a trial at *Nisi Prius*, a preliminary court hearing outside London that might move on to one of the common law courts in the capital if not resolved. Rumour further has it that he appeared with an oversized bag of cases that he had already generated through his own connections. It is impossible to prove the truth of this anecdote, but it was certainly believed by his mid-Victorian biographers and commentators, who would still have a grudging admiration for this way of working.

There is one famous story about his early legal career. Bradford landowner Richard Hodgson claimed to have given Law his first brief and predicted his rise to Chief Justice. In 1780 Hodgson was involved in a dispute about deeds and was the defendant in a trial at York. His opponent had secured the best lawyer on the Northern Circuit, but Hodgson was unable to choose one himself until he arrived there:

> After carefully surveying the big wigs and the faces under them, I remarked to my lawyer, 'I rather like the looks of the young man on our left; speak to him, and inquire if he has any objection to a consultation with a view to a brief; if I am not mistaken there is both sense and law in that head.' The reply to the question was, 'I shall be happy to see you at my lodgings this evening at six.' On being ushered into his room, the young counsel, whose name I did not even know, said, 'This is the first time I have travelled the circuit, and your brief is the first I have had offered: I am but a young barrister, and I think it only fair to give you this warning

He asked the young man's name, and became the first of thousands to make the same joke – that he was pleased to have law on his side. At the trial Law was brilliant, but when the judge inquired about whether this was a correct point of law, he replied: 'Yes, my lord, answered a gruff voice: we are not in the habit of falling before we are knocked down.' [4]

Hodgson then predicted that Law would be Chief Justice. It is, of course, a story told in retrospect, but it rings true.

Law's chief mentor was Justice Francis Buller. Buller's career was similar to Law's: the Inner Temple, training as a special pleader under the leading teacher at the time, and afterwards called to the bar: then a KC and judge on the Northern Circuit. Buller was famous for his hasty and intemperate remarks in court. He was also famous for the ruling that 'a husband could thrash his wife with impunity provided that he used a stick no bigger than his thumb'. The outcry about Buller's ruling did not appear for another century; male dominance meant that it was deemed a common sense ruling, and there was a shocking indifference to interpersonal violence generally. Law was a protege with similar instincts. Another mentor was James Wallace. He was the half-brother of Anne Tomlinson, the wife of Law's brother. It was all going reasonably well, but something a little more dramatic was necessary.

Chapter Four

National Breakthrough

Progress was slow. A Whiggish-inclined lawyer on a peripheral legal circuit with no friends in very high places after the triumph of William Pitt in the 1784 elections could expect no more. Law was influential within his limited jurisdiction on the Northern Circuit, and prosperous. When his work was finished he made the three- or four-day journey back to his home in London, though he was not well known in the capital. He was well protected by his patrons, and with a reputation for hard work and, it seems, a growing reputation for cases involving marine and commercial insurance, the future sounded secure but not terribly interesting. Something needed to change.

His promotion to King's Councillor in 1787 was a massive step up. He was now an officer of the Crown; the salary was a mere £40 a year, but much more money was to be made from the scarcity of 'his majesty's councillors learned in the law' on the circuits – there were only three or four on his. He received a pen and paper allowance and was allowed – and expected – to carry a purple bag, although, of course, Law had been doing so long before that. He was also obliged to represent the Crown on request in the law courts and refrain from opposing the monarch's wishes – this was not a problem for him; indeed, if it were, he would not have been appointed.

His real breakthrough happened in 1788. Campbell suggested that Law had gone to his chamber one morning and discovered a cheque for £500. This was a retainer for being part of Warren Hastings's defence team, and, while the money would have been welcome, the exposure was worth its weight in gold. Over the course of the next seven years he was able to make a legal name for himself on the national stage, take on both the government and opposition and effectively beat them, and finally destroy his reputation as a Whig; and once again, it was nepotism that helped him along the way.

The key to his fortune was the former Governor-General of India, Warren Hastings. Hastings was accused of arbitrary and tyrannical conduct in India, and of corruption. He had left India at the end of his post with £74,000, but this figure was regarded by experts as extremely moderate. Law would have known that a determined man on the make could accumulate money faster than Hastings did in India, and Law knew of at least two other people who had made a large fortune – his brothers Thomas and Ewan – the two brothers who did not become bishops.

Thomas had made a fortune prior to emigrating to the United States. He returned to England for his health in 1791, bringing with him his three illegitimate sons – George, John and Edmund, born of his Indian mistress. Like Hastings, he remitted home much more money than he had ever made in salary while working in India. Ewan Law joined the East India Company in 1763, aged 16, and was able to retire from work in 1782, aged 35, with a load of East India stock and a handsome house in Sussex. He became a nabob, a recognisable type that was not very popular.

How did Edward Law get this job? It was Thomas Rumbold who recommended Law to Hastings, and he was married to Law's sister, Joanna. They married in 1772; he was 35, and she was not yet 20. He was notoriously corrupt, and it is very hard to believe that Law took on this task without knowing it. Rumbold himself had come home from India with a much more impressive £600,000.

Hastings was unpopular in the Commons and received only lukewarm support from William Pitt. Most of Hastings enemies were the Whig grandees, with the not-yet-Tory Edmund Burke leading the charge. Essentially, Law was taking on both political groups simultaneously, with little prospect of defeating them. His defence of Hastings derailed his plan to become a Member of the House of Commons, the natural next step for an up-and-coming Georgian lawyer, and practically guaranteed obscurity rather than fame. It was all a huge risk. Taking on the defence was a brave thing to do. Thomas Erskine had been offered the task first but turned it down on principle – possibly the cowardly principle that he would be in direct opposition to the ruling politicians of the day, which would not have done him any good, or the more noble principle that some of the people involved were his friends. Erskine had always been Law's opponent, and one step ahead of him all the time – this was the first exception.

The impeachment proceedings took place in Westminster Hall. Assembled MPs and peers were all dressed up and the nation was watching; this was not the magistrate's court in Appleby. The process was decided by one generation of Lords and finished by another, said Campbell, only partly exaggerating. A third of the Lords who agreed to take part had died by the end. There were 148 days of proceedings at a time when a treason trial could be completed in a long day. It was a national political marathon, with Law at the centre. He had swapped a seat in parliament doing somebody else's bidding for a national stage. The trial made Law famous; he joined, albeit temporarily, the ranks of the metropolitan elite satirised in the cartoons of Gillray, Cruikshank and Rowlandson. To be lambasted by these popular artists was an acknowledgement of fame. A historian of Georgian print culture tells the story of George Canning, an up-and-coming Tory politician who was absolutely desperate to appear in one of the cartoons that the London public was buying from the print shops.[1]

Law's debut in the booksellers' window came in a cartoon of February 1788 called the *Grand Pitch Battle*, showing Hastings and Burke as a pair of pugilists – a fair comparison given the viciousness and length of Georgian boxing matches and their popularity, which, like the Hastings trial, crossed class boundaries. Alongside Law are Thomas Plumer, another friend of Sir Thomas Rumbold, and afterwards Master of the Rolls, and Robert Dallas, another lawyer known to Law. Law is portrayed as the boxer, with Dallas holding a water bottle. Also featured are Sheridan (carrying sherry) and Charles James Fox. Law was to appear in many satirical cartoons from about 1800, but this was his early brush with fame – and a little bit of a false dawn.[2]

Law's success was procedural at first, and gave him a lasting reputation for knowing the rules in detail and exploiting them for his own advantage. The Lords agreed to hear the evidence on all charges before the defence was called, and the trial proceeded according to all the rules governing the admissibility of evidence in a criminal trial rather than a parliamentary impeachment, therefore giving the accused the benefit of the doubt. It was Law's 1793 speech that made his name. His biographer Campbell suggested that Law was daunted and timid at first, but soon rose to the occasion. It lasted for three days, beginning poorly but ending in complete success. Fellow lawyer Brougham noted the 'finer passages have rarely been surpassed by any effort of forensic power'.[3]

It was more than impassioned, long and forensic. He attacked the famous prosecutors, attacked the House of Commons, and accused Fox of calumny and slander. Burke accused him of insolence and arrogance, showing a little contemporary racism at the same time: 'Let us hope that some of them do not understand the English language, as the insolent remarks we are compelled to hear from counsel would be a disgrace to a Turkish court of justice.'[4]

It is no surprise that Burke turned his back on Law when refusing to shake his hand at the end. Law was no more than a jumped-up special pleader without the basic manners of an English gentleman. The son had tried the patience of Whigs like Fox, Sheridan and especially Burke, the kind of people his father had admired.

In 1795, the House of Lords found Hastings not guilty. The vote was twenty-three to six, a large margin but a small turnout; the Hastings trial had tried the system's patience. The parvenu lawyer had earned a total of £3,000 and seemed to have invested some of it in East India Stock. Law's brother Ewan, who spoke as a witness for Hasting's at the impeachment, made a similar investment. In any case, Hastings was to spend £71,000 on his defence. Only the lawyers won.

Law had made enemies; this vitriol against the Irishman Burke, written by Dallas, was widely attributed to Law:

> Oft have I wonder'd why on Irish ground
> No poisonous reptile ever yet was found:
>
> Reveal'd the secret stands of Nature's work,
> She saved her venom to create a Burke.

He certainly was regarded as doing the most damage, nullifying the clever rhetoric of politicians with legal procedural rules. By the end of the impeachment, Law and Burke had witnessed the French revolution and agreed on the dangers of republicanism and atheism, but they were still not on the same side. Law's role was noted and not forgotten. He had climbed the greasy pole, but he had few powerful friends around him. The short-term fillip looked like a long-term dead end.

Chapter Five

Anne Towry: Bloomsbury Beauty to Establishment Lady

These were the first two wedding announcements in the *Reading Mercury* on 26 October 1789:

> MARRIED: Mr Cole, maltster, aged 73, to Mrs Ward, his housekeeper, aged 24. Mr Cole had been a widower eight weeks.
>
> MARRIED: Edward Law, Esq, of the Inner Temple, to Miss Towry, daughter of George Phillip Towry, Esq.

Neither of these two families had any connection with the Berkshire county town, or indeed Hereford, Bath or Leeds, where newspapers also printed this comedic juxtaposition. The first entry was inserted because it was an oddity, and the second because two quite prestigious families were forming a marriage alliance, and this was national news – even if it had nothing to do with Reading. The first one was meant to be hilarious – a member of the artisan classes who was wasting no time marrying his 'housekeeper', with the ages added on to make it even funnier. It didn't matter too much if the plebs behaved like this, but members of the establishment needed to marry equals.

Did the second marriage meet that criterion? It was the union of the son of a bishop, 39 next birthday, and the daughter of an accomplished navy officer and senior administrator, aged 20. Law married relatively late for an eighteenth-century gentleman, but the disparity in ages, large by our standards, was reasonable for those of the time. Law was, in many ways, not much of a catch. He was small, squat and loud, and when he opened his mouth, he was very provincial. To use a modern phrase, he was punching above his weight.

Who gained the most from the marriage? It would have been a very fine judgement, which would have been the ideal outcome. Politically, they were both Whig-inclined. In terms of heritage, the Towrys were superior, being related (by recent marriage) to sixteenth-century Lord High Chancellor Sir Thomas More, while at the same time the Laws would have been tending sheep in Cumberland.

The father, George Phillips Towry, was one of his Majesty's seven Victualling Commissioners and, prior to that, had a distinguished military career. He did not rely on his salary of £400 per year; he was independently wealthy, having inherited money from his elder brother, who died in battle in 1762. He had done well from his own marriage to Elizabeth More, and had even won £20,000 on the state lottery in November 1770 and bought Foliejon Park in Berkshire with the proceeds. Edmund Law, who died during the courtship period, had occupied an elevated position as a bishop and Cambridge academic, so the sums more or less added up.

All the bishop's sons were high achievers. The ugly son was a sound prospect. His best days were still to come and he was clearly going places. Just before their long and tortuous courtship, he had achieved King's Counsel (June 1787) and been elected a bencher of the Inner Temple. He was already on Warren Hastings's defence team – although in 1789, that was no strong indicator of fortune or fame; indeed, it was a risky decision as he was taking on the establishment with no guarantee of winning.

Who was Anne Towry? Physically, she was everything Edward Law was not. Law eventually asked for the right to court her, and she seems to have refused him on a number of occasions. Only on the fourth occasion did she say yes, and was probably under some pressure from the family. Victorian commentators like Campbell saw his successful pursuit of Anne as another example of his ambition and hard work, a laudable consequence of determined self-help. They were married on the morning of 17 October (all marriages had to be before 12 am until 1868) by special licence rather than three sets of banns, with a ceremony at the father's house with a specially appointed cleric.

Her attractiveness did not diminish over the years. The rumour was that she was so elegant that anyone who passed by their house would deliberately slow down to watch her water her flowers on her balcony. She remained for years the rage of London: 'Even at this date, there remain a few aged gentlemen whose eyes sparkle and whose checks flush when they recall the charms of the lovely creature who became the wife of ungainly Edward Law.'[1]

In the 1790s, they lived in Bloomsbury Square, an appropriate place for lawyers and judges to live. They had thirteen children, of whom three died prematurely, a very similar ratio to his own mother and father. The first child, a boy and an heir, was produced promptly, yet morally, ten months and twenty days after the wedding day. Like his father, he had married slightly above himself but managed to close the gap as the years went by. He also produced a son who became more famous than him. This was the Georgian privileged family reproducing itself along predictable lines.

Not much is known about the quality of their relationship. Joseph Farington, a leading artist and power behind the Royal Academy, suggested that it was not good: 'Lady Ellenborough is a fine woman and much liked. He is said to be, not with the least cause for it, very jealous of her, and his temper is very controlling.'[2]

One highly touted story tells us something about their relationship. It was recycled in books of collected witticisms for a century after his death, and it rather backs up Farington's view. Lord Ellenborough was about to go on the assize circuit when Lady Ellenborough said that she should like to accompany him. He replied that he had no objections, provided she did not encumber the carriage with bandboxes which were his utter abhorrence. They set off together on the 'first day's journey', so it was probably the Midland or Northern Circuit, until an accidental discovery piqued his anger:

> Lord Ellenborough, happening to stretch his legs, struck his feet against something below the seat. He discovered that it was a bandbox. His indignation is not to be described: up went the window and out went the bandbox. The coachman stopped and the footmen thinking that the bandbox had tumbled out of the window by some extraordinary chance were going to pick it up, when Lord Ellenborough furiously called out, Drive on![3]

He had, of course, thrown his own wig out of the window. She had obeyed orders, and her husband had jumped to the conclusion that she had not done so. His failure to take his wife's view into account is all the more surprising because without his wife's business brain, he would not have had a coach to go anywhere. Her correspondence with her husband's coach makers, Collingridge and Rowley, has survived, and she is clearly a force to be reckoned with, especially as this company held a Royal Warrant. In 1808, she wrote to them in the third person, complaining that his Lordship's coach was not ready for his return to town and that her own coach and her barouche (an opened-topped carriage for stylish trips around town) needed to be ready by Friday.

One of Anne's duties was to be charitable. In 1812, one particular act of charity was noted by the newspapers:

> One hundred poor women and children in Waldershare Kent and in its neighbourhood were clothed from head to foot in suitable apparel by the benevolence of Lady Ellenborough, the amiable hostess house. The poor sons afterwards accompanied her Ladyship and family to Waldershare church and returning to the mansion were plentifully supplied with soup to carry to their respective homes, and each of them were further [given] with one shilling in money.[4]

This was Georgian charity in a nutshell; the women and children would be selected from among the blameless poor, and if the women were not widows, then their husbands would be vetted too. It was Lord Ellenborough's cash being used, but the lady of the family is framed with the appropriate feminine value of Christian charity and benevolence. The role of religion is obvious, as is the use of soup; the only surprise is that cash was handed out as it was commonly believed that the poor could only be trusted with charity in kind. The Ellenboroughs must have known these poor people very well or have been able to monitor and control their behaviour.

She had two duties: to be a mother and to be a public figure. One was essentially private and the other public, but as she was a celebrity, both were given publicity. Like other ladies of her rank, she was expected to preside over social occasions and attend them; this was even more important after 1802, when her husband was a public figure. The outward-facing events were mostly routs (drinks, conversation and a little music with a few dozen people – a 'grand rout' could be a hundred or so) and assemblies (dancing, eating, gossiping and match-making). There would also be smaller-scale social occasions and charitable work. Events were highly gender-specific. Men held dinners, women hosted music, routs, assemblies and children's balls. On one occasion, the Ellenboroughs held two events in their house on the same day: a rout for the ladies and a formal dinner for the Lord's political friends. Most of this would be packed into the London season, with other times being spent in fashionable spas or sea-bathing resorts.

The period from 1803 to 1805 took a toll on Anne. It started well in January 1803 when she appeared at court, possibly for the first time as the wife of a hereditary lord, alongside almost every member of the political and religious establishment except her own husband. Ellenborough differed from most members of the Georgian establishment because he had a job that obliged him to be in a certain place at a certain time; this was unusual but not particularly onerous. The legal terms were short and the parliamentary ones not much longer, and for the first half of the year they overlapped, so there was time to do other things, but occasionally it was convenient and acceptable to go without him to major events.

Anne held a rout in early June 1803 at her house in Bloomsbury. It was advertised in the newspaper, not as an invitation but as an example of what the '*bon ton*' (elegant society) were up to; there were five other similar events on the same day under the heading 'Fashionable Arrangements for This Week'. She was seven months' pregnant at the time, a reminder that she was hosting the events rather than organising them. In August 1803 the newspapers reported she was out of danger after her recent pregnancy or *accouchement*, as the preferred term was. It sounded more genteel in French, but it obscured the terrible dangers of childbirth in the Georgian era. In this case, the worst happened, and the child died after a few days. The crisis had taken place when Lord Ellenborough was in Croydon on assize court business. He arrived home a day before the child died.

The newspapers were interested and sympathetic. They reminded everybody that she was a credit to her husband, who was described by one highly partisan newspaper as a 'dignified prop of the British Constitution'. Had she not been linked to such a patriotic bulwark, her sufferings would have been relegated to the level of' 'unfortunate mishaps' that befell all women in the Georgian era. In response to her continuing ill-health, she left for recuperation in Bath in early November 1803; she was still there and no better on 16 December and returned to town.[5]

Anne was successfully delivered on a daughter, Frederica, in April 1805, but tragedy struck again almost exactly four years after the first one when she gave birth to a still-born son in August 1807. Part of the recuperation included visits to Tunbridge Wells, Bath and Brighton. She was away from home in Tunbridge Wells in October 1807; she was out in the carriage with her husband and Lady Donegal when they witnessed a whiskey carriage overturn. Lady Ellenborough did not quite see it, and she was persuaded not to look because of her delicate health. Georgian road accidents could be appalling, with bodies crushed and limbs amputated under the weight of the machines. The injured were placed into Lady Ellenborough's carriage, doubtless to linger in the nearest inn until a surgeon could be summoned, and Mary Berry, the diarist who recorded the incident, walked to Tunbridge with his lordship.[6]

Lady Ellenborough was in Brighton again in December 1807. The *Morning Post* reported that her health was precarious when she arrived but had improved due to warm water bathing. Only the best was acceptable – she patronised Williams Warm Baths. In August, they were praised by *the Morning Herald*: 'Williams Baths are in very fashionable request. Numerous elegantes were in hot water there this morning.'

She had started her recuperation in Bath in early November, with the papers reporting that she was ill and was taking the waters there. At the end of December, she and her husband were at the promenading party on the glazed red-brick pavement at the Steine in Brighton. On later occasions, they also rode in their carriage – their equipage – in the same area. She was bathing and promenading on Christmas Eve. They must have visited as a family; in January 1808 they were still in Brighton, and the children had measles. All this was newsworthy.

Her movements around the country were also reported in the newspapers, under such headings as the 'Mirror of Fashion'. In some newspapers, it was the 'Fashionable World' or the 'Oracle of Fashion' or any permutation. Bath, Worthing, Tunbridge Wells, and the then-fashionable Ramsgate, were popular, but the key destination was Brighton. Thousands of the *bon ton* arrived there in the summer, but only a small percentage were worthy of comment. Lady Ellenborough arrived there in August 1802, and was announced in the local papers as a 'fashionable arrival'. Most followed the example of the Prince Regent, arriving and departing when he did and therefore defining the fashionable session. Few knew him personally, but Lady Ellenborough was in that number.

She was in Brighton on 12 August 1802 to celebrate the Prince Regent's birthday while her husband was still on the assize circuit. One patriotic newspaper reported the excellent news that the prince's bedroom in the pavilion had been altered to allow a view of the Steine from his pillow. Another piece of gossip from the evening meal for 400 was that 'neither His Royal Highness, nor the Duke of Clarence, nor Duke d'Orleans, danced'. Another newspaper announced that the full moon lit up the celebrations even more, almost suggesting that the heavenly bodies were allied to the prince's wishes.

Lady Ellenborough was in Brighton again in October 1802; at this time of year the *bon ton* would be thinking about returning to London, and indeed they were, said the newspaper, until the excellent weather induced them to change their plans; the fact that Lady Ellenborough was *not* doing something was also worthy of news. The whole family was present at a field day for the Prince of Wales's regiment, the 10th Light Dragoons. The Prince Regent was also in his military uniform, which he had designed himself. It was more a change of location than personnel: she would be eating, drinking and socialising with the same people as London as they all made their way down to Brighthelmstone, as some still called it, every August and December. Wilberforce called the resort 'Piccadilly by the Seaside'; this was not meant to be a compliment, but was a reassurance for most of the *bon ton*. He also believed that it was a place to be avoided in winter, presumably because of the company rather than the climate.

Apart from set pieces like this – the military provided a lot of entertainment in the resort towns – there were other novel activities. The Ellenboroughs exact activities are unknown, but they would have included listening to the band on the esplanade, warm bathing near (but not in) the English Channel, visiting the theatre, and attending subscription concerns. Lady Ellenborough had a cultural hinterland; we have evidence that Lady Ellenborough played whist (although the game was so ubiquitous that evidence was hardly necessary). She attended the opera, watched *Don Giovanni* with the children and listened to Handel (which cost her half a guinea). She enjoyed a musical evening at Bartleman's Vocal Concerts at Hanover Square. Her friend Mary Berry accompanied her and spent most of the time judging the audience. Lady Ellenborough may have done the same.[7]

Anne was in Brighton in 1808, as one of the 400 people eating simultaneously at the Pavilion (called the 'Chinese Palace' by its detractors).

An invitation from the Prince Regent was in fact a command, although in reality there is no reason to believe that it was unwelcome. She was not with her husband in December 1815 when the Prince Regent (and his mother, Queen Charlotte) held a concert at the Pavilion; dinner was a 6 pm, and the concert started at 8.30. The queen retired to bed at 12 pm, and then the whole party would take on a different, more decadent hue. Lady Ellenborough was also there on twelfth night 1816 with her husband. Mrs Fitzherbert, the Prince Regent's first and illegal Catholic wife, was present. She was mentioned on most of the guest lists, which also included the Ellenboroughs. Like the rest of the establishment, they knew about the prince's outrageous and unconstitutional marriage in 1785.

At parties the prince was loud, greedy and indiscreet. He told dirty jokes, asked inappropriate questions, and peered shamelessly at any exposed parts of women's anatomy that appealed to him. But he could also be personally charming and attentive, and his love of the arts and literature was real, not an affectation. Both Ellenboroughs knew the Pavilion well, though it is not known what they thought of it. They probably did not concern themselves with the amount of money spent, or the fact that it was finished in 1823 and that the prince had stopped going there a year earlier, losing interest in Brighton and its ungrateful citizens (who by 1816 were hissing him in the street because of his treatment of his wife and child – see Chapter Twelve) and transferring his affections to Ramsgate in a fit of pique.

There were other occasions for merriment on the south coast. Lady Ellenborough (and her husband) were also present when 'reels, waltzes and strathspeys' were danced at Copeland's Assembly Rooms in Dover in November 1811. It was the culmination of a few days of dance, plays, concerts and card parties organised by the Royal Buckinghamshire Militia. At another sumptuous dinner in Dover in the year before, Lady Ellenborough's dress was most superb: it was black lace, richly ornamented with diamonds, and her headdress consisted of a plume of brilliants with a necklace, cross and earrings of the same, reported one admiring newspaper.

In June 1809, her final son, William Towry Law, was born. She had her last child, Frances Henrietta, in February 1812, at the age of 43. By 1813, her two eldest sons were already married. Edward, the heir, had married Mary Octavia Stewart, sister of Lord Castlereagh; Lady Ellenborough and Lady Castlereagh knew each other well and attended the same social occasions. Two years earlier, the second son, Charles Ewan, shocked the family by marrying in Gretna Green, then regularising their liaison three weeks later in London. The jaunt to Gretna in the Georgian era was more about a fait accompli for the disapproving family than a grand romantic gesture.[8]

Lady Ellenborough performed her duty of introducing her daughters to society. In 1806, she held a 'children's ball', and that would also have been training and experience for her daughters and those of her friends. The first mention of a formal event was in 1807 at a civic reception for the Duke of Wellington, when Lady Ellenborough was probably accompanied by her eldest daughter, Mary-Frederica, born in 1796. By 1813 there is more regular evidence that her children started to accompany her to social occasions. One of the daughters appears at a ball in Ramsgate in September 1813 – 'a very fine and beautiful girl' – said the *Star*, in a rare comment about appearance. From that point on, it was the Misses Law in the plural, so the exact number is unknown.[9]

Lady Ellenborough appears to have been more lively and fun-loving than her husband, but that, of course, was a low bar. There are some clues: her reputation as a beauty; her penchant for flower arrangement at their first house on Bloomsbury; but mostly her love of dancing, particularly the waltz. This dance was a little risqué; originally the dance of the south German peasant classes, it involved a man dancing with a woman with his arm around her back, and this shocked respectable society. Lady Ellenborough danced the waltz early enough to be fashionable, but late enough not to shock. She was 'valtzing' again at her friend Lady Keith's in 1814, after attending a function at Lady Derby's. In June 1814, she spent an evening with her husband at Vauxhall Gardens, a place of dancing, overpriced eating, loud music, fireworks and, for some couples, discreet night-time journeys into the wooded and forested areas. Anne would have enjoyed the evening more than Edward.

Lady Ellenborough was seriously ill with dropsy (oedema, as it is called today), from November 1814 until at least April 1815, when the *Carlisle Patriot* reported that she had at one time been on the point of death. Modern medicine identifies dropsy as caused by problems of the heart, liver or kidneys, or malnutrition. We can probably rule out the last one. The main effect was the accumulation of fluid in the body, often in the abdomen but also in the arms, legs and face. It was painful to have, hard to cure, and often fatal. Those who died of it literally drowned in their own secretions.

The Ellenboroughs would have known the implications of long term chronic illnesses like dropsy and gout. Her brother-in-law, John Law, died miserably of gout in 1810, having been in appalling pain for a year. The Prince Regent had gout and dropsy in his final years, which were spent in Windsor in painful misery. Charles James Fox died of it in 1806. When the obligatory reassurances were given to Fox about his recovery, the suffering politician knew the truth. Was there nothing that could be done about the accumulation of fluid in his body? 'No,' was the reply, 'if the water is let out by one vent, it will only be to make room for more.'[10]

Purging and diuretics were one way to recovery, often through quack medicine advertised in newspapers containing poisons like antimony, which not only induced urination but also vomiting, and it was the vomiting that stopped the antimony from killing the patient. Other less painful but less effective methods involved inducing extreme sweating to reduce the amount of liquid being carried. The same effect could be achieved by administering emetics to induce vomiting or using laxatives to expel liquid and waste matter. Her illness could have involved some or all of these things; untreated dropsy was invariably fatal, as vital organs would be compressed until they failed, and it is a reminder that even the privileged life of the rich and famous could be stopped in its tracks by a horrible, debilitating disease. It is to be hoped that Lady Ellenborough would have avoided the worst of this rogue medicine, but the ruling class tended to take the same pills and potions as the rest of the population when faced with a disease that they could not cure. The popularity of pills and potions (vapour baths, fumigations and frictions) was partly because the alternative, tapping, was horrible. Tapping usually involved draining the affected area with a long curved syringe inserted into the navel or abdomen. Like much of the response to dropsy, the process was as dangerous as the condition itself. Knowledge of germ theory and causes of infection was very limited, and tapping many times naturally increased the risk. It is possible that she was not tapped at all, or very little.

In late spring 1815, the newspapers reported a revival in the hopes of her friends, which was shorthand for 'not going to die yet'. However, during this period, she still seemed to be obliged to fulfil her duties. She arrived in Brighton on 3 December 1814, which could be considered a health benefit for a sick woman (although no amount of sea air or bathing could help somebody with dropsy). She also attended the Prince Regent's New Year's Eve Party, so her illness may have been intermittent.

After her illness, her appearance and hosting increased. From about 1815 to her husband's death, she seemed to go to many events on her own or with her daughters. This was acceptable without being usual; in June 1815, she attended, with more than one daughter (the breathless report said 'Misses Law' again), an assembly at the London mansion of Richard Wharton, MP for Durham, given by his wife. There were fruits, sweets and flowers everywhere, and (once again) 200 people. Anne may have enjoyed the evening; there is some evidence that she did, given her love of dancing, but she was on duty that night as well. Her daughters needed to be married off, and that evening in Grafton Street was a chance to meet the right people.

In May 1815, the Ellenboroughs gave a Grand Ball at their house in St James's Square. The newspaper reported that it was the 'first in a series of years' – a possible consequence of her illness, and the fact that the man of the house would never have expected to organise such events. There were 200 people present in three drawing rooms, illuminated by the finest-cut glass chandeliers. The dancing would have taken place in the largest room, saving the others for networking, matchmaking and gossip. Unusually, there was no set period for eating, just constant grazing all night. Everybody who mattered was there: the Prince Regent made a quick visit, and the newspapers listed the guests in order of seniority. Quadrilles were danced, that was traditional, and the waltz, which was quite new. Nothing much happened until just before midnight, and the party broke up about 4 am. The first dance was the Honourable Miss Law and the Dutch Ambassador – this was a marriage market, and the person who paid the bills got to show off their daughter first.

Two weeks later, Lady Ellenborough was entertaining again, this time it was Wednesday, 14 May. This was a rout, a social gathering with drinks and chat starting at 10 and finishing at 12, so most of her guests could go somewhere else and Anne could go to Willis's, another socially prestigious assembly. She was there again two weeks later, once more with two of her daughters in tow. It probably took place within Almacks, the most prestigious assembly of the London season, and by sought-after invitation only.

She organised routs, grand routs and musical evenings. She attended the Countess of Derby's Grand Concert in April 1816 and then went on to the Countess of Jersey's grand rout. Lady Ellenborough attended the ball of Lady Liddell in Portland Place in July 1816. It was highly illuminated, of course, but it was special in that the floor was chalked; this would prevent the dancers from slipping, and anything but white chalk would rub into the shoes. The floor was decorated with flowers and Etruscan scrolls, which would have taken days to do but hours to rub off:

> A great proportion of the company, as is usual, neither danced nor played: their attention was greatly occupied in surveying the tasteful style of decoration displayed around, and they were not a little delighted with the inspection of the landscape paintings (admirable productions) which were in the different apartments, the whole of them executed by the fair hostess.

About two o'clock, supper was announced, which was 'in every respect elegant'. The company sat down at fourteen round tables in the great eating room and the library, 200 people were served at once: 'The rooms rivalled the meridian sun in splendour, and there were innumerable clusters of oil lamps with wax candles affixed to the walls, shedding a pure and tranquil light around. The royal Dukes of Clarence and Gloucester were much gratified.'

Marriages followed, eventually. Mary Frederica (born 1796) married a major general in the army in 1827, moved around the Empire with him and became a minor painter of the Canadian landscape. Their son, Douglas, died at Sevastopol in 1855 during the Crimean War, aged 23.

Elizabeth-Susan (born 1799) was an unpublished poet and novelist who called herself 'ESL'. It seems clear that she had spent some time in cultural pursuits in Italy around 1820. She wrote the three-canto poem 'Giustina', a romance set in Spain, clearly commenting on the tyranny of fathers and the mercenary way they married off their daughters. She married Charles Abbott, second baron Colchester and a naval commander admiral, when she was 37, and Abbott was a year older. She continued her literary endeavours after marriage, changing her name to ESC, but remaining unknown both in her lifetime and afterwards. According to the unpublished memoirs of her husband, she spent her life collecting newspaper reports of her brother's life, keeping house and visiting foreign spas for her health. She did charitable work, of course, with the Royal Naval Female School for the Education of the Daughters of Necessitous Officers of the Navy.

In 1832 Frances Henrietta, aged 20, married Charles de Voeux, aged 30. His family was Irish, had given up on their Catholicism and had made a fortune in India. He was a diplomat and friend and translator of the German poet and playwright Johann Wolfgang von Goethe. Her uncle, George Law, Bishop of Bath and Wells, conducted the service. Voeux died suddenly the next year while on a diplomatic posting to Brussels. Frederica Selina (born 1805) married Henry James Ramsden in 1829, the third son of a baronet and a captain in the army. He was a captain in the 9th Lancers during the time when Frederica's brother Edward was governor-general of India.. Anne Law (born 1800) did not marry until 1841, when she became the second wife of the seventy-one year- old Admiral John Colville.

Apart from a slight artistic bent in the family, a few rather late-in-life marriages, and some possibly rebellious spirits, the daughters married conventionally into the armed forces and diplomatic service. Anne had done her duty.

Chapter Six

Unpopular with Lord Kenyon

When Lloyd Kenyon was appointed Chief Justice of the King's Bench – the most senior position in the Common Law Courts at the time and still the head of the judiciary in England and Wales today – his future successor Edward Law was a nobody who had just received (or was about to receive) his first retainer from Warren Hastings. On paper, Lloyd Kenyon and Edward Law were similar. Kenyon was rough, combative, hard-working and very rude. Kenyon had a hatred of change, even tiny ones, on any subject whatsoever, especially after the convulsions of the French Revolution. His memorial inscription attests to his devotion to 'Religion, Law, and Order'.[1]

Kenyon was born twenty years before Law and joined the Middle Temple on 7 November 1750, a week before Law was born. He joined the Northern Circuit in 1762, eighteen years before Law, became an MP in 1780, twenty years before Law, and became the Attorney General in 1782, once again twenty years before Law achieved that position. In the late 1760s, he became a special pleader, like Law, and made a fortune from his opinions. He was famed for doing so; Wilberforce said he could produce correct opinions, 'as man would crack walnuts after dinner'.

Their career paths look similar, but there was one major difference: 'Taffy' Kenyon, as he was called when he wasn't in the room, was the son of minor Welsh gentry, with no university education at all but lots of early experience of low-grade legal work. He was insufficiently connected in his younger years to attend Charterhouse or Cambridge, and his general (non-legal) knowledge was limited. Campbell suggested that, to his dying day, Kenyon believed that the sun orbited the earth. Law, like other members of the establishment, made jokes about his meanness and lack of general knowledge.

Unlike Law, he had nothing to talk about at dinner parties, which was perhaps another reason why he did not hold them. He was God-fearing, austere, and morally outraged by gambling and adultery, and he was rebuked by the Prince Regent for accurately linking him to gambling clubs. In 1799, he suggested the death penalty for adultery. He was a member of the establishment who did not quite fit in.

This did not matter because Kenyon refused to take part in the social round and refused to spend money. He was a noted penny-pincher, even the deferential press said so at the time. Kenyon was a miser in the ultimate sense that he worked equally hard at not spending money as he did accumulating vast amounts of it. It was rumoured that he only had one handkerchief, and when he suffered from catarrh in court, he wiped his nose on one of his only two wigs. It was said that he wore the same black coat for fourteen years, and eventually it turned green. Kenyon had died with assets of £314,000, all earned through his own efforts, but it was a regular source of embarrassment that he had achieved this with so little grace and spent it with so little style.

However, Kenyon was the boss until the grim reaper had his say, and he made Law's life difficult whenever possible. He was known to ostentatiously stop listening when Law spoke. Kenyon would assault him from the bench using the impunity of a judge in the same way Law would do later. When Law did fill the dead man's shoes, one of his first pronouncements was that he would be more considerate to council than his predecessor; everybody knew that it was more of a rebuke to Kenyon rather than a promise to be a nicer person.

Kenyon was prone to using odd language. Metaphors would escape his competence – he once accused a thieving butler of feathering his own nest with his master's bottles; his use of Latin often had officials scratching their heads. Law was one of the most likely and most able to snigger at his efforts. Kenyon's hatred of Law was made even more unusual by the fact that Kenyon generally had no favourites – apart from Thomas Erskine, who was also Law's slightly more successful and more popular rival. Law was particularly upset that Kenyon would interrupt him in a hostile manner (a little rich considering his own later reputation), whereas Erskine was heard in silence. On one occasion Law had had enough:

> Perhaps, gentlemen, I may, without arrogance assume that I have successfully disposed of the observations of my learned

> friend and that the strong case I made for my client remains unimpeached. Still, my experience in this court renders me fearful of the result. I dread a power with which I am not at liberty to combat. When I have finished, the summation is to follow.

Then he turned to Erskine: '*Non me tua fervida terrent Dicta, ferox.*'

He then made a bow to the Chief Justice, and as he sat down, he added in a low, solemn tone, '*Di me terrent et Jupiter hostis.*'

Law did not translate the last line, but it was not a compliment, and was said because he knew Kenyon could not understand it: 'I am not frightened by your heated words, fierce one. The gods and the enemies of Jupiter frighten me.'

Kenyon did not recognise this as a quotation from Virgil's *Aeneid*, and did not realise it was far from a compliment; he compounded his embarrassment by bowing slightly to acknowledge the remark.[2]

Law always liked an easy target. When at a dinner he heard that Kenyon was at death's door, he remarked, 'Dying? What would he get from that?' Even given the crude manners of the age, this was a bit much. Victorian apologists suggested that he was lightening the news with a joke, but in reality, Law was saying that Kenyon the miser calculated everything. He would have known that Kenyon's son had died tragically six months earlier and may have known that Kenyon had commented that there was room for another as he wept over his son's tomb – but his quip was still hilarious, and there were more of them. His memorial motto after death, '*Mors Janua Vitae*' ('Death, the gateway to life') was misspelt by the printer who left off the final 'e'. When Law heard this, he disagreed: 'Mistake! It is no mistake. The considerate testator left particular directions in his will that the estate should not be burdened with the expense of a diphthong.'

Kenyon was more traditional and paternalistic towards the poor than most of the up-and-coming lawyers and politicians. Help was certainly needed by 1800. Food prices, which had risen slowly but inexorably for years, rose so fast in the 1790s that the poor were feeling the pinch, and mass hunger made its last appearance in British history. Joseph Farington at the Royal Academy banned the use of bread by his pampered students in 1795, not in solidarity with the poor but to stop his precious students from throwing it at each other as a lark. Bread, the stuff of life for the poor, was a way of erasing pencil drawings for the rich. Instead of help, the poor were urged to eat stale bread, use poor-quality flour, or settle for brown bread – which was seen as inferior. The Prince Regent banned bread for the soldiers under his command but then rather missed the point by replacing it with vegetables. His father took to eating inferior-quality bread and gained the unflattering nickname 'Brown George'. The most unrealistic suggestion to the poor was that they buy their necessities in bulk. The poor could not buy in larger quantities because the rich had already done it, both increasing the price and reducing the quantity available.

After the terrible food shortages of recent times, especially the dearths and high prices of 1795–6 and 1800–1, Kenyon believed the poor deserved help from the state to guarantee their basic necessities, and it was the responsibility of the law to uphold this. Kenyon would also have agreed with the establishment view that poor harvests were acts of God and had to be borne stoically, but with the help of the rich. However, he also knew that the system was increasingly rigged against the poor, and only judges such as himself could protect them from parvenu commercial types who had no belief in a duty to the poor and just wished to make money.

Other common abuses were forestalling – preventing goods from coming to market, and engrossing – buying large amounts and breaking them into smaller amounts to maximise profits. Both activities were made illegal by a statute of Edward VI in 1552. After 1772, in a bout of enthusiasm for free and unregulated trade (although the book that inspired it, Adam Smith's *Wealth of Nations*, was still four years away), these commercial transactions were no longer criminal activities.

Sometimes this problem would come to the courts. In *Rex v Rusby* in 1800, John Rusby was accused of regrating – that is, buying food (in this case corn) at a market and selling it at the same market on the same day at a higher price. Rusby was found guilty. Kenyon made his position clear. The 1772 Act of Parliament had, unfortunately, been repealed, but it was still in contravention of common law as it harmed the whole community. If persons of rank were entitled to their comforts, the poor ought not to be deprived of their necessities. The deserving poor who cannot support themselves must be helped, and that was more important than Rusby's profits.

Kenyon was not radical. You did not become the chief legal officer of the kingdom that way. He believed in a social contract between the rich and the poor and obligations that bound them together based on community, tradition and religion. He was not going to let the views of an economist break a centuries-long tradition. Unfortunately, his denunciation of greed did not pacify or reassure the common people, it just emboldened them to protest and increased public disorder. On the day that the jury found Rusby guilty the price of foodstuffs fell, and Rusby's house in London was ransacked and his life threatened. Songs were sung and graffiti scrawled on walls, praising the Chief Justice to the skies, and the politicians looked on aghast; it was not the role of the nation's leading law officer to provide a genteel invitation for the poor to riot. Many members of the establishment honestly believed that it was Kenyon's judgement that had caused the problem, not the price of basic necessities.

Another case that was taking place contemporaneously was *Rex v Waddington* (1800). Samuel Waddington was a rich London businessman who decided to use his money to buy up as many hops as he could in Worcestershire and Kent and, using his monopoly, to sell them on for much higher prices. He was accused of buying hops in advance of the harvest from growers, organising hop merchants to demand higher prices, and spreading false rumours about scarcity.

Waddington hired seven expensive defence lawyers, one of whom adopted both a patronising and combative approach during proceedings in November 1800. It was, to all accounts, very long and very skilfully constructed. His initial argument infuriated Kenyon: hops were not food; a rather specious point as they were used in the production of beer and to preserve food. The lawyer then wished to know what law had been broken – he was sure that his learned friend would tell him that it was still an offence under common law, but they were still being left groping in the dark. A man could put any price on an item that he put up for sale. Trade would find its proper level. High prices led to economy, and imports freely added to supply. This new orthodoxy came from the Wealth of Nations. The lawyer wanted to know: had the learned judge read Adam Smith, who suggested that state interference only distorted the market and raised prices, and had compared persecution of such people with a mediaeval witch hunt? Every country magistrate had, it was implied, and then further implied that old Kenyon did not understand anything new. It was a book 'not sufficiently studied, but well known in this courtroom'.

Then Waddington weighed in in his own defence, but became his own worst advocate. Waddington repeated the comments that would become common for the next two centuries: commerce would perish and the country would be in ruins if men like him were not given free reign. He had not read the room adequately, and then went on to make his defence lawyer pull his hair out by saying that he was not pleading for mitigation but declaring that the crime was not real.

Waddington's argument was clear and quite modern. He was an out-and-out free marketeer; a man had the right to use his capital as he saw fit. Everybody should pursue their own narrow interests and this would, in a miraculous way that was never quite explained, lead to the prosperity of all. The only plausible example was that Waddington admitted making forehand bargains with hop growers, which he claimed helped them with their planning and cash flow. But it didn't wash with Kenyon.

Georgian Juries were not expected to confer for very long before giving their verdict – indeed, they were encouraged to huddle while seated and have the most perfunctory of chats. The system did not encourage discussion or delay. Juries were forbidden food and heat if they chose to go away to deliberate.

Kenyon was convinced that men like Waddington were not good for the poor and told the jury as much: this was human mendacity, not the work of the Almighty:

> It is said that people have no more reason to fear forestalling, engrossing, and regrating than they have to fear witchcraft. It is easy for a man to write a treatise in his closet, but if he would go to the distance of 200 miles from London and observe people at every avenue of a country town buying up butter, cheese, and all the necessaries of life they can lay hold of in order to prevent them from coming to market.[3]

Anybody who believed that it was good for the poor for food to double in price could not have good or God on their side. Then Kenyon quoted from a slightly older authority on human morality, Proverbs 11:26: 'He that withholdeth corn, the people shall curse him: but blessings shall be upon the head of him that selleth it.'

Prosecution barrister Erskine had announced the victory, and pronounced it glad tidings for the poor. The poor certainly supported Kenyon, and a popular cartoon of the time by Isaac Cruikshank shows a giant Kenyon 'flailing the forestallers'. The establishment was outraged. Rusby's house had been attacked in September, and the poor were agitated and liable to riot once again.[4]

The pushy defence lawyer hired by both Rusby and Waddington – the man who pushed Kenyon's patience to the limit and had been defeated by Erskine – was Edward Law. This did not make Kenyon hate him – he hated him already.

Law was to be Kenyon's successor as Chief Justice; there would be no more trials that punished the rich for market manipulation. Three weeks later Law became Attorney General, and after Kenyon died there were no more attempts to regulate the market and protect the poor from monopolists. Law represented the hard-headed future: the new dawn for the poor was a false one.

Chapter Seven

Rising Like an Aeronaut

In 1800, Law was an eminent member of the legal profession with an impressive but increasingly distant reputation from the trial of Warren Hastings. He was rich, but he wasn't famous, and he was approaching 50. Law may have been the coming man in the 1790s, but the reality was that progress had stalled. Up until now, his friends, families and connections had allowed him to climb the greasy pole, but the opposite of that phenomenon is also true. Relying on power, networks and nepotism for advancement was a double-edged sword. When it was working, it provided its own momentum, and people knew it. 'Power and patronage have a natural tendency to produce their own growth, for support is willingly lent to those who are already strong and who can hold out the expectation of returning more than is given.'[1]

But when patronage stops, so does progress; a man with more enemies than friends can make no new friends. Law's career had been launched by the Hastings' impeachment, but that success created resentment now. Law was also the son of a Whiggish bishop, and the Tory administration would eternally hold this against him – and the Pitt government seemed to be holding power eternally. As a gentleman, he only made the newspapers in the marriage, births and deaths column; as an eminent lawyer, only when one of his legal opinions on insurance or commercial law was circulated beyond the legal profession. He was stuck, and he knew it. He had 'crawled along the ground without being able to raise himself from it', he told his friend William Paley.[2]

This is a little melodramatic. Pitt *had* given him something: he was made the Attorney General of Lancaster in 1793. In 1794, he prosecuted the radical Thomas Walker in Manchester for a conspiracy to overthrow the constitution. Walker was everything Law hated, in his eyes, a political monster borne straight out of the French revolution, although when it transpired that a government spy had lied in the witness box, Law organised the consequential prosecution for perjury. In the same year, he prosecuted John Horne Tooke for treason. At one point in the trial, a witness overheard the defendant say, is it possible to get ready by Thursday? Law interpreted this as the first day of the insurrection but it actually referred to the preparation of a pamphlet condemning government corruption. Tooke was acquitted, but Law must have got some satisfaction from the five months Tooke spent in the Tower of London. Law did his bit in the turbulent 1790s in prosecuting the state's enemies, but that was his job.

So, by his strenuous actions, he had rid himself of Whiggery, but Pitt had enough real friends not to need to bother with Edward Law. He would only rise when Pitt fell, and then only if the replacement was more amenable. Pitt was not the only obstacle. Lord Kenyon was not yet dead – not that it was important to Law if he had no friends to promote him into his job.

Law gained his promotion by patiently waiting for the grim reaper to do his job and by awaiting a change in the political landscape. Luckily for Law, they occurred in the correct order. Pitt succumbed first, in 1801, if only temporarily. Lloyd Kenyon expired permanently in April 1802, and the two events in tandem allowed Law to rise. Pitt had resigned because the king would not support his measure of Catholic emancipation, nor even allow the subject to be brought up in his company.

So Law's rapid rise only began at the age of 51, and not a moment too soon. He received his first of many promotions in February 1801. Pitt's replacement as Prime Minister was Henry Addington, later Lord Sidmouth, who appointed Law as Attorney General 'at one bound'. Law had missed out on one step: it was usual for the Attorney General to serve as Solicitor General first, but that job went to Spencer Perceval because that is what Addington wanted. So, Law had already omitted the first step upwards; it was common for ambitious men to decide which political faction would be successful and angle to be their Solicitor General, the first step on the ladder to being a high court judge.

The Attorney General was a government appointment, as it is today, and could change on a Prime Minister's whim, or a defeat at a general election. He was the government's chief legal officer and led prosecutions for the Crown; today the focus is on advice, as a separate body organises prosecutions. The job came with a knighthood and a seat in the House of Commons and was usually a signifier of even better things. Most of Law's legal colleagues had held the post, including Kenyon himself, Garrow, Gibbs, Wallace and Lee from his Northern Circuit days, and John Scott (Lord Eldon). Law would have expected to be Attorney General only for the lifetime of his enemy Lord Kenyon, assuming that there was no change in the political landscape.

Law now found that his abortive attempt to become a member of parliament during the Hastings impeachment was a blessing: most Attorneys General had done a stint in the Commons. Law was spared the humiliation of previous incumbents who had said something radical or even mildly opposed to the government of the day and had it repeated back to them when Attorney General. George III asked Law if he had ever been an MP, and when he received the answer he responded that at least he would not have to eat his own words, like most of his predecessors.

This promotion was a risk; there would be no going back to the Northern Circuit, and Addington reminded him of this. Law was given two days to think about it, but it took him mere seconds: 'I am yours, and let the storm blow from what quarter of the hemisphere it may you shall always find me at your side.'[3]

This was the beginning of a genuine, and genuinely beneficial, life-long friendship. Many of his character insights from this point come from his frank and friendly letters to his boss and friend, later Lord Sidmouth, and much of the national hatred for Law was because he was associated with Sidmouth's draconian policies as Home Secretary. The radicals condemned him as a puppet judge of a repressive state, and later historians quoted these words of absolute and unqualified support as if they were a terrible admission, but as a sentiment, it was par for the course at the time.

Law was responsible for only one major state prosecution during his time as Attorney General, but it was a momentous one. Law prosecuted Joseph Wall on behalf of the Crown for extreme cruelty. It was a disturbing case that created a great deal of interest and indignation, and for the only time in his life, Law found himself in alignment with both the government and the masses, who both wanted Wall to be found guilty and executed.

The trial took place at the Old Bailey on 20 January 1802, and Law opened the case for the prosecution. Wall was accused of the unlawful death of a soldier under his command at the Goree in present-day

Senegal – a disease-infested slaving and trade outpost of the Empire. Benjamin Armstrong, a sergeant in the African Corps, was one of a number of men flogged on Wall's orders. Armstrong, unsurprisingly, had not survived the 800 lashes he had received. Seven had been flogged, three of them received 800 lashes like Armstrong, and in total, three had died.

Wall's charge was that these poor soldiers committed mutiny but there had been no court martial, no official process prior to the offence, and to Law this was the reason why it was a crime. Law was not opposed to flogging in the army *per se*. Wall had turned up drunk at a parade and ordered the sadistic mass punishment. He then left the colony without permission, went into hiding in France and Italy, and did not return to contest the case until his return to England in 1801. There had been a reward on his head of £200 for all of that period, but it was irrelevant until his arrival home to clear his name. He had written a letter to the secretary of state to bring the matter to his attention. Law suggested in court that he had waited until all the possible witnesses were dead. What Law knew, and Wall now realised, was that two of them were still alive.

Perceval (Solicitor General, soon to be promoted to Attorney General) established that these soldiers had done no more than ask respectfully, hat in hand, for their arrears of pay. Had there actually been a mutiny, proven through evidence, there would have been nobody more supportive than Law. In any case, he would be obliged to prosecute for the Crown. It was clear that Wall had behaved appallingly, even by the standards of savage punishment allowed in the army. Armstrong was stripped, tied to a gun carriage, and given twenty-five lashes by a group of five before he died. They worked in teams, used large ropes, and were almost all Negro slaves, according to the witness.[4] Wall's words were thrown back to him by another witness: 'Lay on you black bastards: cut him to the heart: cut him to the liver.'

It tells us a great deal about the racial attitudes of Georgian society that the audience at the Old Bailey were particularly outraged at the 'humiliation' of Armstrong being flogged by black slaves. Using enslaved people to dole out punishment was unheard of.

Subsequent events reveal all the random cruelties of the English criminal system, with additional ones caused by Wall's celebrity and connections. The system had a strange and disconcerting mix of rigid application of the letter of the law, random mercy and unpredictable delay. His death sentence included more or less immediate execution and then a mandatory dissection and the lack of a body for the family to bury. Three weeks was the average time between hearing a death sentence and then receiving any reprieve; after that time, the agony would increase exponentially. The amount of notice might be zero, but he also might see a list of people to be hanged and had to scan it for his name.

His execution was immediately postponed, which was common, but then further delayed by the creation of a petition for mercy from Wall's influential friends, including the Duke of Norfolk, who was related to Wall's sister. These petitions were presented to the king himself and discussed on more than one occasion by the Privy Council, of which Law was a member. Then the execution was postponed a second time. This must have been agony for Wall – even if it is hard to feel sympathy for him, either then or now.

As a new date for his execution approached, 29 January, eight days after the sentence, Wall was informed that he would not receive a definitive yes or no answer before the morning; no news would be bad news, and good news could come at any time.

Wall could have heard the hammering of a scaffold being built outside Newgate at 4 am, for an execution scheduled for 11 am. He seemed to have slept through it, but was woken by the passing of the post coach, one of the few things that could be guaranteed to be timely. His wife gained permission to stay with her husband and wait for those final two hours: some reports say that her hope came from the fact that the Privy Council was meeting again. He was not chained in his prison cell, not even on his last night, though a guard was employed to watch him. 'Time hangs heavily: I am anxious for a close to this scene', he was reported as saying.[5]

The execution was in public; when Wall had been bound and partly blindfolded, he was brought up to the executioner. Three cheers went up from the crowd. The 'brutal effusion of one common sentiment', as one report put it. They were not merely interested or curious: they wanted him dead. However, the state's method of execution was as ramshackle and random as its judicial system. The short-drop method was still in use. The platform dropped, and he was 'launched into eternity', but not transported to it for another half hour. The rope had slipped to the back of his neck, preventing a clean break, and he choked to death. A handkerchief would have covered the convulsions on his face; his legs were not pulled quickly to speed his fate.

The establishment was self-congratulatory. The law applied to all with equal firmness, peer and peasant alike, it was claimed. The usual jokes were made about equity being founded on law. Law himself was tasked with the job of making an example of Wall. While Law was not against flogging in the army – as later events would prove – nor against execution for mutiny, he wished to apply the rules equally to all.

Law was moving quickly now. April 1802 was the most momentous month of his life. Kenyon died on 4 April. He had gone to Bath to restore his health, an almost certain indication of impending death for any elderly Georgian gentlemen: Law replaced him on 12 April, and was created Baron Ellenborough of Ellenborough by letters patent on the 19th, became a Privy Councillor on the 21st, and took his seat in the House of Lords on the 26th. The coat of arms has the motto from the Roman poet Horace, '*Compositum jus fasque animi*', which is officially translated as 'a mind that respects alike the laws of mutual justice and of God', but could be shortened to 'Law and Equity combined'.

His new post was the Chief Justiceship of the Court of the King's Bench, or Lord Chief Justice for short, and CJ for even shorter. He was the senior judge of all the common law courts and thus was at the top of the tree, with three assistants called puisne judges, which derives from the word 'puny', but is still a prestigious position. It remains, to this day, the most senior judicial appointment in England and Wales. It also came with a seat in the Lords, so the Commons was no longer convenient.

His friend and mentor Henry Addington, Lord Sidmouth, noted the transformation:

> Saturday 17 April. The gazette announces that the dignity of a baron is conferred on Sir Edward Law, late Attorney General and now Chief Justice in the Court of King's Bench. His name, style, and title is Baron Ellenborough of Ellenborough in the county of Cumberland. This successor of Lord Kenyon is a man of unblemished character, great mental powers, and profound legal knowledge.[6]

A man called Law in charge of the law began an avalanche of weak puns for the next two decades: the press could not resist: 'a kingdom where Law is Justice must inevitably flourish', punned one newspaper.[7]

His friend William Paley said that Law 'rose like an aeronaut', meaning a balloonist. There were celebrity balloonists in the late Georgian period: it was a brash and colourful activity, and it appealed to all classes. Both of them rose spectacularly, but the simile, you might imagine, could only go so far. Law was never brash and colourful, and his appeal certainly did not cross the class divide, but the rest of the comparison works quite well.

The aeronaut that Paley had in mind was Andre-Jacques Garnerin, who was enthralling Londoners with his ballooning antics in July 1802. He was a Frenchman in London, with the locals cheering him on in a balloon adorned with a Union flag and a tricolour. The Prince of Wales was another enthusiastic fan: he gave Garnerin a special letter that he could produce if he dropped out of the sky in rural Essex, to prove he wasn't a supernatural force for evil. If this sounds like a slur on the intelligence of those living in the sticks, it needs to be remembered that many Georgians distant from the centre of power had a reputation for limited horizons. The well-known story of the people of West Hartlepool hanging as a spy a pet monkey captured from a French warship was believed by the Victorians about their predecessors.

Perhaps Paley's comparison went further than he thought. Both Law and Garnerin had to wait for the weather to change in order to elevate themselves: both men failed at first. Both men prospered because the temporary end of the war in France allowed them to be centre stage – Garnerin could enter Britain, and Law could make it to the top of the establishment – and both men had the support of the Prince Regent if they got into trouble.

The Chief Justice was now an assize judge. Not all justice was dispensed in the capital, that would have been impracticable. Ellenborough and the other eleven High Court justices would perform their rounds of the regional court circuits twice a year. The decision was made at the Treasury Chambers at King's Bench, and it was tradition for the Chief Justice to have the first choice. In the first year of his elevation, Ellenborough decided to travel the Northern Circuit. He took with him as deputy Sir Alan Chambré, Chief Justice at the Court of Common Pleas and formerly one of his drinking companions at the Society of the Bears.

It was a long way to the Northern Circuit, even on England's rapidly improving roads, and Ellenborough, as Law, had done it many times. It was so difficult that often the winter circuit was omitted, and all six counties would only be visited in the summer. It is difficult to work out why he chose to endure it again; perhaps he wished to play the role of the local boy made good. In August 1802, he presided over the Carlisle Assizes and started the habit of a lifetime by giving the jury the benefit of his opinion, even when not legally required. He was glad to be back, he said; he had local connections, which everybody would have known, but that was not the point. He complemented his county compatriots with their relatively blameless way of life. He told the grand jury that they were ideally suited to judge the law and he would be here to advise them, and for perhaps the only time in his life with a jury, he used flattery rather than intimidation: 'He observed that the number of crimes committed in this county, when compared with the numbers committed in other places to which the distribution of justice had carried him, were not in proportion to its extent and population.' This seemed 'most sensibly to affect all present'.[8]

The criminal cases covered were indeed 'not malignant' and it was over in a few hours – another fact that would have lightened his mood. Henry James was found not guilty of stealing £500 of promissory notes; two men were acquitted for stealing parcels; and Robinson Wilson was imprisoned for a year for manslaughter.

Ellenborough had also come with his own agenda, another act to be repeated over the next two decades. Money needed to be spent on Carlisle's courtroom and the local prison. The Carlisle Assize building would not have been purpose built, and Ellenborough complained that it did not increase the dignity of the court or inspire awe in the minds of those in it. The Georgian state did little more than protect property, wage war, and run a post office; outside of the capital, the machinery of the justice system looked unprepossessing.

His other arenas were more fit for the dignity of the law, represented by himself: the Court of King's bench was cramped but intimidating, and the Old Bailey was even more threatening. The judges stood on a high platform on one side, surrounded by a semi-circular phalanx of the court's legal officials. Above the judge's head was a huge sword of justice, pointing down to the presiding judge and making a point in all senses of the word. The witness box was directly opposite, as far away as it could be: you would have to both talk loudly and listen carefully. Ellenborough always refused to speak up because he was convinced he was right about his volume as he was about everything else.

He continued with his lecture on the point of prisons to his Cumbrian jury. He suggested that the first objective of prisons was to deliver punishment efficiently. The second objective sounds more modern: not to harm the health of the inmates. The facilities were poor, there was not enough sex segregation, and this would make bad people worse: 'They who are already tainted become hardened in their iniquity, and they, if any such there be, who have entered those unhappy mansions without taint, come out into society depraved in their principles and conduct.'

This part of the criminal system was literally ramshackle. Nothing had improved four years later. The prison was in a terrible state, according to a report from 1806:

> Commons side, debtors have 4 free wards, 28 feet by 18, and a small room: but they are in a very dirty and ruinous state: with windows opening into the court: formerly they looked into the street. The sexes are separate at night, but together all day.
>
> The wards for felons are 2 rooms, down a step or two: dark, damp, and dirty: one of them, 7 yards by 5, the day room, which serves likewise as a night room, had a window to the street, through which spirituous liquors and tools for mischief might easily be conveyed, but it is now bricked up. The condemned room is only 11 feet by 9.[7]

Carlisle Assizes was remodelled as a purpose-built building in 1808 and the prison in 1827. Investment in prisons and courts was not to improve until the Victorian era; in the meantime, the system continued on the basis of organised random cruelty.

Ellenborough was back on the Northern Circuit in 1804 with his junior colleague, Sir Alan Chambré; the first case was the alleged murder of John Littlewood by Joseph Hobson (this author's fourth great-grandfather). The charge was reduced to manslaughter, and his junior seems to have presided over the assize in any case. Hobson was awarded a year in prison rather than a good chance of execution if convicted or murder – which means I am here to write these words.

Ellenborough visited all the circuits during his career, dealing with both criminal and civil cases. For example, in Essex he was presented by a man called Hudson, who pleaded in tears and was unable to speak, that he had burgled a house in desperation because he was starving. Ellenborough found him guilty, but was merciful. Contrition was always helpful, it proved who was in charge. At the same time, he sentenced a man called Cordun to two years in prison for stealing and fencing six pieces of wood belonging to the king. Ellenborough commented that crimes like this were endangering the Royal Forests. Once again, the punishment was not for the crime committed but for the consequences for property if it was repeated. The philosophy of punishment was not quite as it is today.

Chapter Eight

Protecting Asses and Assets

In 1818, men with nets strolled unchallenged into the grounds of a large house and farmstead in Roehampton. They found the lake and removed all the fish, leaving the small fry to die on the river banks. The rogues escaped by boat and were never seen again. They had got away with it, like most criminals did in the Georgian era. The householder was annoyed. He had recently bought the fine house, which meant he frequently travelled the muddy roads between Roehampton and Westminster, some of which were infested by highwaymen. He would travel with loaded pistols. The era of police patrols and regulated turnpikes had not quite arrived. Crime was a constant: almanacks announced the date of full moons, not for astronomical purposes but to advise about nighttime travel and when to stay at home.

The same gentleman had also had property stolen four years earlier. His bailiff, James Thornton, noticed John Purvis driving three asses through the street. Thornton must have been a new or incompetent employee, as he could not definitely recognise the animals as his master's property, and then swallowed the unlikely story that Purvis had bought them from some local gypsies. Purvis offered to show him the place where they had been purchased, hoping that the bailiff would not bother, but his bluff was called and they visited the 'location'. Thornton was convinced.

The next day, Thornton noticed his master's asses were missing. He retraced his steps, followed the ass prints in the snow (the winter of 1814 was the coldest of the century – soldiers froze to death at the roadside and an elephant crossed over the frozen Thames), and followed on foot seven miles to the Kennington toll booth, where he interviewed the turnpike keeper. It took two more days to find Purvis in a gipsy encampment in Ragmore Lane. The thief was imprisoned in a Clapham watch house but picked the lock. He was tracked to the George Public House in Kent Street, where patrol officer Snow apprehended him dancing with a gipsy princess. Three people were later indicted, and two were transported to New South Wales. This was a lot of effort for 'three asses, one very old'. They were worth £6. The gentleman to whom these fish and animals belonged was Lord Ellenborough.

The weaknesses of the Georgian legal system have already been evident in the treatment of Joseph Wall. The severity of the system is a modern cliché, and the list and extent of the capital crimes is well known, but the unpredictability of the process is a forgotten terror. Death was the theoretical punishment for over 200 crimes in England. In 1803, seventy-six people were executed. There were ten murderers and three rapists, but there was also William Bassett – a postman hanged in Kent for stealing a letter on his rather large postal round between Maidstone and Tonbridge. The system was almost random, and deliberately so; it was part of the contorted pantomime of the Georgian legal system. Legal reformer Sir Samuel Romily noted that, excluding crimes that were almost never pardoned – murder, treason, and counterfeiting – then the death penalty for crimes of property was not carried out on 95 per cent of occasions. Excessive punishments could be remitted if there was enough begging and grovelling from the plebs, and this had the added advantage of reminding them where power lay.

A criminal law system that both condemns and reprieves freely sounds like a system that would destroy its own credibility, but in reality it gave itself a capricious power that was quite an effective weapon. So among the executed in 1805 were Samuel Mitchell, who murdered his 12-year-old daughter Sarah, and George William of Horsham, who stole some horse saddles.[1] Twelve of the sixty-six executions involved theft of sheep and horses; this seems ridiculous among the arsons and child rapists, but it made sense to an establishment that had few ways of protecting their property, and sheep and horses were easy to steal. So the crime needed to be deterred more sternly: 'Men are not hanged for stealing horses, but that horses may not be stolen'.[2]

William Paley was one of the strident voices wishing to maintain the tradition that: 'crimes are not by any government punished in proportion to their guilt, nor in all cases ought to be so, but in proportion to the difficulty and necessity of preventing them.'

Paley first influenced Law as a professor and tutor when they were in Cambridge, and by the turn of the century, he was the most influential critic of reformers like Romily. The Chief Justice did not have to consult his friend's book *Moral and Political Philosophy* because he could chat with Paley over breakfast, as he had a bedroom in Ellenborough's House in Bloomsbury for when the archdeacon visited the capital.

Under the Georgian bloody code, the theft of property worth more than forty shillings (£2) was punishable by death. Britain was a rich country; there was plenty worth stealing, lots of poor and desperate people ready to rob, and no police force to stop them. There is no wonder that Ellenborough and nearly every other member of the establishment thought the extensive use of the death penalty was not just necessary but perfectly logical. A system designed to be cheap also had to be severe.

He may have condoned rather than approved of the vast variation in outcomes for crimes committed; to catch more would have needed a draconian police force, extensively funded and with wide-ranging powers, and there was almost nationwide opposition to this. He knew, as well as anybody else, that juries rarely enforced such draconian punishments, mostly by underestimating the value of the goods stolen. Despite everything, severe punishments were a deterrent. There had been a crime wave since the end of the Napoleonic war: some commentators put it down to the irregular way that the law was administered. Paley expressed it pithily: 'few actually suffer, whilst the dread and danger of it hangs over the crimes of many'.

So Ellenborough opposed nearly every attempt to reduce the severity of punishments, and his chief adversary in this regard was Sir Samuel Romily. Romily saw a lot wrong with these repressive laws but had little success in his lifetime, partly because of the resistance of men like Ellenborough, whose view was still in the majority. His only real success was the abolition of the death penalty for stealing privately from the person – pickpocketing – in 1808, which neither Paley nor Ellenborough opposed.

In 1810, Romily put forward a bill to reduce the penalty for shoplifting under five shillings and robbery from houses and vessels over forty shillings from death to transportation. Ellenborough opposed this because such a change admitted that the existing law was defective, an implication that he could not stomach. He argued that the inability of his critics such as Romily to produce something better proved his point; he feared for the small shopkeeper and modest householder – if the terror was removed from the system, how could they run a business or know that their house was safe? In this, he was at least consistent in his defence of property, no matter how modestly it was held. His view had support as well, and not just from the people at the very top. In a prosperous country where many people owned something that could be denied to them by theft, he could see himself as a man defending the majority, not just the rich. When speaking against reform in parliament, Ellenborough was fond of conjuring up the honest toiling artisan who had little, or the upright rural tenant who lived precariously in a cottage; they needed protection, their poverty was ordained by God, but God would not want them robbed of what they had.

Ellenborough freely admitted that terror was part of the system. He acknowledged that murder and property crime were not equally bad, but by having the same terrible punishment, crime was held in check: 'for if the terror prevents the commission, it promotes the humane object of all good laws, the prevention of crimes'.[3] As the ramshackle and cheap system of law and order could not guarantee someone being caught for their crime, severity was the only remaining weapon.

Ellenborough opposed the use of transportation as an alternative to execution. Many historical sources suggest that his argument was that this punishment was no more than 'a summer's excursion, an easy migration to a happier and better climate', and have gone on to speculate that this was a lie, a mistake, or a joke, but the debate is futile because the full quotation is a lot more straightforward. Transportation was a useless punishment for the young, unconnected and desperate; in fact, it was the opposite: 'My lords the threat of transportation has no terrors for men as these. Believe me, transportation to Botany Bay is, nine times in ten, looked upon as no more than a summer's excursion in an easy migration to a happier and better climate.'[4] Ellenborough, like Paley, fretted slightly that imprisonment and transportation were outside the public eye and served poorly as salutary lessons.

Romily started his campaign with a pamphlet, which Ellenborough read and disagreed with. Romily's diary notes a conversation with Ellenborough reported back to him by Lord Lauderdale, defending the death penalty for theft and rejoicing in the random nature of the process and his joy in making exemplary punishments. Romily reported Ellenborough's thoughts:

> though the instances were very rare, it sometimes became necessary to execute the law against privately stealing in shops, and that he had himself left a man for execution at Worcester for that offence. The man, he had said, when he came to the bar, lolled out his tongue and acted the part of an idiot. He saw the prisoner was counterfeiting idiocy and bade him be on his guard that the man, however, still went on in the same way whereupon Lord Ellenborough, having put it to the jury to say whether the prisoner was really of weak mind and they having found that he was not and having convicted him, left him for execution.[5]

Lauderdale then pointed out that, in effect, the man had gone to his death for pretending to be an idiot in a court of law, one of the few things that was not a capital offence – but Ellenborough could not see his point.

It is normally taken as obvious today that the Georgian treatment of debtors was both brutal and counter-intuitive, yet strangely lax at the same time. Ellenborough supported indefinite imprisonment for debt, and said so when the subject was discussed in the Lords in March 1806, and he had some good arguments to make, which, arguably showed a good understanding of the reality of the times.

In 1806, Lord Holland introduced an Insolvent Debtor's Bill to fractionally modify the harshness of the system. Ellenborough spoke against it. Britain was a commercial and entrepreneurial country that relied on credit and the good reputation it needed. Faith in repayment had to be protected. Strictly speaking, the problem was *insolvent* debtors; there was no shame in having debts, just not being able to pay them back. The rich would pay their bills in three months, six, or even yearly intervals; the tradesmen would be expected to wait. The middle classes would expect similar treatment. Only the poor dealt in cash. If defaulting on debt was easy, then credit would be impossible to get. Commerce and trade, a clear source of the country's wealth, needed to be protected. Sparing the debtor from prison was a bigger injustice than punishing them harshly. Ellenborough pointed out that, five times out of six, a period of imprisonment resolved the problem.

Ellenborough told Lord Holland that the bill was based on ignorance of the present law and the dire unintended consequences of change. He did this regularly, and it did not endear him to his fellow peers.

> It was incredible how injurious the frequent repetition of insolvent acts was to the course of fair trade. The professed principle upon which the bill, in the first instance, proceeded was highly objectionable, namely, that the gaols were overloaded with prisoners. It was his opinion that persons threw themselves into prison in order to take the benefit of an insolvent act: and, therefore, that such an act, in relieving such a description of persons, produced great injustice.
>
> For every debtor that may or may not be culpable, there was a creditor who was probably innocent and had risked a lot more than the borrower; there were twenty fraudulent debtors where there was one vexatious and unmerciful creditor.

This was the voice of Adam Smith; knowing both his *Wealth of Nations* and his New Testament, he also knew that unredeemed debt was a sin forbidden in the ten commandments. It was little different to theft and even his less flinty-hearted predecessor Lloyd Kenyon agreed: 'Bankruptcy is considered a crime, and a bankrupt in the old laws is called an offender,' he had decreed.

To those like Lord Holland, who argued that some debtors were just unlucky rather than fraudulent and the law should try to notice the difference, Ellenborough replied that the suffering of the rare number of innocents was less important that punishing the clearly guilty. For every debtor, there was a creditor or creditors who were less culpable than the debtors. With his slightly jaundiced view of humanity, which is often part of a more traditionalist mindset, he pointed out that many people *could* pay but just didn't want to.

Life was hard for the victims, so it needed to be harder for the perpetrators; there was no question of making life a little easier for both. Prison was the answer. It was so much easier to run away and never be found than it is today, and it was always an option. Lots of people did it, even people at the top of society, running away to the nearest place that was not England

and often, like Beau Brummell, finding themselves living hand to mouth in Calais. It was the establishment that could most easily get away with not paying their debts. In 1857, there were 7,000 English people living in Boulogne – about a quarter of the town's population.[6] Some debtors, such as the Prince Regent, simply asked the taxpayer for more money.

Being a creditor was not easy, even if your debtor stayed at home. The process of obtaining an arrest warrant for debt was time-consuming, bureaucratic and costly. Often, several creditors would have to band together to see a writ for debt issued. The English state provided no assistance with legal costs, and it was a very expensive system for those who were owed money.[7]

One debtor that Ellenborough would have had no sympathy for was John Dickens, father of Charles, who was imprisoned in February 1824 for failing to repay a baker the sum of forty pounds and ten shillings. John had a decent, well-paid, recession-proof job with the Royal Navy yet failed to pay his creditors, and in Ellenborough's view, only the prospect of indefinite incarceration would modify immoral behaviour. It was generally believed that the perpetrator would have family, friends and connections who would help out, and this was often the case. There would have been no motivation to help if the debtor had been living comfortably at home, free from obloquy, and the parents or children less likely to avoid the same by opening their wallets. Dickens junior worked around ten hours a day fixing labels to jars of black boot polish for six shillings a week and never forgot the trauma, but Ellenborough would have approved.[8]

Dickens was held in the Marshalsea, newly built in 1811, and Ellenborough himself was held responsible for debtors at his own prison in Southwark. Life in a debtors' prison was a carbon copy of life outside. Those well connected could still buy privileges, but for those who could not afford to raise money it meant a damp, overcrowded cell. Charles Dickens reported that there was a 'kind of iron cage in the wall of the Fleet Prison, within which was posted some man of hungry looks who, from time to time, rattled a money box and exclaimed in a mournful voice, "Pray, remember the poor debtors: pray, remember the poor debtors!"'[9]

Ellenborough's own prison in Southwark allowed debtors to live outside the walls for a fee. This system of flexibility at Ellenborough's prison was known as the Rules. Wine, beer, coffee and a bakehouse were available at the King's Bench prison, although there was no doctor available unless there was one among the inmates.

Two of the most famous inmates of the debtor's prison were Lady Emma Hamilton and Thomas Cochrane; Cochrane was put there personally by the Chief Justice (See Chapter Twenty-Two). Hamilton ended up there through overspending caused by her attempts to keep up appearances after the death of her lover, Admiral Nelson (a funeral attended by Lord and Lady Ellenborough, but from which Emma Hamilton was barred). When Lord Chief Justice Ellenborough was asked by Hamilton for an extension of the Rules, he gravely replied that he could not see the reason since they apparently extended as far as the East Indies. It was not a perfect system, but it was the best one possible – with one major exception: the problem of personal violence.

Chapter Nine

A law Unto Himself

Ellenborough had no desire at all to weaken the bloody code, and in fact, he strengthened it. While men like Romily were trying to reduce the number of capital crimes, Ellenborough's most famous sponsored Act of Parliament actually increased the number. The formal name of this law of 1803 was the Malicious Stabbings or Shooting Act. It was not about saving property, the church, or the constitution, but an attempt to deter acts of violence against the person. It has to be said that such an act was necessary. This was an age of interpersonal violence that would test the belief in human nature of any member of a modern liberal democracy. Prior to the nineteenth century, most incidents of non-lethal violence, if they were prosecuted at all, were tried before magistrates as misdemeanours, and punishments were light by today's standards. It was certainly a problem that needed solving.

Ellenborough was thinking specifically about Ireland, where acts of violence were common among those resisting what they saw as the occupation of Ireland by a foreign power. It culminated in the 1798 revolt of the United Irishmen, who tried to overthrow British rule and resist the religious sectarianism that the British cultivated. The Irish rebels were doubly united against the British and their attempts to divide them on the basis of religion.

Law had a personal stake: his elder brother John had been an Irish bishop since 1782. John Law's career initially advanced under the patronage of his father, the bishop, but passed to more powerful hands when he aided the Duke of Portland in a legal case by tracking down and interpreting obscure documents. John Law was more like his father in his religious latitudinarianism; on arriving in Ireland, he once ventured that he could not convert the many Catholics around him into Protestants, but he could make them better Catholics by distributing pious literature by acceptable Catholic divines for free. He later, according to one source, admitted that he had been a 'liberal fool' and, later on, in 1798, had to protect his palace from revengeful Irishmen wishing to be free of the rule of Bishop John, the Anglican establishment, and the British.[1]

One horrible form of violence was 'chalking' – slashing at an opponent's face with the intention of leaving a scar as a form of trophy. Such cutting and maiming with an intent to rob, murder or intimidate was already a crime in Ireland. Following the 1801 Act of Union and the abolition of the parliament in Dublin, this law and others needed to be renewed by the new Imperial Parliament. When the Irish Chalking Bill reached the House of Lords, Lord Ellenborough questioned why it should not apply to England. He took on the task of writing a new law himself. The bill that he introduced less than two weeks later contained a range of highly specific offences: 'An Act for the further Prevention of malicious shooting, and attempting to discharge loaded Fire-Arms, stabbing, cutting, wounding, poisoning, and the malicious using of Means to procure the Miscarriage of Women: and also the malicious setting Fire to Buildings.'

Its preamble was a reminder of Law's interest in Ireland: 'Whereas divers cruel and barbarous outrages have been of late wickedly and wantonly committed in divers parts of England and Ireland.'

Ellenborough admitted in parliament that he was adding extensively to the number of laws that attracted the death penalty and that he had created the list merely from his own opinions and experiences. Ellenborough's new law was designed to punish such behaviour with the same ferocity as crimes against property, so there would always be a humanitarian element, even if it was not deliberate. Wounding in an attempt to murder and/or rob would become a capital offence. If killing was the objective and only God's providence prevented it, then it would be viewed as murder. Those who wished to scare people before robbing them would now think twice. Setting fire to your own house for insurance purposes was only a felony if it spread to others, but now it was a felony to do so to defraud insurers. It was also, strictly speaking, an innovation, which Ellenborough generally opposed, but this was an innovation that tended towards severity. Ten new capital crimes were created in total. One awful violent crime that did not come to

Ellenborough's mind was acid attacks, which continued to attract a mere two-year maximum sentence even after the legislation.

His new law became universally known as 'Lord Ellenborough's Act', the only modern piece of legislation named after a person, and its victims followed rapidly. In January 1804, Corneille and Draper were capitally convicted of wounding police constable Boardman with a cutlass as he raided a disorderly house in Hatton Garden. In the same year, 19-year-old Thames waterman Hugh Evans was found guilty under Ellenborough's Act of maiming Elizabeth Palmer. Palmer lived in Tooley Street with her boyfriend; the culmination of a short, bitter feud saw Evans threaten to 'spoil her pretty face'. He was as good as his word, slashing her face until she was unrecognisable. Ellenborough's Act construed this particularly cruel act as attempted murder, and Evans was hanged outside the Horsemonger Road gaol on 2 March. Hanging next to him was David Rose, convicted of bestiality, and like Evans, the only person that year hanged for that capital crime. From that point on, one or two people a year could be expected to hang for cutting and maiming, making it a salutary lesson for anybody else contemplating it. That was the plan.[2]

The new law also heightened the risks for smugglers and poachers, who regularly came into conflict with state officials. Armed resistance to lawful arrest now attracted the death penalty, but the unintended consequence was that both sets of men would be more likely to arm themselves and work in larger, more aggressive gangs. In 1817 Ellenborough also approved of the tightening of punishments for actual poaching to fourteen years of transportation, which meant that night poachers would reach for their guns if arrested.

If a poacher shot with the intention of hitting and then missed, they could still be put to death. Charles Smith was executed by hanging in 1822 as a result of Lord Ellenborough's Act; he had shot and missed a gamekeeper to Lord Palmerston at Broadlands in Hampshire. Smith was hanged at Winchester prison in March 1822 for the crime of shooting his victim in the thigh. Judge Burrows made it clear that this was an exemplary punishment. 'It became necessary to these cases that the extreme sentence of the law should inflicted to deter others, as resistance to game keepers was now arrived at alarming height and many lives had been lost.' A few weeks earlier, another poacher, James Turner was given the same punishment for successfully *killing* a gamekeeper.

These were not the biggest consequences of Law's freestyle law-making. Most of the Act was repealed in 1828, except for the provisions of the last line, which refers to the termination of pregnancy and the killing of infants born alive. Anti-abortion laws do not have a particularly long history in Britain. Before 1803, there were no laws criminalising a deliberate termination before the 'quickening' of the child in the womb, and procuring an abortion afterwards was not a criminal offence. One case below came before Lord Justice Kenyon in 1801. It was an allegation that somebody had procured an abortion. The judge pointed out that this was a civil matter and asked why he was being asked to comment on it in a criminal tribunal. It was not necessarily regarded as a major social problem that needed state intervention; perhaps part of Ellenborough's motivation was that he thought otherwise.

What did it mean to be 'quick with child' in the eighteenth century? Part of the definition was practical – there was a quickening if the baby could be felt by the mother. There was a range of ages for this, but in the Regency period doctors put the period at around sixteen to twenty weeks. After quickening, the soul was believed to enter the body and so there was a person in the womb who had rights. Its first right was not to be executed alongside the mother, even if the latter had committed a terrible crime. This was known as the anatomically incorrect term of 'pleading the belly', and it was a regular though not common aspect of judicial proceedings in the late Georgian period, and of course this continued after the severe tightening up of the law in 1803. This distinction between pre- and post-quickening survived the 1803 Act, it was just that the punishments for both were made more severe. Life now began at conception. A new criminal offence was created for an action that was formerly not illegal. Anybody who,

> wilfully and maliciously administered to, or cause to be administered to, or taken by any woman, any medicines, drug, or other substance or thing whatsoever, or shall use or employ or cause or procure to be used or employed any instrument or other means whatsoever, with intent thereby to cause the miscarriage of any woman not being, or not being proved to be, quick with child at the time of administering such things … shall be and are hereby declared to be guilty of felony, and

> shall be liable to be fined, imprisoned, set in and upon the pillory, publicly or privately whipped, or to suffer one or more of the said punishments, or to be transported beyond the seas for any term not exceeding fourteen years.

Never have two large rambling paragraphs had so much effect on the British and American criminal justice systems; Ellenborough's Act was still influencing the law on abortion in Britain until the 1960s and in the United States until the present day.[3]

Chapter Ten

Against High Treason

Until 1946, execution was the normal punishment in England for treason. William Joyce, a Nazi propagandist and the last to suffer this fate, would have been weighed and the correct length of rope calculated in order to produce a quick end. The methods aimed for instant brain death by snapping the neck vertebrae. The death penalty for treason lingered, unused, until 1998, when it was replaced by life imprisonment.

So it is no surprise that death was the tariff for treason in Ellenborough's time, but there was an added challenge for the ruling classes when the tariff for lesser crimes was the same, so the bloody code was obliged to be even bloodier when faced with treason.

So one morning in 1803, Ellenborough, wearing his black cap with a corner hanging down to his nose, used a form of words that had been used for centuries. It was 2 am, due to Ellenborough's habit of keeping a trial going all night if important people, including himself, had better things to do in the morning:

> Each of you shall be taken from the place whence you came, thence you are to be drawn on hurdles to the place of execution, where you will be hanged by the neck, but not until you are dead, for while you are still living, your bodies are to be taken down, your bowels torn out and burnt before your faces. Your heads are to be then cut off and your bodies divided each into four quarters to be at the king's disposal and may the Almighty God have mercy on your souls.[1]

Something worse than hanging was required, and being hanged, drawn and quartered certainly was. It had been used selectively since 1351 as a fate worse than death. It destroyed more than your life; it was an indication of your utter powerlessness, a stain on your memory and reputation, and reaffirmed the power of the state to deter those who were not alarmed by the prospect of their own death. According to its supporters, there was no more generous act for the nation than this punishment for traitors, as it would deter any attempts in the future. It was an antidote to fanaticism. It was also a mercy to potential traitors; it would change their minds, save their bodies from torture in this life, and save their souls in the next. This was Ellenborough's view.

The Chief Justice had condemned a number of men to this horrible death that morning. The jury had agreed with his direction that they were guilty of treason but asked for mercy, which was ignored. This was a remarkable degree of confidence from a judge who had just taken up his position. It was his painful duty to send them to their deaths, he said. It was an awful warning to others, and their salvation depended on how they reacted to their sentence in the last few days of their existence. Despite all the ritualised regret and reluctance, we should be under no doubt that he relished every verdict, not from personal satisfaction but from the belief that he had done his duty. The *Gentlemen's Magazine* described Ellenborough's speech as 'impressive'.

The main traitor in this case was Edward Despard, who, along with John Francis, John Wood, Thomas Broughton, James Wratton, John MacNamara and Arthur Graham, were indeed executed at Horsemonger Lane Gaol on 21 February 1803.

What had they done to deserve such a fate? The short, and perhaps simplistic, answer is that they had done a lot of naïve and wildly optimistic plotting against the establishment while drinking in various low public houses in London. Over a pint of porter, they discussed universal suffrage, religious toleration and freedom for Ireland. It was hardly a secret conspiracy, indeed the opposite. They were in a busy public house, the Oakley Arms in Lambeth, when they were raided by the Bow Street Runners in November 1802.

They had already been infiltrated by Home Office spies, and their fantasy plans were already known. The immediate objective of these desperate men was to assassinate King George III with cannon as he passed down The

Mall in his carriage, shooting his horse, and seizing the Bank of England and the Tower of London. The other pillar of the establishment was deemed to be the Post Office. As the revolt spread, the plan was to intercept all the post coaches that left for the provinces simultaneously at 8 pm. This seems counterintuitive, but the rebels wanted to spread disaffection and revolt, and the coach was the way news travelled. The rebels knew that the absence of post coaches would prove that something momentous had happened in the capital because the state ran a very effective and well-resourced all-night postal service, and its absence would prove that others were now in charge.

It was no more than tap house tittle-tattle, born of drink, poverty and resentment. The fact that they had done nothing more than talk did not matter. Words were enough, said Ellenborough, 'if they are addressed to persons with an intent to excite and to confirm them in the prosecution of measures which have for their declared object the assassinating or deposing of the king by force of arms'. The treason law of Edward III said that 'imagining' the king's death was enough; more recent legislation had made this clear. In his summing up, Ellenborough acknowledged that it was abortive treason, but he was able to say this because, legally, it was irrelevant and made no difference to guilt.

The trial was a travesty by modern standards. No state witnesses were cross-examined, and one of them was a state spy with the appropriate name of Windsor. The main plotter, Edward Despard, was particularly admonished by the Chief Justice. He was socially superior to the other men and should have known better. Ellenborough made it clear that Despard's fall from grace was greater than that of the other men. Part of his condemnation (literally) was to point out to Despard that he was more guilty than the others because 'born as you were to hopes, intended and formed as it should seem by Providence for better ends and purposes: accustomed as you heretofore have been to better habits of life and manners'.[2] From his ragged and ignorant compatriots, such behaviour could be expected; he was a better person, so his shame was greater.

Despard, an Irishman in the British Army, had a successful career of bravery and loyalty. He had shared a tent and personal confidences with Nelson. The great British hero gave him a character reference in court. They were on the Spanish Main together, said Nelson. 'We slept many nights together in our clothes on the ground we have measured the height of the enemy's wall together.'[3]

They served together, and he declared him to have been a loyal man and a good officer. Nelson was extremely popular even before Trafalgar, having recently returned from his triumph at the Battle of the Nile. But Ellenborough was not deterred, pointing out that the famous admiral's warm words about Despard were a number of years out of date. It was very much in his character to openly contradict the hero of the hour: 'I am sorry to be obliged to interrupt your Lordship, but we cannot hear what I dare say your Lordship would give with great effect, the history of this gentleman's military life.'[4]

Nelson's pleas were the main reason that the jury asked for mercy, notwithstanding his guilt. Ellenborough ignored that as well.

It was the legal system and the treatment of Ireland that had radicalised Despard. He read the *Rights of Man* in Ellenborough's debtors prison at the King's Bench in the 1790s. Ellenborough had read Paine in 1792, just after publication, in order to assess the enemy; Ellenborough would been disgusted by any member of the establishment who was actually convinced by it. He admonished Despard for believing in fantasies. Ellenborough told him that wide differences in wealth and power were natural, inevitable and desirable, and when gentlemen fell for this republicanism and atheism, their degradation was complete.

This all looks like a triumph for the establishment – and it was, as far as Despard and his colleagues were concerned, but the victory had its limits. Ellenborough may have wielded total control over the judicial process, but there was always public opinion, and it had to be taken into account. It was usually easier to pronounce a harsh sentence than to enforce it while maintaining authority. The establishment was afraid of the reaction of the mob to this severe sentence and their own ability to cope with the consequences. The public mood was grim, and people were openly calling it murder. The Southwark magistrate was worried. Nobody wanted to be seen building the scaffold either. The authorities had made the same mistake as Despard, believing that there was universal support for him in London and that a gruesome execution would only inflame them.

The disembowelling and quartering were dropped, but it still needed the Bow Street officers patrolling around Newgate all night and the lifeguards being stationed around the corner to assuage their fears that the men would be rescued by the mob. There was a large crowd – some say about 20,000 and only Nelson's funeral was bigger. The main difference was that this event had to be protected by every law officer in London and beyond, as well as a cordon of horse guards two deep.

Despard was applauded on the scaffold when he refused to die in the accepted manner, which was meekly accepting his guilt and grovelling for forgiveness from the Almighty. He did not flinch at the flimsy coffin in front of him, ready and full of sawdust to soak up the effusions from his severed head. The traditional cry of 'behold the head of a traitor' was used as bloody remnants were shown off, but the event could never be a total triumph for the authorities. His last speech was published for all to read, organised by his wife Catherine, and his body was not dissected.

When he died and his head was delivered to his relatives, Marie Tussaud, herself a refugee from revolutionary events in France, obtained permission to make a plaster cast which went into her London exhibition. It was her first severed head, and her family was amazed and a little aghast at her interest, but with 20,000 people at the execution, she knew a good business proposition when she saw it. Ellenborough might have been mollified by the fact that it exhibited in the House of Horrors alongside a lot of French Jacobins, some of whom may have been responsible for imprisoning Marie herself.[5]

Chapter Eleven

Against Vice

When a society invests so little in crime prevention and detection, social control of the population becomes very difficult. It is even more difficult to control 'vice' – behaviour short of a crime that the authorities would like to see less of but are not in a position to do much about because it was private, consensual, too common, or too convenient to look the other way.

What counted as a vice? In no particular order, it included swearing, profanation of the Lord's Day, blasphemy and obscenity, pornography, prostitution, welfare dependency, illicit intercourse, gambling, and cruelty to animals. More specifically, swearing involved taking the Lord's name in vain, and Sunday profanities included travelling, conducting business, and reading newspapers (the first Sunday newspaper, the *Observer*, caused a stir in 1792). Even more specifically, theatre, fairs, fiddlers, lewd songs, poetry, bull baiting, bear baiting, anything French, pretty dresses, ball assemblies, country music, horse racing, and Shakespeare in the original version.

This is a long list, enough to cause panic in any earnest young clergyman, maiden aunt or sensitive single lady, but not everything was vice. It was a generation too early for the fight against the torrent of alcohol drinking to be tackled; it was still hard-wired into a society where everybody drank excessively and the tax base was dependent on that continuing. The animal cruelty of the poor was looked down on, but animal torture by the rich was not. By the end of the Georgian period, it was increasingly frowned upon to throw stones at chickens until they expired, but it was still aspirational to chase a fox until it died of exhaustion. It is a sign of who was in charge that hare coursing, badger baiting and fox hunting lingered into the late twentieth century, when 'working-class' cruelty was illegal.

The problems of fighting vice were threefold: many of these were hidden or victimless crimes, where those taking part had no reason or desire to snitch to the authorities; secondly, there was a large section of society who did not feel the need to fight such immorality; and thirdly, the rich were just as guilty of many of these vices as the poor, so it was best to leave things alone. For most of the eighteenth century, the establishment had not even tried to intervene to improve morals and deter bad behaviour. The main exception was the gin panic of the mid-century, when the social consequences became too acute to ignore.

A new organisation was founded in the year that Ellenborough became Chief Justice, and it was very indicative of the way the moral wind was blowing. The Society for the Suppression of Vice was founded by Ellenborough's contemporary, William Wilberforce, and was the successor to other similar organisations that had their roots in George III's proclamation against immorality in 1787. Wilberforce was the man behind that as well, and Kenyon, Ellenborough's more pious predecessor, was a member.

What were the concerns of these evangelical Christians? It was the poor that worried them. Their drinking and fornication would damage the productivity of those chosen by God to be the beasts of burden; their self-indulgence would lead to heresy, atheism and a breakdown in obedience. In 1809, Sydney Smith famously dubbed it a 'Society for the Suppression of Vices of Persons whose income does not exceed £500 per annum'. To be fair, while targeting the poor, the Vice Society (another version of their name that they did not like) also asserted that the moral rot had started at the head a long time ago. It had been made worse by the outpouring of radicalism and atheism from the French Revolution and English radical writers like Thomas Paine, which would further distract and confuse the gullible poor. It might have been the rich that were the cause of the moral decay and spiritual barrenness, but they would not be the ones appearing in front of the learned judge. Their method was not to lobby for stricter laws from an establishment that was not quite ready, but to entrap the poor into breaking existing ones. The society acted as a supplement to the police system, often by provoking crimes that it believed would have taken place anyway. For Ellenborough, the former was a positive boon, and the latter was perfectly acceptable. The Lord Chief Justice was against vice, for the poor for sure, and for the establishment selectively, and he did show support for Wilberforce's society when it sallied forth into the courtroom to prosecute bad morality away.

There were differences. The Vice Society was composed of clergymen and their supporters, and Ellenborough was first and foremost a lawyer and a politician. He was not in the business of reforming manners, but he *would* apply the law. He had no time to understand offenders or convince them of the error of their ways. The reformation of criminals was impossible, considering they were the dregs of society. He merely looked for evidence of guilt, and the Vice Society liked to provide it, so they rubbed along. The problem for the Vice Society was that they had to encourage lying to get the evidence, and there was a commandment against that.

Pornography was an acknowledged vice. London had a thriving trade in pornographic prints, and many a Georgian gentleman had a locked drawer in his study to store them. Masturbation was noted in the press as a solitary vice, but only in the context of children, often those confined and lonely in distant boarding schools. It was an adolescent phrase that you grew out of, and if you didn't, it became a vice. In a way, pornography was worse than robbery; with robbery a crime is committed and the evil then ends, but pornography corrupts continually.

One of the first victims of the Vice Society was the Italian print seller Baptista Bertazzi, who hawked filthy pictures around Covent Garden. Bertazzi was approached by one Robert Gray, who asked to see the prints that he had under his arm and, after a long look, judged that they were not quite to his taste. Bertazzi hinted that some items more to his interest could be viewed at his one-room home over a pub in Little Turnstile, where a few days later, Gray purchased six indecent prints.[1]

It seems that the going rate for a first-rate pornographic print was three shillings. That was not the end: Bertazzi suggested a distribution agreement, whereby subsequent prints could be had at half price if Gray introduced him to more customers. Later, Gray arrived with some men, claiming to be East India officers who wanted small prints to smuggle out of the country. Sin was to be exported.

It was a sting. Robert Gray was working for the Vice Society, making a test purchase that would be the *modus operandi* of the censorious state for the next century. The 'East India officials' were police officers and arrested Bertazzi. The case went to trial in February 1803 at the King's Bench, with Ellenborough presiding. Ellenborough allowed the prosecution a long speech in which the defendant was described as a demon in human shape, intent on the destruction of humanity. The Lord Chief Justice was also relaxed about the fact that Gray was a paid spy and would have warmed to him further when Bertazzi's defence managed to make Gray admit that he had previously worked for the state as an agent provocateur against Manchester political radicals and Irish nationalists. It later turned out that he was a full-time officer of the Vice Society, earning £100 per year.

This was not Mr Gray's first entrapment. Robert Gray was doing the same thing six months earlier under a different judge, but the King's Bench referred it back to the magistrates: 'the defence … rests upon the character of Gray, who is the informer and probably the only witness on this occasion and was therefore regarded as circumspect'.[2]

Ellenborough was more flexible. He had no problem with paid informers and agents provocateurs; he sent Despard to his grave on similar evidence and was willing to do so again.

> If a person induced another, who was innocent, to commit a crime, in order to be his accuser, that was a crime of the highest enormity, but if a person be in a habitual course of committing a crime, and it be difficult to detect him, then to produce a declaration of that which may lead to his detection is not a crime but a beneficial service to the community.[3]

This was an admission of the feebleness of the system and that it needed all the help it could get. Ellenborough also gave the green light for more cases like this: 'I thought it was necessary only to say as much to prevent misconception.'

Bertazzi was found guilty of stirring up lewd and unchaste thoughts among his majesty's subjects, but there were fewer cases like this as Wilberforce had a conscience even if Ellenborough didn't. Wilberforce eventually stopped using paid informers.

The case of *Hope v Dubost* shows Ellenborough once again crusading against filth. The case was brought by art collector and connoisseur, Thomas Hope. Hope was an accomplished and powerful man, the master of his own field, whose opinions on art were taken extremely seriously. He was also very unattractive, conceited, and lacking in tact. His wife, Louisa Beresford, was the opposite: 'Mrs Hope is an Irish beauty – her mouth and teeth are particularly striking. Her husband, on the contrary, is incredibly ugly – if you were to see him in a dream, you would never wake again.'[4]

In 1810, Hope fell out with French painter Antoine Dubost, over the price of a painting, just as Ellenborough was to do in his own quarrel with Lawrence and his own beautiful wife. Dubost responded by painting *Beauty and the Beast*. It was ostensibly a scene from the Arabian Nights, unconnected with his row with Mr Hope. It was in fact a revenge picture portraying Hope as a big-eared, hairy dwarf chimpanzee, gurning and stupid, surrounded by a box of jewels that had been used to purchase Louisa, who was looking away in horror as he holds on to her by the hand. The facial expressions alone made the slur obvious. All of London society understood the point being made. Rich ugliness had bought delicate, innocent beauty.

One of Louisa's relatives was outraged and took action. Louisa's brother, the Reverend Beresford, arrived at Dubost's exhibition in Pall Mall one Saturday morning, paid his entrance fee, and slashed the picture into unrecognisable pieces. The idea of ugliness for Mr Hope was a given, but the idea that his sister had sold herself in return for security was unconscionable. Dubost took Beresford to court and asked for £1,000, compensation for the artwork, and the lost entrance fees of those who had wished to be scandalised by it. This sum may have been optimistic, but the painting was definitely worth more than the £5 that Lord Ellenborough awarded him.

Ellenborough had no sympathy for him; the painting was just another form of libel, like a book or a pamphlet, and deserved to be suppressed. He said that it would have been suppressed and the sale banned if they had taken the legal route and appealed to the Lord Chancellor. Dubost was French, and there was plenty about him to dislike. He had lived happily in Paris in the 1790s when the revolutionaries were in charge, had come to England with little, and had been supported by Thomas Hope. Here was a needy Frenchman who did not know the meaning of loyalty.

Why £5 rather than a flea in his ear? The artwork was also private property, which Ellenborough felt duty-bound to defend. Beresford did not deny the destruction, so Ellenborough suggested an amount to the jury that compensated him for the wood, canvas and colours only. The jury got the hint and offered the foreigner a token sum.

There is one vice where the rules were different. It was a vice that they were prepared to prosecute if it came to light, but would rather have kept in the shadows. It had no name, except as an euphemism. This was the crime not to be named among Christians: the unnatural crime; the abominable offence; the Italian vice; the crime at which nature shudders; the crime that is subversive of every idea of virtue and manliness. The vice whose middle letters were removed in print to avoid moral contagion was b-----y. [5]

The crime was called sodomy, and it was an offence that left the establishment rather perplexed. While today we might see the consensual version as a victimless crime, the eighteenth-century view was that it was an evil act, a sign of moral degradation. It was literally a sinful action, not linked in the mind with a sexual identity or natural-born proclivity. The word homosexual was not used, and there was no recognised gay community. Sodomy was just something very bad that men did to animals, women and other men. It was unpopular with all classes; if you were put in the pillory for it, expect your life to be in danger from the fury of the mob.[6]

Sodomy was difficult to prosecute. Blackwood's Law Commentary said that sodomy was such a terrible crime and so easy to lie about that only the very strongest proofs would be accepted. There needed to be witnesses to the event, which had to include penetration and ejaculation in order to be a felony that attracted capital punishment. This meant, in practice, an unwilling partner, a stranger coming into the room at the wrong time, a police raid, or somebody involved who turned king's evidence. The latter two were much more common.

It was the French Revolution that frightened the establishment into believing that the working man was organising behind their backs and were up to no good. Sodomy was not the most obvious manifestation, but there was the occasional moral panic. In 1806, such a conspiracy came to light when Lancashire magistrates uncovered an organised club of men in the ordinary town of Great Sankey in Warrington (then in Lancashire). They were mostly semi-skilled or skilled artisans; they often had wives and children. They met every Monday and Friday in a house owned by 69-year-old Isaac Hitchin to have consensual penetrative sex, or – in the words of the trial of Joseph Holland – that horrid, detestable and abominable crime called b-----y'.[7]

There had already been mass arrests in Liverpool and Manchester, and men had been prosecuted and were awaiting execution. Indeed, it was Ellenborough who sent one of the conspirators, Thomas Rix, to the scaffold. There was more activity to be nipped in the bud and more men to catch, but the Home Office, under Sidmouth and influenced by Ellenborough, made it clear to the local Cheshire magistrates that they should stop their investigations, despite there being many more to punish. What was going on? What had they seen that frightened them so much into, essentially, looking the other way?

The problem was, they were unsure of what they would discover. The guilty who had been punished were not just corruptible plebeians. Five men in total were executed, including a member of the middle class. Joseph Holland was worth £40,000 a year and was a gentleman, and there were rumours that members of the gentry were involved with the group, even members of parliament.

The truth is that such activity scared the establishment. The Great Sankey men were not effeminate 'mollys' meeting in London pubs and clubs. In its more extreme forms, the 'molly subculture' saw men take on female identities with female names, and mimic females in marriage and childbirth. That it mocked the very basis of a male-dominated society was bad enough, but the sheer ordinariness of the 1806 case was a horror in itself. Sodomy did not need the publicity in case this moral outrage caught on; and, of course, its proponents were not all members of the lower classes. There were exemplary punishments for some unfortunates, but some sleeping dogs were left undisturbed. Vice was complicated.

Chapter Twelve

The Broad Bottoms and an Indelicate Investigation

Ellenborough could have been forgiven for thinking that he had reached the zenith of his career in 1802. Nobody in the legal profession was more influential; all but a handful of the Commons were his inferior, and he was a peer in both senses of the word in the House of Lords. He could expect to stay at this level until death – this had happened to his immediate predecessors, Mansfield and Kenyon. Yet the political disturbances of 1802 which had sparked his rise reoccurred in 1806, when a change of government and the behaviour of the royal family pushed him even further up the establishment, increasing his power but to the detriment of his reputation. Ellenborough crossed over to becoming a politician and a courtier, and generally speaking it did not turn out very well for him.

In 1806 there was a hiatus in government, filled by what we would call a coalition, given the (largely sarcastic) title of the 'Ministry of All the Talents'. It was easy to be cynical about them, as they seemed to be three different political factions with nothing in common other than their desire to take power after the death of William Pitt. Again, one of the beneficiaries in the final, fatal fall of Pitt was Ellenborough.

Ellenborough was invited into government by the leader of one of these groups, Lord Sidmouth, who wanted some allies around the cabinet table and insisted on his friend Ellenborough, despite him being Chief Justice. No Lord Chief Justice had been in the cabinet before, apart from Kenyon's predecessor Lord Mansfield. High Court judges were always a de facto political appointment, but having one in the cabinet actually making laws was rather flagrant. Mild critics suggested he could not do either of his new roles well; more severe ones said it was an unconstitutional power-grab and a foreboding precedent. Even his ally Lord Eldon, a man who knew – and was prepared to say – that all judicial appointments were political was against it, but his only solution was to leave it to Ellenborough's sense of decency to make the 'right' decision. This appeal to conscience worked about as well as it does with politicians today.

Ellenborough explained his position in a letter to Perceval. He was yielding 'with considerable reluctance' to the wishes of others, he said, and had put limits on his power, which rather suggested that his opponents may have had a point: 'I have stipulated expressly not to be present at the consideration of any criminal questions or questions in any degree connected with the particular subjects of my jurisdiction.'[1]

He followed this up with the agreed coalition line: 'You know I daresay that the Cabinet is only a Committee of the Privy Council and that there is no subject which comes before them upon which the Crown might not already require me to advise in my capacity of privy counsellor.'

He was not interested in politics, especially the amount of work involved, but he would do it anyway: 'I have disposition little enough to devote myself to politics and have no curiosity to gratify in reading dispatches. To the extent to which my convenience may be broken in upon by allowing myself to be occasionally summoned to extraordinary councils.'

And then his trump argument – his prince requested it: 'I make a sacrifice to the request of one who has a right to ask of me any sacrifices which are not inconsistent with public duty.' His only proviso was that he would under no circumstances support political rights for Roman Catholics.

Such dual appointments to cabinet never happened again, and later in life Ellenborough seemed to regret the decision, but at the time, as ever, he brazened it out. It did his reputation little good. Ellenborough was seen as a man who had turned his coat, a Whig who had become a Tory and was now joining a mostly Whig government. Being a Whig had kept him from promotion by Tories; now *not* being a Whig had made him super powerful in a Whig government. One of the faction leaders was Charles James Fox, who had joined the Whig club in 1784, a year before Law, and they would have inhabited the same political space – the same Fox who was his enemy at the Hastings impeachment, but now Fox was his friend again. From an outsider's view, it was hard to see Ellenborough as a man of principle. The satirical cartoonists had a field day – 'two heads are better than one', said one, portraying Ellenborough as a two-faced creature looking in opposite directions at once.[2]

At first he was offered the post of Lord Chancellor. This was a political post, and one that would take him away, permanently, from his lucrative position at the King's Bench. It may also have crossed his mind that his present post earned him more and could not be taken away with a change in the political fortunes of his friends. Thomas Erskine became Chancellor instead. Ellenborough seemed to have both suggested Erskine for the post, and predicted that he would not prosper in the long term – and he was right about the last point. Ellenborough had finally and definitively overtaken his rival.

The new Prime Minister, Grenville, wanted the new government to have a broad bottom – that is, political balance – but their opponents took the phrase to describe the way they used up the state resources. There was an unseemly squabble over positions and paid posts which created a bad start. James Gillray portrayed them all as thirty-two rapacious piglets sucking the mother pig dry while farmer John Bull looked on in despair. Among them was a pig in a wig, Ellenborough himself, clambering over others to get more than his fair share, with the heading 'MORE PIGS than TEATS or the NEW LITTER OF HUNGRY GRUNTERS.'[3]

The government itself was short-lived, lasting no more than a year. It was fractious and argumentative, a reminder that coalition does not necessarily guarantee unanimity. It did have one major achievement, and that was the abolition of the slave trade in the British Empire in 1807. During the debate, Sir Samuel Romily had told the Commons that 360,000 Africans had already been sold into slavery or perished in the sea, a figure that shocked but was almost certainly an underestimate. Ellenborough was opposed to the trade in human beings. This was a common view of many mainstream politicians, although both the Prince Regent and the Duke of Clarence opposed it. He also differed from Lord Sidmouth – the man who had put him into government – who was suggesting postponing a decision into the undetermined future:

> Lord Ellenborough said he was sorry to differ from his noble friend Lord Sidmouth and yet he could not help saying that if after twenty years during which this question had been discussed by both houses of parliament their lordships

> judgments were not ripe for its determination he could not look with any confidence to a time when they would be ready to decide it The question then before them was short and plain. It was whether the African slave trade was inhuman, unjust and impolitic. If the premises were true we could not too speedily bring it to a conclusion.[4]

The peers voted forty-two to twenty-one in favour. Wilberforce was gratified to note Ellenborough's support (and less surprised at Erskine's, always was regarded as more 'humane'). The king also wished it, and it would have been interesting to see how Ellenborough would have voted if he didn't. The majority of 108 in the Commons was solid, but not overwhelming. The real force behind 'the most glorious measure that had ever been adopted by any legislative body in the world', according to Lord Grenville, was Ellenborough's friend, enemy, and then friend again, Charles James Fox. Fox was also the man who had to appear in the Commons to support his elevation to the cabinet. This rather shows the fluidity of establishment politics: both men opposed the slave trade and that was the limit of their agreement – yet they worked together for a year, with Ellenborough rediscovering some respect for his former opponent.

The main domestic event – achievement would be the wrong word – of the Ministry was the so-called 'Delicate Investigation' of 1806/1807. It was a very indelicate attempt by the Prince of Wales to rid himself of his wife, Caroline of Brunswick, something he had fervently wished for from the moment he met her. By 1806, the Prince of Wales had reached the end of his tether in trying to detach himself from the Princess of Wales. He encountered great difficulties, because the people still liked her. George III still liked her too, and getting any kind of legal separation was both constitutionally and politically impossible. She was one of the most popular members of the royal family, made even more popular by the atrocious treatment of her by a very unpopular husband. Ellenborough stood by his prince, despite his appalling behaviour, and was ready and able to take part in an investigation designed to discredit her.

The prince tried the extreme gamble of framing the princess for high treason, for which he needed the active support of the leading men of the establishment. This included the Prime Minister, Lord Grenville; the Lord Chancellor, Lord Erskine; the Lord Chief Justice, Lord Ellenborough; and Lord Spencer, the Home Secretary. They were known as 'The Prince's

Friends' and Ellenborough lived up to this name, at the expense of his own morals and principles.

Something had to be done, and Caroline had made herself a very easy target. Her unpopularity with the prince was not just a selfish peccadillo of the prince himself. She was unkempt, flirty and, in her boredom, badly behaved. She lived in near-exile in Blackheath; she was isolated and resented not seeing her daughter, but there seems no doubt that she behaved in an unseemly manner with the men she invited to her home, up to and including extra-marital sex. It was alleged that Caroline had given birth to a male child, William, four years earlier in 1802 by one of her lovers. The possibility of this being High Treason was a bit of a stretch; this boy could be used to challenge her legitimate child Charlotte's right to the throne, but it may have worked to intimidate her into leaving the country or allow a separation. It was all made easier by the princess half-pretending that the story was true, allowing one of her ladies in waiting with a pre-existing grudge to turn resentment into a serious allegation.

This assault on Princess Caroline was called the Delicate Investigation, but it was neither; indeed it was a legal disgrace presided over by the two most senior legal officers in the land, Erskine and Ellenborough. It followed no known legal process. Caroline only suspected that it was taking place when her servants were removed for interviews. Other witnesses were visited in their own homes, and obliged to take an oath; Lady Douglas was slightly intimidated when she was summoned to Downing Street to give hers. Servants of the princess were equally worried about being summoned to London to do the same, but the main difference was that Lady Douglas was given a £200 annual pension by the prince after her evidence. The comments of the witnesses were merely summarised – there were no verbatim reports of the questions and the answers, which meant that the evidence was merely the recollections of the interrogator.

It proved to be suspiciously easy to prove that William was the son of Sophia and Samuel Austin, that he was born in Brownlow Street Lying-In Hospital in July 1802 and that the princess had adopted him. By late July the papers were reporting this as fact. There was still no attempt to allow the princess to make her own case. They were gathering mud under the guise of investigation, and enough of it stuck. Caroline could not rebut the charges because she was unaware of them during the process or afterwards; the case concluded on 14 July and the findings shown to the princess on 11 August; only then could she write to the king with her plea of innocence.

How this could be reconciled with Ellenborough's ferocious defence of procedure in court is a difficult question to answer without coming to the conclusion that he was putting the interests of the prince above that of proper legal process. It was of course, the king who ordered him to do it, which was a useful fig leaf, but it was the prince that led the attack. Indeed, one of the prince's objectives was to turn the king against her – the only part which did not succeed.

Ellenborough seemed to have continued to be coarse and direct even through this 'delicate' process. As a public figure, he was often the butt of political cartoons and one famous one shows quite pointedly a book in his pocket called 'A New Dictionary of the Vulgar Tongue'. He seemed to have excelled himself during a cabinet discussion of the final report of the investigation by making a joking reference to Caroline's hair. It was in the possession of Captain Thomas Manby, who had a of souvenirs from this Princess, including a small lock of hair that, it was claimed, could have come from no woman's head. Ellenborough, ever the lawyer, said that this hair was only evidence if it could be compared to 'the record to which it was originally annexed'.[5]

The report concluded that the princess had not given birth to a child in 1802. She had bought him for £1 from Mrs Austin – regarded as irregular but not something to openly condemn. They went on to add that: 'evidence had been laid before them of other particulars respecting the conduct of Her Royal Highness such as must especially considering her exalted rank and station necessarily give occasion to very unfavourable interpretations'.[6]

The report was clear that there had been an irregular relationship with Captain Danby, and this could be assumed to be adultery unless proved otherwise. It is hard to see which was worse here – the lack of natural justice, or the impossibility of proving a negative. The king himself was sympathetic to the princess but could not receive her in court after her de facto admonishment. The prince had got much of what he wanted, and Ellenborough had played his part.

It would be unfair to say that Ellenborough politicised his post at the King's Bench; it was always a semi-political post, the occupant decided by politicians as proxy for the monarch, but Ellenborough made it more

Above left: Bishop Edmund Law. (Wikipedia Commons)

Above right: Edward Law, Lord Ellenborough. (Yale Centre for British Art)

Above left: William Pitt, no friend of Edward Law. (public domain)

Above right: Lloyd Kenyon, no friend of Edward Law. (Library of Congress)

The Trial of Warren Hastings. (Public Domain)

The Grand Pitch Battle. (Public Domain)

Right: The Prince Regent. (Look and Learn)

Below: Another version of the Prince Regent. (Wikipedia Commons)

The Court of the King's Bench. (Wikipedia Commons)

The King's Bench Prison. (Public domain)

Charles James Fox. (Public domain)

Gout and misery. (Wellcome, London)

Above: Carlton House. (Public domain)

Below: The stables at the Pavilion, Brighton. (Yale Centre for British Art)

Transportation to Botany Bay. (Wikipedia Commons)

Cold Bath Fields House of Correction. (Public domain)

Bloomsbury Square. (Yale Centre for British Art)

Slums of London, 1800. (Wellcome, London)

The home of a poor curate. (Yale Centre for British Art)

The home of a rich judge - St James' Square. (Yale Centre for British Art)

Governor Wall Case. (Wellcome, London)

The torture of Louisa Calderon. (Internet archive)

Palace of Westminster by Joseph Farington. (Public domain)

The Assassination of Spencer Perceval. (Public domain)

A favourite of Lady Ellenborough – Vauxhall Gardens. (Metropolitan Museum of Art)

A favourite of Lady Ellenborough – the waltz. (Wellcome, London)

PEACE and BREAD

The REPUBLICAN-ATTACK.

STREET RIOTING IN 1795

Gillray's Caricature of the Attack on George III., on his way to open Parliament, October 29th

Above: An attack on the King's Coach, 1795. (Look and Learn)

Left: The Dangers of Crim Con! (Wikipedia Commons)

Right: Tom Paine. (Wikipedia Commons)

Below: The Life and Times of William Hone. (Wikipedia Commons)

Above left: Anne Law, Lady Ellenborough. (Cleveland Museum of Art)

Above right: Princess Charlotte. (Wikipedia Commons)

Above left: Princess Caroline. (Wikipedia Commons)

Above right: A young William Wilberforce. (Public domain)

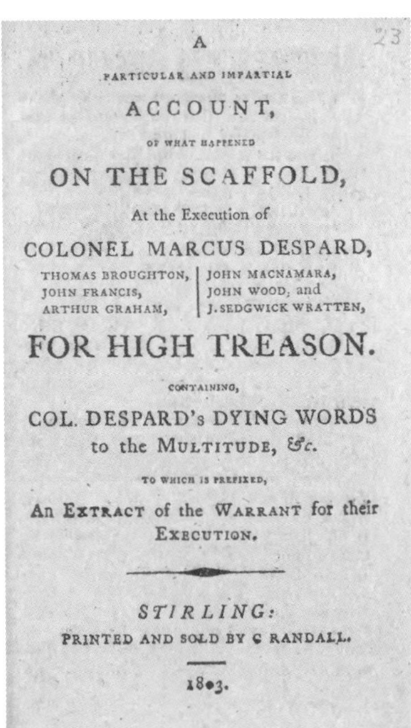
A

PARTICULAR AND IMPARTIAL

ACCOUNT,

OF WHAT HAPPENED

ON THE SCAFFOLD,

At the Execution of

COLONEL MARCUS DESPARD,

THOMAS BROUGHTON, JOHN FRANCIS, ARTHUR GRAHAM, JOHN MACNAMARA, JOHN WOOD, and J. SEDGWICK WRATTEN,

FOR HIGH TREASON.

CONTAINING,

COL. DESPARD's DYING WORDS to the MULTITUDE, &c.

TO WHICH IS PREFIXED,

An EXTRACT of the WARRANT for their EXECUTION.

STIRLING:

PRINTED AND SOLD BY C RANDALL.

1803.

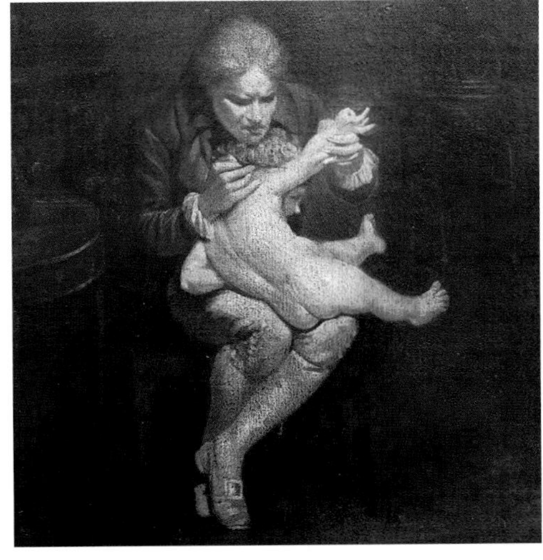

Above: Edward Jenner vaccinating his son. (Wellcome, London)

Left: The Despard Case. (Wikipedia Commons)

Above: Polite society. (Public domain)

Right: Suicide of Lord Castlereagh. (Public domain)

A Prison Hulk. (Public domain)

Hanging outside Newgate. (Wikipedia Commons)

so. Another problem for him when he left government was that any loss for the Crown that he presided over was seen by some as Ellenborough now being in opposition, an impression that was probably untrue but was made possible by the fact that he had once been in government. Sir Vicary Gibbs, doing his stint as Attorney General, allegedly said that 'we shall never get another verdict for the Crown while the Chief Justice is in opposition'.[7]

Gibbs was sarcastic, arrogant and bullying, so this may well have been a light hearted comment, but the whole episode had done nobody any good, including the Chief Justice.

Chapter Thirteen

Humanitarian?

Ellenborough's faults and foibles seem obvious to the modern reader, but a bit of caution is needed. The first, of course, is anachronism; Ellenborough was a man of his class and represented the establishment of the time; to condemn Ellenborough is to condemn most of society – which can be self-affirming to the modern world-view but is not history. It is possible to start with a piece of positive news:

> I have always felt a great abhorrence of the mode by which these unfortunate creatures are torn from their families and country, and have doubted whether any sound policy could grow out of a system which seemed to be so vicious in its foundation: but I am extremely alarmed at the consequences of disturbing it, particularly in the present convulsed state of the world.[1]

In this letter to William Wilberforce in June 1802, Ellenborough accepted that the slave trade was not morally acceptable to him. Ellenborough goes on to say that he is clear that, notwithstanding the law as it stood, trading in human beings was not God's will. However, like many social conservatives in a period of political turmoil, he used the argument that 'now is not the time'. Wilberforce described the letter as 'truly pleasing', believing that when the time was right, Ellenborough would vote in favour of abolition in the House of Lords – and he was correct. It was to be only five years away.

Yet he was no humanitarian in the broader sense. He was not liberal, forgiving or tolerant. He did not wish to ameliorate punishments of the guilty or reduce the burdens on the poor. They were God-given; slavery was not. He would never have heard the term 'human rights', and if explained to him, would have argued that the rights people had were correct and sufficient, with the possible exception of the plantation slave. When he heard humanitarian views in the Lords from Whig aristocrats or radicals in his court, his least offensive reaction was a sneer.

So, it is a great surprise that Ellenborough has been praised in our time by what are now regularly called 'human rights lawyers'. Lord Ellenborough's judgements have been used in the twenty-first century in an attempt to protect refugees from the state's attempts to deny them access to public funds. In 2003 there was a legal dispute between the then Labour Home Secretary David Blunkett and the legal establishment about the attempt to deny asylum seekers housing and social security benefits. Legal judgements are based on precedents, many of which are from eminent judges. This one is regularly quoted: 'The law of humanity, which is anterior to all positive laws, obliges us to afford them relief, to save them from starving.'

So, if there is no active legislation to the contrary, then the state has to promote a person's basic right not to starve. This actual sentence was not part of the judgement but an *obiter dictum*, an opinion that can be used as a precedent. So 'Ellenborough's Law of Humanity' is a staple in all English law books and led to this Supreme Court ruling: 'I would hold it unlawful to alter the benefit regime so drastically as to inevitably not merely prejudice, but, on occasion, defeat, the statutory right of asylum seekers to claim refugee status.'[2]

In 1950, the European Convention on Human Rights was drawn up; it was based on the English common law, and Ellenborough deserves some of the credit for applying this humanitarian principle to the common law canon 150 years earlier.

The case that created the precedent was *Rex v The Inhabitants of Eastbourne*, although it was the two poor law commissioners of Eastbourne who were in the dock. As destitution rose in Britain, so did the cost of looking after the poor, and local overseers were becoming increasingly paranoid about the people living on their patch, so Justices of the Peace around the country started to evict paupers who were not locals.

The story began with the German national John Borchert, who had arrived in Britain in the early 1790s, possibly displaced by war in Europe. He married Eastbourne girl Anne Tutt in 1795 and set up shop as a baker. John clearly had no wish to be a burden; he worked as a baker in Seaford, rented a house and paid a respectable rent, but eventually moved his business to Eastbourne to make a better living – a desperate act, as it made his welfare situation very complicated.

Ann Borchert and her four children, John (6), Mary (4), Sophia (2), and Ann, a baby, remained in Seaford and so became a potential charge on the parish, and so the justices of the peace ordered her removal to Eastbourne, where she had been born, and the inhabitants of Eastbourne objected. Rather than worry about whether they would starve, the two parishes squabbled, and this led to a ruling at the King's Bench about the rights of foreigners to welfare.

Ellenborough and two other judges decreed that the hard-working German immigrant had earned the right to welfare, and in any case, it made no sense to allow people to starve – in the absence of any regulations to the contrary, that was the humane approach. The conclusion was humane, but the animus was respect for the law. If one line of the Poor Law Act had specifically excluded refugees from its benefits, he would have allowed John Borchert to starve. Ellenborough's virtue was his insistence on applying the law – if this helped poor people, then that was a detail rather than a principle.

Borchert clearly remained poor, despite Ellenborough's ruling. While returning home to Seaford from Newhaven a few years later in appalling weather, he was struck by lightning ('the blazing fluid', as the newspapers called it) 'He was instantly deprived of life, his habiliments being torn from his body, which was left nearly naked and scattered in numerous fragments around him.'[3]

Both his travelling companions survived. Because of his tragic death, we know what he was wearing: a coat, waistcoats, breeches, stockings and a shirt. His 'silver' watch was opened up and exposed as a cheaper brass or copper body. He was never rich, and nothing is known about Anne and the children, but he died with human rights given to him by Ellenborough.

Another area in which some credit needs to be extended to Ellenborough is his attitude towards the Jewish population. The anti-Jewish prejudices of Georgian Britain were as real as modern antisemitism, moderated – if that is the word – by an absence of the specific paranoid conspiracy theories that darken our age. There was bad feeling and resentment at both their poverty *and* their riches, usually solid evidence that a persecuted minority could do nothing right. The racist trope of Jewish cunning definitely existed: their views were flexible, they were rootless, and they owed little allegiance. They were money lenders, receivers of stolen goods and not producers of anything. The media drew attention to Jews. A man named Smith in a stagecoach accident would be 'the Jew Smith'. It was the same, and more so, in the law courts. If a Jew got the taste of his own medicine, then the newspaper headline had a celebratory exclamation mark.[4]

To be a Jew was unfortunate, and religious conversion was a charitable act similar to the help given to fallen women and the industrious poor. The main engine of this philanthropy was the London Society Promoting Christianity Amongst The Jews. Its aim was 'the benevolent purpose of rescuing the unhappy Jews from the state of moral degradation in which they find themselves'. One of their key members was William Wilberforce. Similarly, the death-bed conversions of Jews were noteworthy. It was good news, a vindication of the truth of Christianity, and was greeted with glee and gloating.

There was a general view that even the 'harmless' Jew could not be allowed to get above himself. In 1782, the liberal Anglophile clergyman German Karl Philipp Moritz toured England. After his visit to London, he took the stagecoach to the village of Richmond, and, en route, the coach stopped at Kensington to pick up more passengers and fill the pockets of the driver with undeclared fares. A Jew applied for a place and wished to have one of the more comfortable seats inside the vehicle. This would not have bothered the passengers on the inside, as silence on short journeys was the practice for both Jews and gentiles alike. What really bothered Moritz's fellow travellers was the fact that there were places free on the more dangerous and uncomfortable outside seats, but the Jewish gentlemen had opted for something better. They could not help thinking it preposterous that a Jew should be ashamed to ride on the outside, as they added, 'he was nothing more than a Jew'.

Ellenborough seemed to lack an active antisemitic animus. Some radicals, such as Cobbett, lauded today, were very anti-Jew. In Ellenborough's court, the application of the law came first, no matter who the defendant was. In one case, in 1811, Ellenborough presided over the case of *Lindo v Unsworth*. The defendant was being sued for failing to complete his business obligations. In mitigation, the day in question was Yom Kippur, the holiest day in Judaism, and nobody of that faith was working in his counting house, but the tasks were completed at the first possible opportunity the morning after. Ellenborough ruled that it was impossible for a Jew to perform work on a holy day, as it was for a Christian on Sunday, and this ruling has become a form of precedent: 'the law merchant respects the religion of different people', but the real step forward was the comparison of the two holy days and the assumption that they were of equal worth. He was not the only Georgian judge to grant concessions when Jews had been called to appear on the Sabbath or a holy day, but it put Ellenborough on the side of the angels in this matter.

Another case of 1807, *Young v Wright*, involved a Mr King – a witness identified as Jewish ('of the Jewish persuasion' it announced coyly, but at least in this case it was relevant). He had evidence in the case of fraud involving a bill of exchange, but his evidence was challenged on the basis of his admission that in the past he had sworn his oath on the New Testament rather than the Old, which had been allowed since 1744. The Attorney General, Vicary Gibbs – perhaps the only person ruder and more reactionary than Ellenborough himself – made the antisemitic point that as a Jew, Mr King had rejected the four evangelists but used them under oath when it suited him, so as a Jew, his word could not be trusted. Ellenborough made no negative comment to the jury, merely asking if they gave Mr King the Jew any credit; in the end they did not, but that was their prejudice, not his.

Ellenborough's house in Roehampton was purchased from a Jew.[5] The Goldsmid brothers Abraham and Benjamin were the first Ashkenazim Jews to gain the acceptance of the British establishment in about 1795, when they started to finance the British war effort and gave money to Christian charities. The family made their money through trading of bullion, navy and exchequer bills and negotiating British and foreign bills of exchange. Their immense wealth meant that they were mostly exempted from Georgian antisemitism. The mob were unable to throw stones at them and abuse them in the street, and the establishment could not socially exclude them because they were vital for the war effort. They were absolutely vital for bankrolling the war with Napoleon, so they were much more than tolerated. They lived in aristocratic splendour at Roehampton and entertained the king, Prime Minister Pitt, and the national hero Horatio Nelson. Government business was discussed, and a top Paris chef and their own kosher catering staff were employed, demonstrating that the Goldsmids managed to negotiate a fine line between assimilation and maintaining their own identity. Benjamin played the game by actively involving himself in charity. He founded and briefly ran the Naval Asylum as a favour to the monarch. His great wealth and open-handed generosity earned him the title of 'The Benevolent Jew', although there is a hint of prejudice in the phrase, which seems to modify with an unusual adjective a value not normally expected with the noun.[6]

Like many such rich risk-taking pioneers, Benjamin suffered from the twin plagues of gout and commercial failure and, in 1808, hanged himself in one of his many bedrooms at Roehampton. He strangled himself with the silk cord that was used to lever his immobile body out of bed in the morning. The jury found a verdict of lunacy, which meant that the family's inheritance was saved. There was an increasing tendency at the beginning of the century for the rich and famous to be spared a verdict of suicide. The same tragedy happened again two years later, when his brother shot himself in the throat due to similar commercial pressures.

It was significant that Ellenborough had bought a house from a Jewish family. It would have been the subject of gossip, and was mentioned in the newspapers. Apart from the social implications, there was a suggestion that Jews could not own property. The 1290 expulsion law had never been repealed; nobody would be more aware of that than the Chief Justice. Property that was not owned could not be passed on. It has been suggested that Benjamin held his property through a gentile proxy, and no doubt Ellenborough would know this too, but what he did was still remarkable.

He accepted that Jews could own property, just as he accepted that they could abstain from work on a Jewish religious holiday without punishment or swear only on the book of Moses without their integrity being questioned. Ellenborough stood for the rigorous and fair application of the law, no matter what the consequences. An absolutist government would have found him a formidable enemy.

Another example of apparent humanitarian animus was the trial of the former Governor of Trinidad and Tobago, Sir Thomas Picton, accused of torturing the 13-year-old Louisa Calderon. She was a 'free mulatto'(in the terminology of the time) who was under the protection of the British crown. William Garrow led the prosecution and gave a harrowing account of the life of a poor mixed-race child in the colonies. She was in a sexual relationship at about the age of 11 with her keeper, Pedro Ruiz. Garrow's plan was to convince the jury that, in the words of a local newspaper recently, 'Louisa's only crime may have been her being a young, nubile girl, forced by poverty to live as the concubine to an old man'.[7]

She was accused of being involved with another man, Carlos Gonzalez, in a plot to rob Ruiz of cash and gold. Her arrest and torture were ordered by Picton after she was arrested, but she did not admit guilt. There was no other evidence. A new word was invented: 'Pictoning' – a form of torture in which the victim has one arm tied by a rope that runs through a pulley connected to the ceiling, while the other arm is tied to one of the feet so that the leg is forcibly bent upward at the knee. The other foot is then positioned so that a toe rests on a spiked piece of wood as the weight of the whole body is lowered onto it. It was meant to cause extreme pain rather than permanently cripple, as it was usually a punishment reserved for soldiers – although it was possible to lose a leg if the procedure was not done properly.

The torture – and the word was used in Picton's order – outraged one section of the public looking for justice, and titillated a more prurient element. A pretty teenage girl, scantily dressed and tied up, was shown in lots of illustrations, some coming from court reporters, others from an overactive imagination. Garrow pointed out that torture is not legal in England; as the judge, a man whose respect for the law as it stood was greater than his desire in principle to stop the torture of girls, Ellenborough would have picked up this point. The opposite argument was that torture was permitted under Spanish law at the time of the first British occupation and had not been repealed, and that the black population was treated worse – noses were split and hands amputated, for example. Ellenborough saw no precedent for torture to establish the guilt of another person; if torture *had* been allowed by authority, Picton would have been freed, even if feelings might revolt

If the law was harsh, then Ellenborough followed suit. The 1808 verdict of *Baker v Bolton* showed Ellenborough at his very worst, or very best, depending on opinion. Mr Baker and his wife, married for thirty years and with twenty-two children, boarded a coach owned by the Bolton company. The driver was drunk; he must have been very drunk for the fact to be noted, as all coach drivers were drinkers. The Bakers were on the outside, and the highly inebriated coachmen took the wrong route and crashed his vehicle into a house in Putney when he should have been in Wandsworth. In the random lottery of consequences when a body is thrown on the ground from the top of a stagecoach, Mr Baker's wife (omitting the first name for women in newspaper articles was common) snapped her thigh with the bone protruding so badly that she had to be laid in a cart and covered in straw. At St George's Hospital, her leg was amputated, and she languished for a month before dying.

The Attorney General (Vicary Gibbs) asked for liberal damages, but these were denied. Mr Baker was given £100 as compensation for his own cuts and bruises, an acknowledgement that his wife had helped greatly in running their public house in Charing Cross, but nothing to compensate for her painful demise – as 'death put an end to their relative situations to each other'. The death of a human being could not be complained of as an injury; that was the law.[8]

A man of Ellenborough's standing would be expected to be charitable, and he fulfilled that role well. From 1806 until his death, he was the Vice President of the Bloomsbury Dispensary. Like most late Georgian charities, money was raised through subscriptions, with senior members of society acting as patrons, to create an endorsement and encourage those further down the social scale to join and thereby associate themselves with their betters. Patrons were advertised in order of social seniority: Ellenborough was third, after the obligatory aristocrat as lead (in this case the Duke of Bedford) and a member of the bench of bishops (in this case the Bishop of Chichester, John Buckner, who had a house in Wigmore Street and was also Rector of St Giles-in-the-Fields, so would have seen the deprivation in the area).

Monies were raised in various ways: annual and lifetime subscriptions; annual sermons and dinners; and one-off appeals to the general public. All contributions were well advertised in the newspaper. Ellenborough's lifetime subscription would have cost him ten guineas. He would have contributed to the charity sermons (prayers beforehand and a whip-round afterwards) and annual dinners at large public houses such as the Freemasons Arms. Dinner was early (on the table at 5.15 precisely, as promised in the yearly advertisements every April) because it was going to be a long night of eating, drinking, toasts (i.e., drinking), singing, and entertainment. They were not cosy gatherings; they were held in a 'superpub'. Admission was half a guinea, and there would be a collection. The 1805 dinner provided food, drink and entertainment for 150 people. The Duke of Bedford made a speech; he vacated the chair, leaving the deferential audience wanting more, and was replaced by Robert Thornton MP and by Mr Fitzmaurice on the union pipes. The advertisements promised 'no collections' after dinner, which really meant no collections when everyone was drunk and incapable.[9]

Money was spent on the poor, mostly tenants of the Duke of Bedford, who was the patron of the society. Like all charities, the benevolent rich were daily under the terror that somebody undeserving should receive help. They needed a letter of recommendation from the officers at 62 Great Russell Street; they needed to be free of the stigma of parish relief, and they needed to be grateful. They had to be the deserving poor, who, by accepting charity, also accepted their place in society. Ellenborough believed this, but then so did everybody.

Unusually, subscribing does not seem to have given you the right to nominate people for treatment yourself; this was quite common. Another London charity that Ellenborough would have known about was the Lying-in Charity for Delivering Poor Married Women in Their Own Habitations. Another ten guinea subscriptions allowed the nomination of eight women for free childbirth at home. Afterwards, they were obliged to go to church to thank God and visit the charity to thank their betters.

Much of this was typical; charity was voluntary, local, and hedged around with caveats, but the Bloomsbury Dispensary was a pioneering one. It was famous for its emphasis on inoculation with cowpox to prevent smallpox. Unlike illness, no letter of recommendation was needed; it was clearly seen as a public health measure. The society had organised free clinics for the poor every Saturday since at least 1802. This was remarkably forward-looking when Jenner's first successful experiment had been a mere six years earlier and variolation, as it was called, was still controversial. Jenner worked with the Bloomsbury Dispensary himself. Jenner was Superintendent of Vaccination at the time of Ellenborough's death, and it is highly likely that they would have met.[10]

Conspiracy theories about inoculation abounded, and Ellenborough rejected them all. He was a scientific Chief Justice. Ellenborough did not believe that the mixture of human and bovine elements would produce monsters, nor that disease was God-given and that preventing it would be unacceptable to Him. He did not pretend or imagine new diseases that would appear as a consequence, or pretend that did not work. His own son, Edward, put forward the case for compulsory vaccination in 1840, perhaps persuaded by the fact that neither he or any of his siblings had suffered due to their father vaccinating his children.

He was well ahead of his time in this regard: anti-vaccination, with the concomitant conspiracy theories, would be powerful in Victorian Britain. Jenner's effigy was still being burned in Banbury as late as 1877. In 1813, there was an attempt to make vaccination compulsory, and Ellenborough opposed it from the House of Lords. However, it was not vaccination that he opposed, but compulsion. Jenner was furious with Ellenborough: 'Why should Lord Ellenborough or any earthly Lord sanction the continuance of small pox when the Lord of all has commanded us to get rid of this pestilence?'[11]

This was intemperate and unfair of Jenner. Ellenborough accepted that it was a public health benefit by saying that a crowded city like London needed such a measure, but he would go no further. His view that the beneficial effects of medical intervention were probably temporary was a mistake shared by large proportions of the population. He acknowledged the progress of science, but believed that the common law and the common sense of parents, such as himself, was enough.

Ellenborough was able to prove his point in 1815, when Sophia Vantandillo was indicted for carrying her smallpox-infected child John through White Lion Passage in Paddington, 'through which his majesty's subjects passed'. The defence argument was that it was not an offence under common law and was rejected: she had committed a public nuisance, not just by the danger of infection but by the distress caused to passers-by who stepped away into a dangerous road to avoid an infected child. Ellenborough believed that the three-month stint in the Marshalsea was a common-law solution to a problem. He did not believe in a humanitarian approach to the rules; he simply applied them as they were.

Chapter Fourteen

Influence and Money

To cut to the end of the story, Ellenborough died in 1818, a very rich and famous man. His legacy was not caused by frugality in life – there is no evidence that he hoarded money or was a miser. The artist Joseph Farington loved gossiping about money; in the month before Ellenborough's death, he incorrectly stated that Ellenborough was thought not to be rich because he lived liberally. Farington knew how much money he earned, and how much he paid for his house at Roehampton, but he did not know the full implications of his other sources of income or his influence with the royal family.

By 1812, Ellenborough had been at the top of the establishment for a decade, the money was rolling in, and most of his unpopularity was still in the future. In any case, he was popular with the man who mattered, having done him a great service during the so-called 'Delicate Investigation', and with both of them knowing that they would need each other just as much in the future.

His salary as Chief Justice was £5,500 a year. He would have been paying a 5 per cent tax on all income above £150 as his contribution to the war effort. This was a property tax introduced by William Pitt to defray some of the £20 million a year that the government was borrowing to fund the war against France. There is no evidence of any complaints on his part; it was a temporary war tax whose abolition was promised when Napoleon was defeated. When the time came, Ellenborough voted to remove it in a rare show of defiance to the Tory government (which he loyally supported after 1812) who thought that the country's finances were so bad that it should be retained.

This headline salary was only the beginning of his income. He had other jobs under his control that could be sold to the highest bidder or given to friends and family. Most of these jobs were sinecures – jobs with impressive sounding names but which involved either no real work, or work that could be devolved on others while keeping almost all of the money. By the end of the Napoleonic era, there was an increasing outcry about such sinecures, but those who enjoyed them regarded the money as just another part of their income and the business of nobody but themselves. In 1812, MP Sir Francis Burdett calculated that Ellenborough received £8,993 in sinecures. The Chief Justice's sinecures could feed 300 families for a year, it was claimed. Another political enemy, William Cobbett, looked again at the figures and concluded it was an underestimation of nearly £1,000.

One sinecure under the control of the Chief Justice was the Chief Clark of the Court of King's Bench. The post had been changing hands for hard cash since the middle of the seventeenth century and Ellenborough was offered £80,000 from an outside source but granted it to his son instead. This post became vacant in late 1811, and Ellenborough acted quickly, according to a plausible story told by his biographer William Townsend. The judge was riding through Hyde Park when he was informed of the vacancy, dismounted at a house in Knightsbridge, and executed a legal document filling up the office lest he should die before appointing his preferred candidate. One of the perks and obligations of holding power in Georgian Britain was to use one's influence for the benefit of the family. The happy recipient was Edward Law junior, his eldest son, bound to be more famous than his father one day but who needed a leg up in 1812.

Ellenborough's eldest son and heir was born in 1790 and was destined for a career at least as glittering as his father, and Ellenborough did as much as he could. In the same way that Ellenborough did not want to be a theologian, young Law did not want to be a lawyer. This turned out to be a good thing, as the new position entailed very little work. It suited Ellenborough as well, as the father kept the actual receipts and only bequeathed the monies to his son in his will, as he did with other forms of property.

Law junior held the post until 1838, when changing views meant it was abolished and compensation offered. In the meantime, he earned £8,000 a year, took fees for his work, and the family took the interest on the money placed with the court by the suitors. One of his jobs was to appoint minor officials and receive fees for that; one of them was Charles Law, another son of the Chief Justice.

Ellenborough stoutly defended his right to these sinecures: should his salary be reduced, he was asked? 'No: reduction of salary must proceed on the ground of diminution of duty. Now, as nothing ever has been done in that office it is impossible that less could be done in it in future.'[1]

In a letter to Spencer Perceval he pointed out that not only were these prerequisites a matter of law, but they were no different from ecclesiastical benefices and positions, such as those his own family had benefited from, and abolishing them would follow next if his perks were removed.[2]

The year before his underserved advancement, Law junior was in Sicily – almost the only place you could visit in Europe in a time when Napoleon dominated Europe, and this was because it was secured by the British military. This was his real interest, but his father did not allow him to follow it. He liked Eton but not the University of Cambridge, and he claimed that his tutors only cared about the war and its soldiers when it pushed up the price of port after a military defeat.

Having been denied a full-on army career, Edward junior compromised on being a 'military statesman', and for that he would need a seat in the Commons. He would also need a connection to the Foreign Office, and he completed both in one bound in 1813. He married Lady Octavia Stewart, sister of the foreign secretary, Castlereagh, and became an MP for the Cornish rotten borough of St Michaels. The marriage allowed Law into the foreign office and looks like a cynical career move; it seems that both families were initially opposed. Entry into the Commons was equally fraught; he became of age at the end of 1811, and it took nearly two years to find a suitable seat. This was his third attempt, and he needed the influence of his father's friend, Lord Sidmouth.

His new constituency of St Michaels was a rotten seat in a rotten county with a rotten system. It had two members of parliament and was fought over by two rival families of equal strength, who each nominated an MP to avoid a ruinous contest. Edward Law junior was elected without troubling the electorate of eighteen. A few decades earlier, the electorate had been thirty-nine, but the landowners had been demolishing the houses of people who had the vote to make their manipulation of the seat easier. When the constituency of St Michaels was abolished by the 1832 Reform Act, the electorate was seven. There was no more rotten county than Cornwall, which had forty-two members of parliament, forty for the boroughs and two for the county before 1832, compared to Yorkshire, which had two for the county and none for the new towns and cities of Leeds, Huddersfield and Bradford.

Law junior was unable to take part in the 1818 election. The voting took place over a week in the summer, chosen from a six-week period, as was the tradition. Law was in Italy with his wife, who was trying, and tragically failing, to recover from TB. Ellenborough did not think it was worth the money to get his son back into parliament; the king was ill, his death would trigger a general election, and even the small investment would be wasted. Law junior, of course, would inherit a seat in the Lords on his own father's death, and by 1818, Ellenborough probably knew that date might be even closer.

Law junior had a successful career after his father's death. Apart from his support for Catholic emancipation, he was as reactionary as his father and shared the same personal defects. In parliament he was always vehement and not always master of the facts, and he was both talented and arrogant – 'certainly a clever young man, perhaps a little conscious that he is so' commented one.[3]

He did not support the extension of the vote in 1832 and had a poor view of the working classes: 'this country does not want philosophers from the loom nor statesmen from the spinning Jenny,' he said.

Ellenborough left £240,000 in his will. His wife was well looked after and could look forward to £2,000 a year to live on. She received nearly all of the furniture in the house in St James's and most of the artwork and decorations, except certain prints which he had kept in his dressing room, hinted Leigh Hunt's *Examiner*.[4]

The house in St James was sold to provide annuities for his other children. His eldest son, Edward, was also well provided for. He received the house at Roehampton and most of its contents and £2,000 in cash – there was no annuity like there was for the dowager Lady Ellenborough, as the implication was that he would make his own way in the world; his most important gift to his son was the peerage and the power that went with it.

Law's other sons prospered after his death. Charles Ewan, the second son (born 1792), was favoured with the legal sinecure of clerk of *nisi prius* at the King's Bench in London and Middlesex, had a distinguished legal career, rising to Recorder of London, the senior circuit judge at the Old Bailey hearing trials of criminal offences. He was also an MP for the continuing University of Cambridge seat and was often returned unopposed.

William Towry Law (born 1809) took two of the other three routes, first in the army and then holy orders. He subsequently became chancellor of the diocese of Bath and Wells, and he joined the Catholic Church in 1851. Henry Spencer Law (born May 1802) was a barrister at the Inner Temple, served in the Lifeguards, and became the private secretary to his brother Edward. Two of his children became the fifth and sixth barons Ellenborough.

Every year of Ellenborough's adult life was a twelve-month period of defending the status quo. 1812 was a particularly busy one, with two libel trials in which Ellenborough was victorious over two long-standing enemies of the establishment who had hitherto escaped 'justice'. Both trials led to crushing punishments for his enemies – and they were his enemies, as he took the attack on cherished institutions very personally.

The year started with another sensitive issue – an update on the mental health of King George III. His condition had become so severe that he was unable to fulfil his constitutional function, and by the Regency Act of 1811, an attenuated version of his authority had been passed to his son George, now the Prince Regent. The law that made this possible was not signed by the monarch; a convoluted legal way was found to get around this, to which Ellenborough consented. Sometimes only extreme flexibility could maintain the system.

Ellenborough was a member of the Queen's Council, who had the job of meeting with His Majesty every three months and reporting back on his condition. The newspaper reports on the king's health did not vary very much, which was a source of frustration for the general public, but it reflected reality. This one was from a few years later, in 1818: 'His Majesty has been very tranquil through the last month and continues to enjoy good bodily health, but His Majesty's disorder is undiminished.'[5]

Ellenborough also received daily reports in the government red box, which on the whole were not much more revealing, although we know from other correspondence that the king could still recognise and acknowledge Ellenborough and missed him on the occasions when he was absent. Eldon, the Lord Chancellor, was the other member of the council who was neither a medic nor a cleric, and the whole group generally reported that he was unchanged and no less likely to recover. It was the doctors who made the decision, and the clerics and politicians who confirmed it.[6]

This meant that the Regency, less than a year old in January 1812, would continue until the death of the monarch. Ellenborough was the centre of the establishment now; he decided who ruled.

Ellenborough had three brothers living in Britain; one of them, Ewan, seemed less ambitious than the others and so Ellenborough did not need to help him; perhaps as a result, Ewan lived in his brother's shadow. The two men were close, as events would show. It is clear that Ewan was later defined by his brother's ascendant position in society, as the *Sussex Advertiser* reported in 1813: 'on that day, I dined with Ewan Law, Esq, (Lord Ellenborough's brother) at Horsted Place'. In August 1810, when Ewan's daughter Maria married Sir George Clerk, she was described in the marriages section of the *Gentleman's Magazine* as 'the niece of Lord Ellenborough'. When he died in 1829, he was described as the 'elder brother of Lord Ellenborough'.

Ellenborough had two brothers who took their father's advice and went into the church: his elder brother John and his younger brother George. Up until Ellenborough's decision to join the legal profession, they both had similar backgrounds: Charterhouse, Cambridge, and then the promotion by their father. Both were more liberal and tolerant than Ellenborough, but that was a low bar, and they did very well in the church.

John died in 1810 after a successful career as a bishop in Ireland, but George needed his brother's help. While he was defending the reputation of the Prince Regent in 1812, he would have noticed a vacancy in the See of Chester, caused by the elevation into the next division of bishoprics of Dr Bowyer Sparke. Ellenborough clearly believed that Chester would be an ideal post for his younger brother and must have been openly lobbying for him, because on 11 June he received an apologetic note from the Prime Minister, Lord Liverpool. Liverpool had been Prime Minister for three days, and, as the Prince Regent's fifth choice and with an unstable coalition behind him, it was not expected to last very long. Liverpool told Ellenborough that his brother was not to be the new bishop, and the post instead would go to Gerrard Andrewes, Dean of Canterbury. Andrewes was highly thought of, and it was his turn to be promoted. Six of the seven previous Deans had been promoted to a bishopric, and the only exception had died in office.

Liverpool's letter is defensive and apologetic, as would be expected when a powerful person is disappointed. 'You will readily believe that in our present situation, it is a most material object to me that the first bishopric should appear to the world to have been filled up at my recommendation.'

It was almost a plea: 'I am new, so I need to look strong.' Liverpool went on to say the prince had informed him about his anxiety about the promotion of his brother. In effect, Liverpool promised him the next bishopric to become available.

Ellenborough was too directly connected to the Prince Regent, and Liverpool too weak, for this to be the end of the matter. He wrote back to Liverpool the next day to say that he was mystified: the prince had thought his brother's promotion was a sound idea ('received with the most gracious condescension'). It was a shame that his brother was not better known; he is as clever as the Dean of Canterbury, although admittedly 'does not equal him in the talent for public speaking by which the Dean is so eminently distinguished'. He has been a benefit to the state and has never asked for anything for himself. Ellenborough threatened to take it personally and drag his resentment around in a way that would not benefit Liverpool's shaky government – in the nicest possible way, of course. He goes on to say that he has never asked for any preferment for himself, and this was true, but it was also not the way that establishment nepotism worked. Somebody else lobbied for you, just as Ellenborough was doing now.

This passive-aggressive missive was only the overture to the main event: Ellenborough decided to be a snitch and go over Liverpool's head to the man who very reluctantly appointed him. On the same day, probably before, he wrote to the Prince Regent, including a copy of Liverpool's letter – a Georgian version of the malicious email 'cc'.

When the letter was received, Ellenborough was at the midpoint of a trial in which two journalists were accused of calling the prince fat, useless, immoral and vain. It would be Ellenborough's skilled job to argue that this truth was false and send them to prison for libel. This must have made some impression on the prince, as a few weeks later George Law was consecrated Bishop of Chester. It seemed that Andrewes was offered it first and turned it down due to his advanced age – at 62, he was quite old for a first appointment to the bench of bishops – but the fact of the matter was that superior forces defeated him. George Law would take his place on the bench, an unelected lawmaker like his brother.

Liverpool's initial promise to promote him when convenient was not nullified by this promotion. George Law rose to the next rank in 1824, being translated to Bath and Wells. In 1818, his own son was promoted into a top post as soon as a vacancy arose; meanwhile, in Ely, Bishop Sparkes was behaving in the same, accepted way, appointing his family to posts in the diocese: 'you could make your way through the dark streets of East

Anglia, it was said, by the number of small sparks on the road'. In another 'coincidence' that shows how the system was organised, the new Bishop of Chester in 1828 was John Bird Sumner, Edward Law junior's tutor at Eton.

George Law had a mixed record as a bishop. He set up one of the first theological colleges outside of Oxford and Cambridge Universities; he had his father's sympathy for the deserving poor, but he is not particularly celebrated in Somerset. He was fond of long holidays; he liked Bath (there is a picture of him in the Pump Room); and he had aristocratic connections in Western Super Mare and helped to develop the seaside resort. He suffered the same fate as many people in a job until death: his effectiveness declined rapidly in the last years of his life, to the detriment of his reputation. He assisted at the coronation of Queen Victoria in 1838, turned over two pages at once in the order of service, and told the queen that the service was over. She retired to an anti-chamber and had to be recalled: the Archbishop of Canterbury had already put the ring on the wrong finger and given her the orb and sceptre at the wrong time. The Bishop of Durham wandered off completely. This is the quality of public servants that can be achieved when the appointment is gained through nepotism.

Chapter Fifteen

Ellenborough Against the Libellers

Ellenborough abhorred libel; the reflective person of our age may agree with him and wonder why he developed a bad reputation for prosecuting it so vigorously. However, in his time, libel was not merely the telling of untruths. In 1804, Ellenborough had defined libel as that 'which tends to incite the discontent of the people, either by calumny or design, to bring the established authorities of government into disesteem'. So a malicious lie that was published widely could be a libel, but so could the truth; it followed that the truth of a statement was not a defence against a charge of libel. This was not the view of the Chief Justice alone: it was the view of all of the establishment.

The whole area was ambiguous. You were allowed to make general statements about the state of the nation. Ellenborough said so himself in 1809 when the Attorney General argued that this statement by newspaper owner James Perry was libellous: 'What a crowd of blessings might be bestowed on the country in the event of a total change of system. No monarch indeed, since the Revolution, will have so fine an opportunity of becoming nobly popular as the successor to George III.'[1] Ellenborough instructed the jury that Mr Perry clearly envisaged the continuity of the monarchy and was observing that life was not perfect, both of which were obviously correct and not libel. It was acceptable for citizens to discuss all public policy freely but temperately, as long as there was no malice and no threat to the present system – a decision that would always be down to the courts and therefore to men like Ellenborough. It was not really much of a concession to free speech.

In 1812, there were two major treason trials where Ellenborough endeavoured to protect two key areas of the establishment. In March,

Ellenborough was out fighting to defend God against the writings of Thomas Paine and the publication of his work by radical publisher Daniel Isaac Eaton. In that case, libel was defined as holding a blasphemous opinion.

The second libel trial of 1812–13 was his attempt to protect another layer of the great chain of being from the gutter press and their seditious libels aimed at the Prince Regent. It was the Hunt brothers, journalist Leigh and publisher John, who were made an example of when they launched a verbal assault on the Prince Regent in March 1812. Tired of all the flattery in the client press, the Hunts wrote a humorous piece calling him a lying, cheating, gambling, adulterous, greedy, irresponsible waste of space who had achieved little substance despite a life of privilege.

The protection of the Almighty on 6 March 1812, did not start smoothly. Ellenborough was informed that Eaton had opted to represent himself. This always annoyed his lordship. It was inefficient, disrespectful to the court and its procedures, and meant that he would have to listen to the views of the defendant in their own words rather than be filtered by the self-censorship of the defence council, who were afraid of him. An efficient Georgian judge controlled everything: the law was complex, the lawyers could be brow-beaten, and the jury could be steered to the correct conclusion.

Eaton was also late. Ellenborough, after checking that the correct procedure had been followed and that Eaton had been informed of the trial, started without him. Ellenborough was regularly complimented on his rigorous application of every rule, but this was no inconvenience when people of his own class actually made the rules in the first place. Eventually Eaton turned up, and his plan, as Ellenborough feared, was to use the trial for publicity.

Eaton had evaded the establishment's revenge for more than two decades. He was regarded by some as the 'Printer to His Majesty the People', a concept that would have perplexed and infuriated Ellenborough in equal measure. He had been found not guilty twice before, in 1793, for publishing the works of Thomas Paine. He knew the stakes were high: he had been imprisoned in 1804–5, and now he was in court for publishing a blasphemous libel, part three of Paine's *Age of Reason*, in which the author, among other things, rejected the literal truth of the Bible and the religious practices and beliefs of the established church. Paine had been a pain in the side of the establishment since the 1790s, when his *Rights of Man* suggested to the working classes that they had a part in the rule and wealth of the country by natural right rather than by the British Constitution. Later, to no one's surprise, he turned out to be a religious dissident as well.

It was Attorney General William Garrow who led the defence of the omnipotent, omniscient creator. The prosecution case was verbose but boiled down to two points. The first was theological – that the purity and integrity of the Holy Scriptures must be maintained, which made sense as this was a blasphemy trial; the second was perhaps more telling: 'if this sacred thread was broken, what would happen to other great bonds – between master and servant, prince and subject, man and man, all of which were supported by religion?'. This chimed well with Ellenborough and his class: anarchy was just around the corner unless the line was held against incorrect and fantastic opinions.

Defendants accused of blasphemy were assumed to be liars. In Ellenborough's view, Eaton and his like subverted the whole system simply by speaking under oath. Even liberally inclined Garrow wondered on what basis Eaton could even speak in his defence truthfully when he was obliged to take an oath he did not believe in – a problem that would plague atheists and deists in English courts for another fifty years.

All words in an English court were directed at the jury. The twelve men in court would be carefully selected – a 'special jury', used in all libel trials. They would be of higher than average social rank on the basis that they would be intelligent enough to detect a libel and leap to the defence of the true religion established by law. It also conveniently and intentionally meant that twelve London merchants on this special jury would have nothing in common with a rabble-rousing poor publisher.

The whole basis of the accusation was unfair: Paine was no atheist; he believed in a first creator but rejected both the form of Christianity that existed and the established church that supported it. He merely wanted a free discussion of the matter. Whether Eaton himself believed in Paine's ideas was not relevant; publishing them was enough. Radical booksellers and publishers like Eaton were always in the crosshairs of the establishment. Even those poor people who sold radical newspaper pamphlets in the street were prosecuted for publishing them and treated accordingly. Like a social media post today, it was equivalent to a publication.

Eaton read out the whole book in dispute. Ellenborough warned him not to do it, as he could not bear to hear blasphemy – rather prejudging the case.

When Eaton insisted Ellenborough issued an obvious threat: 'Begin Sir, the first word and read until the last, but you will recollect that you will take the consequences.'[2]

This is one of the paradoxes of Georgian libel trials: in an attempt to discourage blasphemy and sedition, the offending material had to be read out in open court in order for the patriotic jury to be offended. It was always a difficult moment in a libel case, and most establishment newspapers obliged by abandoning their verbatim reports at this point. The next prosecution evidence was the successful 'test purchase' of the text, something that would remain the final piece of evidence in blasphemy and libel cases for another century. A Mr W. Bell Raven deposed that he had bought a copy of the offending book at Eaton's shop on 12 October last.

However, the court heard the 'blasphemies' (as Ellenborough called them throughout the trial – so much for impartiality), and Ellenborough took the criticisms personally, as if God were somebody he knew. Much of the press took the same view: according to the *Newcastle Journal*, Paine's book was 'a libel against God, against the founder of the Christian religion'. Perhaps at this point Ellenborough might have thought about his father, who would have dealt with Paine's irreligious comments with patience and calm, and perhaps with sweet reasonableness.

Eaton complained that he could not hear the judge very well, but Ellenborough was uncompromising; he was speaking perfectly clearly, and that was the end of the matter. This is how Ellenborough dealt with complaints: it was his court, and he did not debate. So, when Eaton demanded a theological discussion as part of his defence, the Lord Chief Justice was annoyed. Ellenborough told him that any evidence that contradicted the scriptures was, by definition, not evidence. Paine called Jesus an 'exceedingly good and virtuous man, but nothing supernatural or divine', and pointed out that the God of the Old Testament was unrecognisable to that of the New. It is no wonder that Ellenborough was determined to get him for atheism.

Ellenborough interrupted constantly, pushing the defence off course by denying the validity of evidence and provoking sycophantic laughter with such bon mots as 'your defence is an offence'. Ellenborough more or less told the special jury that this was blasphemy and awarded Eaton eighteen months in Newgate Prison and an hour in the pillory. Ellenborough was fond of the pillory as a ritual humiliation for the likes of Eaton, who were setting themselves against God. On one level, the modern observer may query why the omnipotent creator of the universe would need the deterrence of his enemies being pelted with insults and manure. Ellenborough and people like him did subscribe to this, but their main problem was the arrogance and presumption of those who would hold these ideas and, even worse, propagate them.

The Hunt brothers were next in the firing line. In 1812, Leigh Hunt had written and John Hunt had published a description of the Prince Regent's character which ended like this:

> a violator of his word, a libertine over head and ears in disgrace, a despiser of domestic ties, the companion of gamblers and demi reps, a man who has just closed half a century without one single claim on the gratitude of his country, or the respect of posterity.

Eaton and Hunt were similar in many ways: they were both bookish, literary men. Ellenborough was one of the 800 who sponsored Hunt's first book of poetry, written between the ages of 12 and 16, and entitled, accurately, *Juvenilia.* It was also supported by Pitt, Fox, Nelson, Jenner, Wilberforce, Sheridan and even Lord Eldon. Both men had both been through the courts before and suffered for their beliefs, but the differences were greater.

While Eaton sold pamphlets to radical artisans from a stall in Ave Maria Lane near St Paul's, the Hunt brothers were part of a radical set of artists and progressives. They were the original North London types, several cuts above Eaton and his supporters. The Hunts were leaders of the so-called 'Cockney school' of writers and intellectuals, including Keats, Shelley and others. Hunt's newspaper, the *Examiner*, with its other emphasis on poetry, theatre and literary criticism, was not aimed at the struggling poor. Their paths would never meet. Shelley, who supported both Eaton and Hunt, was a friend of Hunt, not Eaton.

Ellenborough was familiar with the Hunt brothers and their newspaper. It agitated for the abolition of the slave trade, political rights for Catholics, reform of the bloody code and parliamentary reform. They opposed the corruption of the system and were happy to use Ellenborough himself as an example. It sold for ten pence, beyond the pockets of the poor fools most susceptible to libel. On the front page of every edition, Hunt pointed out that half the cost of his newspaper was stamp duty and implied that this taxation existed not to raise revenue but to suppress radical thought. However, the severe attitude of Ellenborough was noted by even neutral observers: this was the fourth attempt to send the Hunts to prison, and it was not going to fail.

The prosecution of the Hunts showed that the ruling classes were coming out fighting for the prince. Perhaps it was a good move, as both Eaton and Hunt were implacable foes of the government. When the brothers appeared before Ellenborough at Bow Street, they pleaded not guilty. Hunt knew both that his journalism was true and, in the eyes of the law, a libel: 'No one can accuse me of not writing a libel. Everything is a libel, as the law is now declared.'[3]

Their defence council was headed by Henry Brougham, who knew better than anybody how elastic the libel laws were. He was not a man Ellenborough would want to see in his court. Brougham was no less a member of the establishment than the judge and their careers were similar – Brougham joined the Society of the Bears in 1817 and to this day, their joint commemorations are to be found in the Hall of Lincoln's Inn, which they both attended. The difference was that Brougham made his fame and fortune defending radical causes rather than propping up the establishment, of which he remained a member. Ellenborough would have had no time for him, although the opposite was not true. Brougham developed a respect for the Chief Justice despite everything.

Somebody that the Chief Justice did have time for was the Prince Regent. They were very similar. Both were unpopular with the masses, and neither cared. Both were tolerated by those who thought them politically necessary or hoped for some preferment. The similarity went deeper: both, when powerless, were presumed to be Whigs but became Tories when they ascended to influence. It was not quite the same: Ellenborough became a Tory and then gained power, while the Prince Regent shocked the Whigs that brought him to power by retaining his father's Tory friends. This made the prince unpopular with the Whigs, who were relying on him for power and preferment, and the radicals who hoped for change. One of those Whigs was Henry Brougham. Another two were the Hunt brothers, who were accused by their enemies of being motivated by frustrated ambition when the Prince Regent deserted them in 1811, and there was truth in that.

Brougham's defence was brilliant but brutal. In order to save his client, he had to present him in the worst possible light. Leigh Hunt was pale, tall and tousled and looked younger than his twenty-seven years; this helped Brougham's defence that he was still that schoolboy poet, just a little older and no wiser, whose friends were books and whose contact with the real world was minimal. Hunt said these terrible things about his prince because he was a bit puritanical, a bit fanatical, and a bit naive in his wish to make the world more moral. He was a nobody; our government had 'not to fear the paper shot', Brougham said.

Brougham came as close as he could to the modern defence against libel – that it was true. He also knew of course, that the truth was inadmissible evidence. The Prince Regent was in debt; it was public knowledge. The fact that he was associated with rogues and demi-reps was proved by two facts in the public domain: the successful conviction of one of his friends for adultery and their subsequent appointment to the prince's household. Brougham knew what he was doing; in a letter prior to the trial, he told Lord Grey, a fellow Whig, that the defence would be a thousand times more unpleasant than the libel.[4]

According to Brougham it seems that Ellenborough employed his usual tactic of undermining the defence with his own interruptions; Brougham's account suggests that Ellenborough did not have much luck with this. Brougham claimed that his two-hour speech was interrupted unsuccessfully by Ellenborough, who failed because he lost his temper. We cannot necessarily trust Brougham's version of events, as he shared one characteristic with Ellenborough – a massive ego and high self-regard. But we have evidence from Sir Colin Bell, who had a friend who was there: 'The interruption of his lordship was frivolous but necessary at the same time, for Brougham was carrying the hearts of the jury … the jury were forgetting themselves! Lord Ellenborough in the meanwhile was chafing in rage, restless bursting with bad humour.'

Eventually, the Chief Justice's bad temper and attempt to intimidate the jury would backfire. But that was not this day; it would come more or less exactly five years later.

Brougham's final flourish was this: *these are hard truths, but are they not truths?* The inference was that other papers had said the same thing – so why were the two brothers here now? And what about the hundreds of salacious cartoons saying the same thing? It was so well done that the professional and personal resentment towards Brougham was suspended. 'The barristers who have been so often oppressed by him forgot their jealousy of Brougham in the pleasure of seeing one who would not be repressed.'[4]

In his summing up Ellenborough proved his loyalty to, or perhaps his dependence on, the Prince Regent. Loyalty to his friend and patron was going to take rigorous mental gymnastics, but he managed it. Some of it was plain verbal manipulation – *should the country be dominated by such libellers as the defendants, or should it be protected by the rule of law?* he asked the jury. The *Examiner* thundered afterwards: 'he did not put the question, he begged it'.

The main problem was the charge of licentiousness and adultery. Everybody knew this was true. The prince's adultery was undeniable, so the Lord Chief Justice said nothing, but the establishment needed privacy and protection from the press. Who would take up public service if they were persecuted in such a manner? Ellenborough believed that by protecting one victim of libel, he was looking after the 10,000 people who would be spared the same fate by the force of a salutary example. But he could not maintain this position without downplaying aristocratic vice.

He already had a reputation for favouring the privileged, and this just added to it. Ellenborough suggested that such a charge could be regarded as a misfortune, and there were some circumstances that would soften it down. It was sometimes a lie as well, ignoring the fact that the Hunt brothers had made nothing up. Ellenborough reached his shocking apogee on the subject of friendships with adulterers. He admitted that the convicted adulterer, the Marquis of Headfort, was a part of the prince's entourage. Other monarchs had done something similar. Adultery was a misfortune; 'I chose to call it by that name, circumstances may render it venial.'

At this point, Ellenborough gained a reputation for being soft on adultery, especially when it concerned the male aristocracy. The Delicate Investigation proved that he did not extend his compassion to women. The nation noticed. A friend of the Hunt brothers, the poet Thomas Moore, made the point obvious with a poem making the common pun on Ellenborough's name. In part one, the gentleman's proposal to a lady:[5]

Come fly to these arms nor let beauties so bloomy
To one frigid owner be tied:
Your prudes may revile and your old ones look gloomy,
But, dearest, we've Law on our side.

Each stanza ends the same way, decrying adultery as venial or a misfortune, aping the Chief Justice's language. His mistress replies with a better knowledge of the realities if political power:

> Hold, hold, my good Sir, go a little more slowly:
> For grant me so faithless a bride,
> Such sinners as we, are a little too lovely,
> To hope to have Law on our side.
>
> Had you been a great Prince, to whose star shining o'er 'em
> The People should look for their guide,
> Then your Highness (and welcome!) might kick down decorum--
> You'd always have Law on your side.

The Brougham effect was obvious when, to Ellenborough's fury, the jury withdrew to consider their verdict. It may only have been twenty minutes, but it was the principle that mattered. Brougham thought that Ellenborough had behaved so outrageously that he was 'in a scrape, or next to it', but that was wishful thinking.

The Hunts were guilty, but sentencing did not happen until February 1813, and terms of imprisonment were inevitable. Ellenborough and two other judges declared that the brothers, by destroying the respect due to the constituted authorities, had committed a grievous crime. The message here was clear: respect did not need to be earned when the leading personage of the establishment was concerned.

The Hunt brothers remained silent through the sentencing, believing-correctly- that the judgement and sentencing were forgone conclusions. They thundered through their newspapers instead, and their main accusation was that the Chief Justice could not be impartial. Ellenborough was a member of the Regent's Privy Council. 'Consideration alone should have persuaded your Lordship not to unite two offices in one person, each of which prevents the proper discharge of the other and the just reputation of both.'

Ellenborough was a politician in all but name; he ate and drank at the Pavilion and Carlton House at the expense of the Prince Regent, and they had done each other innumerable favours. Hunt probably did not know about Ellenborough's lobbying for his brother but would not be surprised. The implication was that power had corrupted him:

> Will your Lordship venture to assure us that there has been no real change of late years in your character and opinions, – no change between Mr Law and Lord Ellenborough, – no change from the untitled advocate, who vindicated the general cause of independence and resisted the overbearing temper of his superiors, to the titled judge, who is for promulgating the most aristocratical and unconstitutional opinions

The *Examiner* could not always keep up this high constitutional tone; it wondered where the famously gourmand Chief Justice kept the sauce for his Turtle Soup and was ready to talk about Ellenborough's natural daughter (but only when he was dead). It also speculated rudely about how the Prince Regent would spend the money extracted from them by the court. However, the sentence was enacted.

Chapter Sixteen

The Rusty Machinery of Suppression

The triumph of the establishment over the hostile press seemed complete. Both sets of libellers were in prison, and nobody with any influence cared very much. One headstrong young poet was incandescent about the Eaton verdict and equally angry about the lack of pushback from it. He wrote a 4,000-word rebuttal to the whole trial. It was vitriolic: 'You persecute him because his faith differs from yours. You copy the persecutors of Christianity in your actions, and are an additional proof that your religion is as bloody, barbarous, and intolerant as theirs.'

Religion was an opinion, and blasphemy was a victimless crime. The Lord Chief Justice was a bigot and a hypocrite. The writer finishes with an aspiration that was beyond his time and possibly ours:

> The time is rapidly approaching, I hope that you, my Lord, may live to behold its arrival, when the Mahometan, the Jew, the Christian, the Deist, and the Atheist will live together in one community, equally sharing the benefits which arise from its association, and united in the bonds of charity and brotherly love.[1]

This was the work of a young Percy Shelley. His furious missive was both a terrible libel on Ellenborough and a misunderstanding of how the law was formulated. There was no natural born right for a person to choose their own religious views: there were laws to be enforced, and, notwithstanding Ellenborough's extreme partiality, that was exactly what had happened. Shelley certainly knew the real consequences of blasphemous libel when he ensured that his own pamphlet, *The Necessity of Atheism*, remained anonymous.

Shelley's rebuke was published in Devon by a local publisher, who initially produced one thousand copies and then destroyed most of them in a fit of well justified panic. The content had been noticed by the typesetters and discussed in the Whig and Tory taverns of the north Devon metropolis of Barnstaple. Fifty copies at most made it to London, and almost nobody would have read it – and even fewer people would take it seriously. It only became well known long after the event. By the 1860s, it could be read and appreciated by audiences who now recognised the existence of religious plurality – but that didn't help Daniel Eaton in 1812.

This was not Shelley's most famous contribution to the struggle against the establishment; this came later and is still fondly remembered by radicals today:

> Rise, like lions after slumber
> In unvanquishable number!
> Shake your chains to earth like dew
> Which in sleep had fallen on you:
> Ye are many – they are few

Written in 1819, Shelley's editor withheld the poem from publication out of fear of the response from the authorities. That worried man was Leigh Hunt. The opposition to the establishment was not a large number of ferocious jungle animals but a small number of North London intellectuals, whose influence at the time can be overrated.

It looked like a combination of the flexible libel laws and the dragoons could keep the ruling class in their pre-eminent place, but not all was as it seemed. The system itself was under strain and was undermined in a way that 20-year-old poets could not achieve. At first glance, the libel trials of 1812 and 1813 looked like clear victories for the ruling classes, but on close inspection, those triumphs were a little ambiguous and possibly even a chimera.

Hauling up miscreants to public courts had its dangers. In the English system, it was possible for the radicals to win, as both Daniel Eaton and Leigh Hunt had proved before 1812. The other less obvious danger was that it gave heretical views an airing. When Henry VIII was awarded Defender of the Faith by a grateful Pope Leo X for refuting the ideas of Martin Luther in 1521, he did so by quoting and then rejecting his ideas, allowing them even more publicity. This was still the problem in the nineteenth century.

This explains why Ellenborough was angry when Eaton or any defendant represented himself: they would, and did, aim for maximum publicity for their own views. A defence council would have to use legal arguments, which were already fixed in the state's favour, and possibly face the learned gentleman in court a week later, when their defendant from seven days ago had already been forgotten.

When Daniel Eaton was arraigned in 1795 for publishing the second part of *The Rights of Man*, the official document summarised Paine's views nicely: 'It cannot be proved by what right hereditary government (meaning, among other things the said hereditary government of this kingdom) could begin, neither does there exist within the compass of mortal power a right to establish it.'

It is true that the vast majority of the press did not repeat the libels from the court proceedings. They glossed over the details to protect the sensibilities of the reading public and instead cast aspersions on the plaintiffs. The *Nottingham Journal* suggested that the best place to lock up Daniel Eaton was with the other lunatics. But there were always others who would repeat the contents verbatim. English law allowed fair, plain and honest reports of trials, so Eaton produced one, earned some money from it, and was able to get his views across. The state did burn books and destroy inventory – this happened to Eaton and many booksellers that stocked Tom Paine – but it was on a hiding to nothing in the long run.

The Hunt brothers reminded the world of every Ellenborough bias and partiality in the *Examiner*; when they were sent down on 6 December 1812, they said nothing in court because they would have been interrupted and silenced by the three judges; they saved their vituperation for their newspaper. Thanks to Lord Ellenborough's persecution, the circulation of the *Examiner* rose temporarily to 10,000.[2]

Similarly, Eaton tried to hand out copies of the *Age of Reason* at his 1812 trial. Eaton himself was able to write up his own version of events, written after he completed his full term in prison. His view was clear, as was his sarcasm. Ellenborough had interrupted him constantly: 'a most memorable instance of his lordship's liberality and disinterestedness'; the jury was packed, the judges venal, and the legal officials corrupt. All of this was designed to protect the established church, described brutally as 'the calcined rubbish of bigotry and superstition'. These high-profile libel trials could not stop ideas from spreading.

In the case of the Hunt brothers, the situation was even more desperate. Unlike atheism and deism, which were minority interests, the idea that the Prince Regent was a fat waste of space was already current. The Hunts and their lawyer, Brougham, claimed that the large gap between the trial and the punishment was to give a chance for the brothers to make a deal with the state – a promise to keep them out of prison if they were to desist from publishing. This method had been used before, and it suggests that the main point of legal action was not to obtain justice but to stem the tide of criticism. On both occasions, the inducement was dependent on not attacking the Prince Regent. Massive concessions had to be made: no real effort was put into the reputation of members of parliament, being neither monarchy nor deity, and most attacks on the establishment in the satirical cartoons of the time had to be ignored. Limited resources had to be directed towards show trials for selected individuals.

The three weapons against libel were prison, pillory and monetary punishment. They worked quite well to oppress and suppress the specific offender but did nothing to stop the general offence. Daniel Eaton's time at Newgate would have been just as awful as anybody else who had no money, but the idea that prison would silence journalists was unrealistic; this was Eaton's third term of incarceration. He managed to keep on publishing, even writing a critique of the abuses and corruption at Newgate while a prisoner there, for which he was threatened with yet another stretch when he came out. The prosecution was never pursued because of his health; he died in 1814, penniless, in the great tradition of English radical booksellers.

Prison punished Eaton because he was poor and his health was broken. It worked less well for the Hunt brothers. Ellenborough did get revenge on the Hunt brothers when he committed them to prison, but the victory was fragile. They became the heroes of the type of movements that Ellenborough was trying to stop in its tracks. Both Hunt brothers were relatively wealthy men and were able to use the established system, condemned by Eaton and others, of buying comforts in prison; a system which Ellenborough presumably accepted as part of the natural order of things. Hunt had a comfortable room, books, flowers and wallpaper depicting roses on a trellis. He met his family and fashionable friends and continued as editor of the *Examiner*. What is less well known is that prison exacerbated his pre-existing hypochondria, and he lived in genuine fear of encountering some of the other inmates, whom he knew were not all poets and literary critics.

He reported constantly hearing 'the chains of felons', and every day he met 'with persons, who for aught he knew were guilty of the vilest crimes'.[3]

When Ellenborough sent William Cobbett to Newgate in 1810 for writing against flogging in the army, the punishment worked quite well as a deterrent. Just before his conviction sentence, Cobbett wrote to the authorities, offering to quit journalism altogether, so prison was not taken lightly. The initial fine of £1,000 was a considerable amount. Even with friends to contribute, it would always be a strain on the finances. Another problem with being fined is that your other creditors call in your debts, making your cash flow worse. A hefty bail of £3,000, extending for seven years after release, was also a way of restraining future activity. Although conditions in prison could be mitigated with money, eight guineas a week in Cobbet's case, the money still had to be found. He could continue to write, but he could not look after his farm in Hampshire or see his wife and children. Cobbett himself said that everybody regarded it 'as a sentence of death'. Cobbett came out of prison angrily convinced of the rottenness of the system, but it did not stop him from escaping to the USA during the crackdown on political dissent in 1817 (see Chapter Twenty-three).

The pillory worked less well on libellers, but then it worked less well on everybody. Eaton's visit to the pillory did go as Ellenborough planned, according to the eyewitness, Henry Crabb Robinson:

> Walked to the Old Bailey to see D.I. Eaton in the pillory, As I expected, his punishment of shame was his glory. The mob was not numerous, but decidedly friendly to him. His having published Paine's 'Age of Reason' was not an intelligible offence to them. I heard such exclamations as the following: Pillory a man for publishing a book – shame!

The mob knew little or nothing about Paine's book or freedom of religious thought. Instead, they cheered him on and tried to give him something to eat and drink.

The pillory turned the mob into judge and jury. A crime was only social humiliation if the mob agreed. If the crime was understandable, extreme, or salacious, then they were more than willing to play their part. When Joshua Viggers was pilloried at Cornhill as part of his punishment for sodomy in September 1810, he was at first pelted with eggs, mud and potatoes, but later in the hour he was assaulted with stones and blinded. A pillory holds the hands and head in a fixed place and is not the same as the stocks, where your most vulnerable parts can be protected by the hands and arms

A number of spectators then climbed on a nearby balustrade, which then collapsed, and many were rushed to St Bartholomew's hospital with cracked skulls. The nearby streets of Poultry and Cornhill were blocked, and their shops were closed. There was no doubt who was in charge during these exemplary punishments, and it was certainly not the establishment. In the case of Joshua Viggers the mob could be relied on to be cruel, but if they did not understand the crime, they were likely to be apathetic. More and more people were noticing that it was a lottery; Charles Dickens, for example, described the pillory as 'a wise old institution that inflicted a punishment of which no one could foresee the extent'.[4]

The weaknesses of the pillory as a punishment were soon discussed more widely. In 1815, the pillory was in the dock, so to speak, with many members of the House of Lords pointing out that it was an unreliable punishment. The Earl of Lauderdale, proposing the bill, pointed out that sometimes the masses were the ultimate arbiters when a pillory was set up in the street. He mentioned Eaton by name and others who were lauded by the mob instead of humiliated, and went on to show how those accused of unnatural crimes were in danger of the death penalty because of what an enraged mob would throw at them.

Ellenborough was next to speak. He moderately supported the pillory but objected most to the fact that nothing of the same severity had been suggested to replace it. He also suggested that Eaton had been pilloried outside Newgate not to threaten his life but to protect him if the crowd turned nasty. The Pillory was degradation, but degradation *salvis tamen membris et vita*, which he failed to translate. Ellenborough's view was that it was not a good argument about the punishment to say that it was performed badly and that if Eaton or anybody else was provided with food, drink, or an umbrella, then it was due to officials not doing their job properly. The pillory had been introduced in 1269 by Henry II, said Ellenborough, showing off his legal knowledge as ever. In his mind, that trumped any practical problems with the punishment. He could not comprehend the idea that any law could become a dead letter.

He accepted that the pillory was better for some crimes than others but refused to agree to limit it to perjury and fraud. He rejected once more the notion that the punishment had to fit the crime, a commonsense point today but still an area of debate in 1815. The punishment could never fit the crime, especially when the unwashed hordes were the jury, judge and executioner. Earl Stanhope pointed out that if he and Lord Liverpool had both been pilloried for libel during the passing of the Corn Bill, then 'the Noble Earl would have been confoundedly pelted, and I should not'. Everybody listening in the Lords knew that Ellenborough would have been stoned to death if the mob had their way.

Despite the practical problems of the fines, imprisonments and pillorying, the key problem for those trying to suppress free speech was constitutional. The laws governing free speech in England were the most free in Europe. There was no mechanism for pre-publication censorship; it had broken down in the 1690s and could not be brought back. Criticism of the king and his ministers was allowed without prior permission. Ellenborough said as much himself: 'Gentlemen, the law of England is a law of liberty and consistently with this liberty we have not an imprimatur; there is no such preliminary licence necessary.[5]

Here lay the problem: where to draw the line? In the Regency period, it was men like Sidmouth who were drawing it, and allies like Ellenborough who made it stick. This vagueness worked on one level, as it allowed the establishment to take action when it felt under stress or attack and was able to choose its victims carefully, and it had had success with Eaton and the Hunt brothers in 1812.

There were still embarrassing failures, and this was partly because of the jury system. They had considerable power – much more than they knew and much more than Ellenborough was willing to admit, particularly in cases of libel. Despite Ellenborough being very likely to *tell* an English jury that any libel was proven, thanks to the 1792 Libel Act of Ellenborough's old frenemy Charles James Fox, a jury still had the right to *decide* the matter. It also had the right to conclude that the evidence of publication was not identical to libellous intent. Judges were given discretion to merely advise the jury, and Ellenborough never failed to do this, and juries – often selected for their pliability – seemed to accept this. Although this happened in 1812, it was not guaranteed in the future.

The other potential problem for the establishment was that the membership of the jury was often manipulated in the government's favour, and there would be great jeopardy if that advantage was ever removed.

In theory, the system was elaborately fair. A book of eligible jurors was compiled, and names were chosen at random. In total, forty-eight names were pricked, that is, chosen by opening pages anywhere in the book. Defence and prosecution had the right to weed out people they objected to. A maximum of twenty-four could be rejected, and then a random twelve were selected. This seems admirable, but the system was still rigged; the state had more resources to sniff out radicals and artisans, and in any case, the system was not always random – it was abused by the use of special juries in serious cases of treason, blasphemy or sedition. Even after such selection of juries, the state did not always get its way: if the system was challenged more, they would succeed less often.

Finally, there was no legal future in conflating libel with personal hurt feelings. Later in life, Leigh Hunt pointed out that he was sent to prison for saying that the Prince Regent was very fat, a truth that stared everyone in the face. Ellenborough and the two other judges who sentenced them made it clear that Hunt's writing must be libellous because of motive rather than truth:

> no man filling the character of a good subject could, with any motive but a bad one, print a libel of this description, attacking and vilifying the head of the government of the country: because the individual occupying that station, standing at the head of the government of a nation, is not to be held up in public newspaper, in the manner you have held up the prince regent, as an object of detestation and abhorrence, which you endeavour to persuade your readers that he is.

Nobody needed persuading, but to say so was libel. The system relied on compulsory respect for one flawed man. The charge continued:

> It behoves those who are entrusted with the administration of criminal justice to protect that government under which we all live, and to support the head of that government, without which the present state of society could not exist.

It went on to say that an attack on the prince, like attacks on God, would dissolve bonds. Libel was not really about truth and falsehood, but about statecraft.

As king, George descended into further degradation, and he died unmourned and unloved, as the *Times* reported:

> There never was an individual less regretted by his fellow-creatures than this deceased king. What eye has wept for him? What heart has heaved one throb of unmercenary sorrow? … If he ever had a friend – a devoted friend in any rank of life – we protest that the name of him or her never reached us.[6]

It was hardly surprising that it became increasingly difficult to defend the status quo. A system that relied on compulsory respect backed up with ineffective punishment was not going to last. Ellenborough would live long enough to see the system humiliate him.

Chapter Seventeen

Against Adultery?

There are three reasons to believe that Ellenborough had premarital sex. First, all men of his class did – even the ugly ones like Ellenborough. Second, there were rumours at the time and names were put forward; third, and most convincingly, the details of his will, which left money to his 'natural daughter'. This was Elizabeth Thornton, born in 1782 when he was 32 and unmarried, so she was not a product of adultery, though it was an example of how an ungainly, unattractive rich man from the ruling classes had leverage with women. Her existence was known about during his lifetime – the Hunt brothers mentioned it in their newspaper during the 1812 libel trial, and Ellenborough openly left her money in his will. His gamekeeper in Roehampton shared the same surname, so may have been related to Ellenborough's daughter.

Although Ellenborough himself was probably not guilty of adultery, his premarital sexual behaviour was probably quite typical of his class and gender. The Georgian view of adultery was ambiguous. In theory, they were against it, but in practice, they would lap up every detail in the newspapers because, as well as being terrible, it was also very interesting. Recourse to legal action was mostly done by the prosperous establishment, so the plebs were allowed a glimpse into the private lives of their betters. Hundreds of newspaper columns were devoted to it.

Criminal conversation, or crim. con. for short, was a civil not a criminal case, despite its name. It was up to the injured party to claim compensation for what Ellenborough called, in the case of *Railston v Bedingfield*, 'loss of domestic comfort and conjugal enjoyment'. This sounds crude and reactionary, but it reflected exactly the view at the time. Wives and families were property assets that adultery would destroy, and the guilty had to pay compensation. As with everything, there were class distinctions. Adultery by skilled artisans with no glamorous backstory was worth a couple of lines in the newspapers, but anything with rich or famous people was worthy of lots of newspaper columns.

Ellenborough presided over many examples of sexual immorality at the King's Bench, and his views, unsurprisingly, more or less mirrored the views of the establishment, with the proviso that it was the application of the law that interested him and not the salacious gossip. He was generally thought to be unsound on crim.com., being neither very consistent nor very condemning – unlike Lord Kenyon, who once suggested that adultery should be a capital offence. It was widely believed at the bar that he tended to suggest lower fines than most, and his reputation for being soft on the subject was cemented in the Hunt libel trial of 1812.

Some of the best examples of criminal conversation attracted their own pamphlets; in particular, *Parr v Benson* in 1808 had all the key ingredients of a good yarn. In December 1808, at the King's Bench, the Liverpool merchant Thomas Parr accused Ralph Benson of criminal conversation with his wife, with Lord Ellenborough presiding. The first fixed point in the process was the claim for compensation. James Allen Park, Ellenborough's former compatriot from the Northern Circuit, demanded £30,000 for his client Parr, knowing full well he would not get it. He had to start high, otherwise, the marriage was clearly not worth much. The second reason was that compensation could only fall from this point, as the plaintiffs would try to minimise the reduction. So Ralph Benson put in a plea of not guilty, and the struggle over money began.[1]

The rules were clear; Ellenborough knew them better than anybody and would be calculating a compensation figure in his head as the trial proceeded. The greater the wifely asset, the greater the compensation required, and the judge would advise the jury on how much of the initial outrageous sum should be granted. In another case, Charlie Flowers sued a Mr Lewes for criminal conversation with his wife while he was imprisoned on a hulk at Greenwich. Lewes claimed, and the wife confirmed, that he did not even know she was married. Such a marriage was clearly worth nothing, so Ellenborough told the jury to set compensation at a nominal one pound.

The first rule was that there had to have been a marriage before there was adultery. The cleric who married Thomas Parr and Mary Wood deposed that he married them in 1798. Had this personal witness not been available, the existence of a marriage would not have been taken for granted; witnesses would have been sought who had heard the banns read out. The cleric went on to assert that it was a happy marriage, yet he had seen them only twice or so in the last decade, thus creating doubt in the jury's mind about the truth of their statement. It was a foretaste of how disastrous Parr's civil prosecution would turn out to be.

Mary Parr was not on trial. She was neither required nor allowed to speak. She was not even present in the room. Parr had to prove that his marriage was a valuable asset that Benson had destroyed, so paradoxically, he had no motivation to attack his wife's character. It would be the defendant's lawyers who would try to do that. Compensation would rise if it were a happy family home with a loving father. This was proved (though not impartially) by the second witness, Mr Wilkinson – Parr's confidential clerk. Parr looked after his children and loved his wife, who in turn loved him back – until Ralph Benson came along. Benson first gained ascendency over her mind, then seduced her. She was the weaker vessel, manipulated by pre-planned malice; although her own actions had consequences, Benson was ultimately responsible. This was a standard approach: men were wicked, and women could not help themselves.

The next level was the breach of trust; the better the two men were acquainted, the greater the treachery – as Ellenborough said in another trial: 'hospitality abused and friendship betrayed' exacerbated the offence. Wilkinson continued:

> The plaintiff was a man of a very friendly and convivial disposition and frequently had gentlemen's parties at his house as is much the custom at Liverpool at which the defendant used to be one of the number. Upon every occasion upon which Mr Benson was present he used to sit next to the plaintiff's wife whom the witness represented to be a beautiful young lady.

Mary Parr was attractive, so the loss was greater. Parr had invited Ralph Benson to his house in good faith, and Benson had pursued his wife with malice aforethought. Yet the prosecution case had a problem, ably exploited by William Garrow. They were 'convivial bottle companions', by which we can infer that the men got roaring drunk. On more than one occasion, it transpired that Benson had slipped away from the all-male drinking parties after supper to lurk about in another room, despite Benson liking a drink as much as everybody else. As the defending barrister, it was Garrow's task to muddy the water and reduce the amount of compensation. His question to Wilkinson was designed to prove that Parr knew what was going on and did not mind too much.

> When the sons of Bacchus or the toping companions were together at Mr Parr's and when one of them said what the devil is become of Benson? Is he gone already did not Mr Parr say, No no he is not gone, he is only with Mary?

Benson never reappeared, clearly exchanging his night with the 'sons of Bacchus' for something else that was more to his taste.

These drunken evenings started in 1802. This was a crucial point: it was only year five into a claimed 'ideal' marriage. Parr's wife had been unfaithful. Parr knew but didn't care, was too stupid to understand, or was too weak to do anything about it. The words 'only with Mary' were the killer admission. So the marriage was not that great and literally not worth fighting for. The constant reference to drink was not part of the character assassination of Parr, not only because Benson was equally guilty, but because what we might regard as excessive now was normal then, although perhaps more so in Liverpool – such things were 'much the custom in Liverpool'.

Ellenborough did not interrupt much; this was not about the security of the state – but he did wonder aloud about the value of this marriage. He did not like 'that species of friendship which consists of eating and drinking and conversing with a man and his wife, after it is apparent that such a wife has dishonoured her husband'. Parr should have put a stop to it. He was on trial as much as Benson.

Parr's counsel went on the attack, proving he was a good father to five lovely children, now robbed of their mother by the callous Benson. Mr Carrass, a local merchant, opined that Parr appeared uncommonly kind towards his children. However, it turned out that he did not know the extended family at all, merely exchanged cards at the doorstep, aping his betters. Equally unhelpfully, he added that he had attended Parr's evening parties and seen nothing between Benson and Mrs Parr.

Also mentioned by Parr's lawyer was that his wife was the daughter of another respectable Liverpool merchant, but one who did not bring a very large dowry to the marriage. It was a love match as well. Another prosecution point was that Mrs Parr had not been shackled to an old man; she was 18 and he was 30 when they married, which was not considered an age gap at all, and the vigour of the marriage was proved by the number of children. Eighteen was also considered old enough; a few years younger and even Georgian judges started to have doubts. In the 1811 crim. con. case *Dougherty v Wyatt*, Ellenborough ruled that a 15-year-old marrying girl without parental permission was a form of seduction that nullified the value of the union and destroyed its legitimacy.

Part of the attraction of the crim. con. case for the salacious public was the revelation of first-hand evidence. The public, press and pamphleteers loved these details of crumpled and dirty bedsheets and couples found in flagrante. Jane Hughes, servant, deposed that she had seen Parr and Benson 'in the act'. Mr Parr spent all day at his counting house; that could be guaranteed. Men like Parr did not knock off early from money-making and come home unexpectedly. One day in 1805, when none of the servants but herself were at home, she knew that Mr Benson was in the house about noon:

> She [the witness], having soon afterwards occasion to go to the kitchen, where Mr Benson was, in order to get some potatoes, then heard her mistress's voice crying out, 'Don't Benson, don't Benson don't! This excited her curiosity, and she went up straight into the room where they were and discovered Mrs Parr her mistress lying upon the sofa and Mr Benson in a situation not to be described.

Then Mrs Parr asked if there were any cakes for tea, which failed to distract Jane Hughes from unfolding events. Jane called Benson a dirty devil, which she had known for years but with no hard evidence. Now she did.

The flagrante was never described in detail. When Benson's hand was on Mrs Parr's knee and then moved upwards, a 'curtain of delicacy' was drawn on the issue by all the journalists. Most of the time, the newspapers did not describe the act, which did not put people off reading about it – they came for the human drama; better pornography was available for those who wanted it. Reading about the misdeeds of the rich and famous and watching them destroy each other in court was entertainment enough.

The evidence mounted up. Mrs Parr accompanied Benson to the Shrewsbury Races in 1806; they occupied beds in the same room at the White Lion, and the room dividing curtain was absent because it was out for washing – a reminder about how basic accommodation was even for the wealthy. This was bad enough, but Mr Parr was sleeping in a nearby room too – he knew what was going on. Servants at the inn thought that Mrs Parr was Benson's wife, and when they discovered the truth, they joked about it. Not much of a man, and not much of a wife.

The certainty of illicit intercourse was the key. Innuendo would not do. In another case, the defendant's counsel pointed out that the wife in question had been seen walking the streets of Canterbury with a man, not her husband. Ellenborough pointed out that that was not enough; it had to lead to something else, and that something else would need evidence. If such conduct were to be deemed culpable, it would cut off all of the innocent intercourse in society. This was not 'Muslim Turkey' he sniffed, displaying his own prejudices..

Mathematical certainty was sufficient. In a different case (*Gardner v Jadis*), Alan Gardner was regularly away as a captain in the king's navy, bravely doing his duty, stressed Erskine, trying to up the plaintiff's compensation. Erskine claimed crim. con. had taken place between Henry Jadis and Gardner's wife Maria. Gardner had last seen her on 30 January 1802 when he sailed from Spithead on the *Resolution* and did not return until mid-July. When he returned, she was pregnant, but he was unable to ascertain how far gone she was, and she was unable to tell him so they had separated. His wife gave birth to a baby boy in secret, the heir to his fortune, on 9 December, suggesting conception in early March. Gardner's legal team still felt the need to find servant's evidence of blinds drawn during the day and disordered beds. Ellenborough, in his summing up, said that he did not need the witness evidence because the mathematics proved the adultery perfectly well.

That was not the case in *Parr v Benson*. Crim. con. as early as 1805 had been proved, and Ellenborough told the jury he believed that the crim. con. had started during the drunken evenings of 1802. It was now

December 1808. Why had Parr not acted much earlier? Was this even her first adultery?

This was a pertinent question. Being the second seducer was much cheaper than being the first. In another case the same year, Ellenborough proved the point. Solicitor Jesse Gregson tried to obtain compensation from Thomas Theaker for a criminal conversation with his wife, Grace. Theaker was his coachman, so the shame was seen to be greater because of the class disparity. Gregson's demand for compensation of £10,000 turned into a forlorn hope when the defence was able to prove an earlier seduction by a Mr McTaggert, once again from a servant's evidence. Just like in *Parr v Benson*, servants and maids in inns were often crucial in their evidence, as only they had experience to know how many people had slept in a bed and what they had got up to there. So Grace Gregson's adultery was not caused by her weakness and malice aforethought by Thomas Theaker, but by wanton lust – and with a coachmen at that. Extreme immorality rendered a wife worthless, as another Ellenborough summing up made clear:

> this woman was only waiting for seduction. She invited it: she went out on a signal from a man in the open street, who called at her house as if it had been a common brothel. The damages ought to be moderate. Adultery was a most pernicious crime, and it ought to be punished: but in the present instance the jury would consider, while they compensated the injury of the husband, that they were only to estimate it as the loss of a wife, who was little better than a common of the town.[2]

Gregson was awarded £200; he later went on to prosecute the original seducer and received a shilling. He seemed to have been a solicitor with little knowledge of the law.

Continuing with *Parr v Benson*, the prosecution had an ace up their sleeve, which they played at the correct point. Had Parr suffered because of his wife's behaviour? If so, the compensation would rise, and his delay in prosecuting Benson would be explained. His brother recounted that in 1807 he had had a manic episode lasting seven months during which he ranted and raved furiously; however, it was also disclosed that he had had a similar episode in 1790, so it was not his marriage that was driving him mad.

His earliest brain fever was caused or exacerbated by working eight days, day and night, to elect his friend Banestre Tarleton to be MP for Liverpool. During the 1807 attack Mary did not stay and care for her husband; she took one of the children with her and moved to Benson's home in Shropshire, where they lived in open adultery.

Another method of pushing up the compensation was to stress that the defendant could afford it. Benson was richer than Parr; this should have made no difference when guilt was being established, but it would affect the amount of compensation asked for. Sometimes the plan was to bankrupt the defendant, so it was no surprise that the prosecution brought this up. The prosecution suggested that the figure of £30,000 was appropriate because Benson had recently inherited a fortune from the death of his father. Moses Benson had left his son £10,000 a year and a magnificent Shropshire mansion, which still stands. This was Lutwyche Hall, where the adulterous couple moved when the husband went mad. So the price of adultery was three times the annual income and disgrace. This argument had a ring of practicality, but not legality; in an earlier case, Ellenborough ruled that it was not the defendant's ability to pay that decided the payout, but the strength of the plaintiff's case.

Ellenborough summed up: Benson was guilty (not Mrs Parr, whose behaviour only mattered in the sense that adultery was an act for two), and it was up to the jury to decide whether the plaintiff was consenting to his disgrace. The trial was over in seven hours, and the jury took ten minutes to award Parr a mere £1,000, which represented a total defeat for the plaintiff. The verdict meant everybody was a loser: Mr Benson was found guilty; Mrs Parr would live in penury and limbo for the rest of her life, remaining married but living away from her family; and in his victory, Parr would look like a complete idiot forever, and no doubt his melancholia would return. It was a wonder that anybody went to trial with their dirty linen, but they did.

In the longer term, the ultimate winner was Ralph Benson, largely because he could not be shamed. His life continued to be unorthodox. Benson had a reputation in Liverpool for his own wild parties, hosted by his Irish wife. He was elected MP for Stafford twice, in 1818 and 1826, to a constituency of artisan shoemakers, an electorate of around 500 who, like any other, wanted to be bribed. In 1835, he was convicted of not paying his taxes.

These events unfolded in Liverpool, the home of the slave trade, which was only abolished in 1807, and there is no doubt that both Parr and Benson made their money from buying and selling human beings. Moses Benson started as a captain of a slaver and was associated with sixty-seven journeys in the 1770s. Parr's friend Banestre Tarleton, for whom Parr had risked his health in 1790, was a nationally famous anti-abolitionist. Ralph Benson, born in Jamaica, was against the slave trade but still lived on the proceeds in Shropshire. Buying and selling human beings was not a consideration in this trial; the value of a woman in a marriage was being calculated.

Chapter Eighteen

The Public Ellenborough

Ellenborough was well-known. He did not live in a bubble, isolated from the general public. None of the Georgian politicians did; they mostly mingled with the general public without security. This is why John Bellingham was able to assassinate Prime Minister Spencer Perceval in broad daylight, by simply stepping in front of him in the lobby of the House of Commons and shooting him in the heart. It was a murder rather than an assassination, as the perpetrator had business grievances, not political ones; Ellenborough was a friend of Perceval and must have wondered if he was next.

It was also relatively easy for the plebs to accost the ruling classes at work or in the street. The Court of the King's Bench was a relatively small space, and Ellenborough would be able to smell the poor as well as see them. Courts were public forums without security checks, and all that was needed for entry was a shilling sweetener for the doorman. In July 1815 a Dorset man who had walked to London accosted Ellenborough at work at the King's Bench and started to regale him with his complaints. More worryingly, he claimed to be the son of King Solomon. The *Manchester Mercury* reported that the 'poor maniac' was removed 'with difficulty'.

Ellenborough also occupied the same spaces as the common man. He may well have been sheltered from the poor until he attended university in Cambridge, but after that, they would have been everywhere. Even Cambridge had its town and gown. When he was at Lincoln's Inn, he would have made speeches in the smoke-laden atmosphere of Coachmaker's Hall. Law is known to have spoken in the presence of a closely packed assembly of 'politicians, idlers upon town shopmen, and open to spouters in every rank of life'. His dining and betting club, the Society of the Bears, met at the Crown and Anchor, and Serle's Coffee House. They may have had a private booth or room, but all of society was here, and not all of them would like lawyers or be like them. After 1802, he would have been recognised on any London street.

So, everybody knew who Ellenborough was, and everybody knew where he lived. The addresses of all members of the House of Peers were published in annuals and almanacks, such as *the Gentleman's and Citizens Almanack*. A visit to any modest subscription library would reveal his address in St James Square: something that would alarm modern celebrities. You could not threaten the establishment by doxxing them, they were already easy to locate. His addresses would have been well known in the provinces. The annual list of stagecoach routes, *Cary's Iterinary*, would list the names of all the houses of the famous that could be seen from the road, and Ellenborough's addresses in Surrey and Kent were among them. It was meant to reduce the boredom of those travelling ten miles an hour on the bumpy roads. The locations of the famous were not a secret for the media to keep; it was a sign of their sense of security that it was advertised for the public to gawp at.

It seems that his voice and manner were well known too. In 1812, the actor Charles Mathews made the rash decision to imitate Ellenborough on stage in the play *Love, Law, and Physic* at the Theatre Royal, Covent Garden. Charles Mathews was a dramatic draw, but in this play about lawyers, his part was small, and he was invited to 'fill up for himself' as the character of lawyer Flexible. He had a remarkable ability to mimic the speech, mannerisms and faces of others, and in his one-and-only performance, he did an impression of Ellenborough.

His biographer claimed that the crumpled face, slouching movement and nasal twang were instantly recognised by the enthusiastic audience. As he reached the judgement seat before each trial, he would begin to breathe heavily, puffing his cheeks in and out like a boxer approaching the ring: 'You would suppose he was going to snort like a war horse preparing for battle.' Mathews had a lopsided mouth, which also helped the impersonation along. A later relative continues the story:

> the effect was quite astounding to him for he had no idea of its being so received. The shout of recognition and enjoyment indeed was so alarming to his nerves so unlike all former

> receptions of such efforts that he repented the attempt in proportion as it was well taken, and a call for it a second time fairly upset him albeit not unused to loud applause and approbation.[1]

The call for a repeat of his Ellenborough, after no call for the repeat of his Erskine or Garrow, shows how well known he was compared to his rivals, and Mathews's fear about performing an encore shows that he knew he was in dangerous territory. The story was featured in the press the next day. The papers informed him that he would never be able to speak again in public without ridicule, which was a definite problem for a high court judge.

His biographer believed Mathews immediately realised he had made a mistake and would have quickly decided not to do it again. This was October 1812, and Ellenborough was about to send the Hunt brothers to prison for as long as possible (Leigh Hunt was a great fan of Mathews, as was Charles Dickens, who saw him later in his career and who inspired his own hobby as a mediocre actor and playwright); to provoke Ellenborough was dangerous.

His worries were confirmed, according to his biographer, by a faux-friendly visit from an unnamed eminence – probably the Lord Chamberlain – who advised him not to do it again. Ellenborough would not normally let such pin pricks concern him, but being the victim of laughter that he could not control was a step too far. On the second night, the audience came, waiting for the spoof, and Mathews was in a quandary. When it failed to materialise, they all shouted, 'Imitation! Imitation!' The story goes on to tell us a lot about the Georgian theatre:

> A gentleman rose above the rest in the pit and demanded to know why Mr Mathews omitted the latter part, and by what authority he was prevented from giving the imitation of the learned judge. This was followed by loud cries from the rest of the audience of answer the question! Mr Mathews inquired of his interrogator what learned judge he meant. The gentleman declined giving the name but another nearer to the stage contrived in a low voice to pronounce the one alluded to.[2]

This was a form of mob rule; it was worse in fact – he was trapped in a densely packed room with the braying audience, and no dragoons would come to help him. He respected the constitution and all judges and regretted any accidental offence caused, he was reported to have said. But then he repeated the act, imitating lots of judges but omitting one in particular.

The Prince Regent invited Mathews to Carlton House to repeat the performance. Mathews would have been terrified; his offence could not be that serious, so what reason would there be for a summons? It transpired that the Prince wanted a repeat performance of the first night, immediately yet spontaneously, in the presence of twenty courtiers and the Duke of Clarence, his brother. His Royal Highness was a fair mimic himself, and his brother could do a fair Lord Eldon. Mathews was forced to go through the monologue again: 'It was not so well that you should produce Chief Justice Ellenborough on the public stage, but here you need to have no scruples.'

The Prince Regent could do what he wished, even putting his idle diversions before loyalty to an ally. Ellenborough would, of course, have accepted this.

Chapter Nineteen

The Private Ellenborough

The problem of this chapter is in the title heading. What was he like, and what did he do, when he was not being a judge, and how much was this behaviour different to men of his class? We know something, but not much – but what we know makes sense. We will take for granted his knowledge of the law, his impatience with the intellectually indolent and his work rate and all-round intelligence. What else is there?

It was said that he led a moral life, and that seems true. Apart from one child out of wedlock, he led a relatively blameless life for a man of his class. They are so many moral failings that he could have indulged in, but did not do so. Apart from a little silly gambling at Lincoln's Inn, he did not bankrupt himself by mindless rounds of faro or other games. There seems to have been no adultery or regular mistresses after marriage; he was a good father and conventional husband.

There were vices. Ellenborough was as greedy as any similar man of his class. It was an age where the Georgian gentleman ate and drank to excess, and then took pills and potions to combat the effects of their own greed. We know he liked turbot with lobster sauce. Most British people would never have seen or eaten a turbot. The lobster and the consequent sauce also appealed to him, to the extent that it was said, partly as a joke, that he was as biased towards lobster fisherman as he was partial to their catch. In one legal case he found in their favour when they asked for exemption from the impressment laws. Deep-water fishermen were excused from being impressed into the navy, but this did not apply to fishing for the lobster, which was found in shallow water. Ellenborough combed the law thoroughly, found an instance of the word 'fisheries', and decided that the law against impressment was absolute.

His enemies often employed the image of his slavering over a bowl of soup, but not, of course, any soup. The most prestigious for the high-living nobility and gentry came from Barbados, in the shape (metaphorically and literally) of the turtle, or more precisely, from its tender meat. Fresh turtles were advertised in the newspaper, with a time and date when they were available. It took a lot of turtles to make a soup, and it was a sign of wealth to the elite, and of greed to their opponents. It was the number one soup for the establishment, and it was Ellenborough's favourite. Royalty enjoyed turtle soup; it was the only hot item on the menu when 900 people, led by the Duke of York and all of his brothers bar the Prince Regent, celebrated Wellington's victory at Vitoria in June 1813. Radical papers like the examiner imagined Ellenborough growing even fatter at the Prince Regent's table, 'breathing benevolence over the turtle soup'.

Ellenborough also enjoyed alcohol. Drink was hard-wired into the system: five pint-sized bottles of fortified wines or spirits made you a 'five-bottle man', a phrase never used for Ellenborough, but he certainly drank a similar amount. His enemies went further; he was a voluptuary. Farington, a now forgotten artist who collected gossip about the great and the good at both first and second hand, said that he was, according to James Boswell junior: 'remarkable for indulging himself in eating high dishes and rich food, and that in great quantity. He also drinks freely, both abroad and at home.'

Farington reported that John 'Black Jack' Sylvester, the Recorder of London (senior circuit judge at the Old Bailey), was a famous voluptuary at the table but was easily outdone:

> He had heard of Lord Ellenborough as being a great voluptuary in eating and, altogether, a sensual man. The Recorder of London, Sir J. Sylvester, indulges much at the table, but in eating turtle at a table with Lord Ellenborough, Sylvester fairly acknowledged that he had been outdone by his lordship.

At one Assize dinner, Ellenborough is reported as refusing fowl and demanding beef, and being told by Joseph Jekyll that he would like the beef because it had been well hung. Jekyll was a lawyer, poet and famous wit, and he knew Ellenborough well.

Was he interesting company? Another witness gives a qualified yes. Farington, far from an admirer, said that he was 'an entertaining companion at the table, full of anecdotes and information'. He certainly took some part in the social whirl: 'We expect the Ellenboroughs, the Berrys, Charles Moore, and Rogers, none of whom have any particular attractions in your eyes, and yet there are some good heads and some good hearts amongst them, though few of the faces are worth looking at.'[1]

We know from the diary of Mary Berry that Ellenborough and a son were in Tunbridge Wells on 17 October 1807. He was staying with a family friend, Lady Donegal. A letter written from there shows that he had been in residence since at least 22 September.[2] His exact reason for being there is unknown, but his wife was unwell and this may have been part of her recuperation. Tunbridge Wells was second only to Brighton as a resort for the rich and famous. When there were no royal obligations, Ellenborough seemed to like the more sedate and traditional Tunbridge Wells.

Mary Berry dined the next day at Ellenborough's temporary accommodation in the spa town. It was common to rent houses for holidays, which tended to be long enough to make it worthwhile. The rich did not stay at hotels – even the word was hardly known. Mary was a bit of an intellectual bluestocking and enjoyed clever conversation. The lord was regarded as 'quick and clever' – arguably more intellectual attributes than sociable ones. Three days later, they met again at what sounds like a rather desultory card party, the kind that ate up much of the gentlewoman's spare time, while Mrs Berry talked to Ellenborough and Charles Moore, who was the son of a recently deceased Archbishop of Canterbury. At another dinner, Berry described Ellenborough as very lively and amusing on law matters, which is possibly not much of a compliment and possibly meant he was very boring on anything else.

In a later meeting, Miss Berry's opinion of the noble Lord was deteriorating: 'The day was very fine, and the walk was very pleasant. Lord Ellenborough has plenty of conversation, and though his mind is a coarse one, his language and expressions are sufficiently free from that fault.'

Further entries proved that Ellenborough could play whist and made a four with Lady Donegal and Lord Erskine. An evening of cards with family and friends was one of the most sedate ways of spending an evening; there is no evidence at all of anything more dissolute. His other main activity, outside that organised by his wife, was the dinner party, of which there were many, combining all the main elements of his life: politics, conversation, eating and drinking. This was typical and contained a compliment for

Ellenborough at the end, but also involved the Chief Justice spending time with people he did not get along with, notably Lord Holland. Mary Berry again: 'I dined at Lord Ellenborough's Company [with] almost the whole of the former ministry, Lord and Lady Grey, Lord and Lady Lansdowne, Lord Grenville, Mr Thomas Grenville, Lord John Townshend, Lord Holland, Duke of Norfolk, Lord Hartington', and Lord Ellenborough himself, the greatest speaker.'

Ellenborough would have spent about six weeks a year on the road, travelling to the various assize courts in England. These local courts with local juries would be headed by a senior London judge, who would do a provincial circuit twice a year in February/March (Lent) and July/August (Trinity). By 1800, it was a tolerable journey by private carriage, and it was relatively common for judges to take their wives with them. Lady Ellenborough seemed to have accompanied him only once, which suggests that the noble and learned lord was content with the formal hospitality of the local officials when he was away from home.

When the judge arrived in the town (for example, York or Lancaster for the Northern Circuit), they would be greeted by a civic reception led by local dignitaries who were responsible for their safety, and then isolated in private lodgings, not so much for their own protection but to keep them away from jurymen, defendants and witnesses, most of whom would be having a sociable time in local inns on the proceeds of court and client fees. It was a lonely couple of weeks away, and for many people, company would have been welcomed.

Ellenborough expected the deference due to him, and all the London judges were the same: 'When he went, as judge, to the assizes at Maidstone last summer, he was much offended at the disrespect shewn him by there not being proper attendance when he approached the town. [3]

He would expect, at the very least, the High Sheriff of the County and a company of smart soldiers, a big welcome dinner at the best inn in town on the first evening, and a solemn sermon in a prestigious church on every Sunday of his visit. When Maidstone disappointed him, he lectured them vehemently, and the violence of his demeanour seemed to have rooted people to the spot. He then berated them for not reacting 'You hear what I say to you with petrified insensibility,' he bawled.

He was physically very awkward. He had a habit of entering court walking like a crab, while puffing out his cheeks like a war horse preparing for battle, although an actual physical battle was the last thing he was capable of. During the French invasion scare of 1803, he was part of a militia of lawyers who would buy themselves a gun and bayonet (as his friend Lord Eldon and rival Thomas Erskine did) and pretend to be soldiers against revolutionaries in France and nearer to home. This panicky period was jokingly referred to as 'the scarlet fever', and Ellenborough was a useless but keen participant. Rumour had it that he did not know his left foot from his right, despite it being explained to him patiently by his social inferiors. He was eventually thrown out for being awkward and unathletic; he could not even walk in a straight line from spot to spot – it was more of a parabola. When they were being reviewed by the king in Hyde Park, Colonel Erskine confided that they were all lawyers; the king suggested that their predatory training in law would be ideal preparation. The other joke was that they knew how to charge, and if they were told to stand at ease, they would sit on the grass. The king suggested that they be named 'the devil's own'.[4]

What about his health? It seems that he suffered from gout all of his life, from an early age. In 1794, his brother Ewan reported that 'Edward is labouring hard and I hope laying up well for that time when the gout and infirmities will call for rest.'[5]

This did not make him unique: his brother Ewan suffered even worse than Edward, and Pitt had gout (he was prescribed spirits to cure it, showing how entrenched alcohol had become). In 1809, Ellenborough's gout was so bad that he had to be helped to and from his seat at the King's Bench.

As a member of the elite, your address mattered. The move to St James's Square in 1808 was a little more unconventional. He had been the first common-law judge to buy a house there, as most lived within walking distance of Lincoln's Inn. Even moving out of Bloomsbury was an unconventional act. It was a huge house, and Ellenborough boasted as much in his typical manner: 'Sir, if you let off a piece of ordnance in the hall, the report is not heard in the bedrooms.'[6]

Another personal story about the noble lord comes from the letters of the portrait painter Sir Thomas Lawrence. Lawrence is responsible for the most famous portrait of Ellenborough. The picture has become the standard illustration of all historical references, but Lawrence managed to disguise his sitter's ungainly limbs by shoeing him in his legal robes and regalia and focusing on his face, making him look dignified and severe: 'The broad and commanding brow, the large and regular features, the projecting eyebrows dark and shaggy the stern black eye from which flashed not infrequently indignation or contempt gave a character of gravity not unmixed with harshness to his countenance.'[7] His biographer Townsend implied that Lawrence did Ellenborough a favour by making him look attractive; it is certainly the image that has survived into the present, but Ellenborough was to show no gratitude at all.

Lady Ellenborough had had a celebrity portrait created a long time before her husband. Joshua Reynolds had painted her in 1789, but the picture had been lost at sea. In 1811, Ellenborough commissioned another portrait of his wife, to be done by Lawrence this time. The result was a head-and-shoulders rendition, essentially a portrait sketch in which most of the canvas was unpainted and the work looks unfinished, at least in the eyes of the person paying for it. For the art lover, it was prized as an example of inventive and modern portraiture by a fashionable genius, but that was not Ellenborough's view.

Lawrence demanded a 50 per cent deposit – the 'half price' – before starting any substantial work. This was his normal practice, and many less eminent painters made similar demands. Lawrence wrote to Ellenborough on 12 August, just after the first sitting, and asked for immediate payment; Lord Ellenborough wrote to Lawrence, complaining about the total cost – his own picture had cost eighty guineas, while in a mere four years the price of his wife's portrait had risen to two hundred. He omitted the obvious fact that both men had become richer and more famous during that period. Lawrence was the pre-eminent portrait painter by 1810, had become the official court painter and had moved into impressive apartments in Russell Square. Ellenborough could afford to pay, and Lawrence could afford to decline the commission.

Ellenborough also pointed out that the two portraits were to be the same size, thus making it even less of a bargain. He also refused to pay the one hundred guineas deposit. Distinguished military men and members of the royal family had readily agreed to this request, but not Ellenborough; he set his own deadline: 'This sum, Lord E, will however pay the moment the picture of Lady E is finished and sent home, and it depends on Mr Lawrence how soon that shall be.'

It was August, and the London season was ending. If the portrait was not completed soon, then there would have been nobody in town to admire it. Lawrence was famous for the slow speed of his artistic endeavours, and Ellenborough's letter was a rebuke to a tradesman rather than a negotiation with Britain's most prestigious painter. His letter went on: It's a quiet time of the year; paying a deposit would slow things down; you are a well-known procrastinator; and you could get around this stipulation by just getting on with it:

> The payment of a large deposit beforehand operates so much and so generally to the delay of the performance of any work and particularly to the completion of pictures that Lord Ellenborough feels extremely indisposed to accede to the proposition suggested in Mr Lawrence's letter. Mr Lawrence may render it a stipulation of no importance by completing the picture very soon at this season of comparative leisure.[8]

Lawrence decided to dispense with the Lord Chief Justice's patronage and wrote to Lady Ellenborough. He was too scared of the consequences of telling her that her husband was a boorish, bullying philistine – perhaps she knew already, but he could not say it. Instead, he wrote to her to call the whole thing off, citing artistic problems. When Lady Ellenborough went to visit him on the same day as the letter arrived, he was 'not at home'. She wrote a peeved letter to him asking for a smaller, or less complete picture – something that she could at least show off to her friends. After a studied delay of two days, he declined to continue with the project.

At this point, Lawrence seemed to be ruing his rudeness to two people so powerful, and wrote to his friend Joseph Farington for moral support. Lawrence had previously been implicated in the 'Delicate Investigation' and it had got to the point where he'd had to make an affidavit declaring himself innocent of any dalliance with the princess. He was aware that Ellenborough had not only collected the evidence, but had also decided what it meant.

It would seem that the green-eyed monster might have played some role; the physical differences between Ellenborough and Anne were obvious, perhaps more so when depicting them in paint. Lord Ellenborough knew that Lawrence was an acknowledged old flirt. He was unreliable with pretty women, never married, and had lots of affairs behind him.

The first portrait, unfinished, was gifted to a friend, and, as Lawrence's fear increased and his resentment diminished, he indicated his desire to start a second picture. Lady Ellenborough used all the power, and implied threat of her husband's power, in her letters – she hoped to have 'the opportunity of telling Lord Ellenborough that he is in Mr Lawrence's debt'. On their next sitting, Lawrence reported that all she wanted was to assure her husband that the portrait had begun.

Art was not a priority for Ellenborough – for a start, there is no evidence he had been abroad on the grand tour to widen his cultural horizons. He visited France briefly in 1775 and toured Scotland with his friend Paley, but there was no extended travel in pursuit of cultural artefacts. In 1809, the gossipy Farington reported second-hand that Ellenborough had failed to impress at a recent Royal Academy dinner held in Pall Mall. He seemed quite hard and insensible to art, was only interested in the size of the room, and showed his real priority by asking how many people could be fed so quickly. It was a lavish feast, and that's why he was there.

The sum of his cultural hinterland was modest at best. He was a trustee of the British Museum and a member of the Society of Antiquities. His role at the museum was *ex-officio* and more or less compulsory, and it is hard to know his true level of interest. In 1806, he attended a concert of ancient music, a regular royal event, at Hanover Square. These concerts were traditionalist in tone and were forbidden by statute to play modern music; all compositions had to be at least twenty years old. They were more commonly known as the 'King's Concerts' because he patronised and enjoyed them, and it is hard to know whether the only reason Ellenborough attended was because of the royal presence.

His main country seat was Waldershare House, near Dover. The Ellenboroughs were living there most summers after 1811. Joseph Farington said he was pleasant with his neighbours, actively liked their society, and dabbled in agriculture – which was exactly how a gentleman from London with a seat in the country was expected to behave. This was a rented house belonging to the Earl of Guilford, for which the Ellenboroughs paid £200 per annum, according to Farington. It was not uncommon to rent houses, even at the highest level of society, and Ellenborough initially rented his mansion in St James's Square London for £1,200 a year.

Kent was a popular place for a country seat, and Waldershare House was perfect. 'The house is magnificent, the furniture elegant, and the library capital,' said an advertisement from 1804.[9] It came ready furnished – most did – and there was the option to rent more land around it, with rent-paying tenants and a pleasure garden. In an age where the poor were suffering, there was unlimited fruit and vegetables available from a full-time gardener who had sublet the kitchen garden and hot house. It was well stocked with game, a meadow and as many horses and cows as the owner would wish. A later advertisement claimed that it was for a nobleman or a gentleman of great fortune: Ellenborough was now both of those things. The house was good enough for the royal family – the Prince of Wales and the Duke of York stayed there in 1811.

In about 1814, the family bought Roehampton Lodge, which became their main family home outside London. Despite its name, it was a substantial property with one hundred and fifty acres and was also a working farm with tenants. The village was a small collection of villas and country houses, a place like Putney or Wimbledon, where successful men had built a refuge from the mob and the stink of London. The movement of the family was regularly followed in the newspapers. On 27 October 1817, the *Morning Chronicle* reported that the family had returned from France, spent a day in London, and then repaired to Roehampton. The family spent Christmas there in 1817, and the *Morning Herald* reported that a large company of fashionables had been invited over to Roehampton on the day after Boxing Day.

Chapter Twenty

In the Courts

From a modern perspective, Ellenborough was a nasty, sarcastic piece of work. On first sight, the motto of our subject seems to have been Law first (in both senses of the word) and other people's feelings nowhere. He had an appalling temper, certainly. James Boswell junior described 'Ellenborough as the worst-tempered man living'. Joseph Farington called him 'the violent judge' – violent not because he condemned people to painful punishments, as all judges did, but because of his way of speaking to people. He bullied juries, witnesses and legal officials, was arrogant, overbearing and prejudiced, and rushed justice to save time. Even his obituaries, normally riddled with the normal bias when a member of the establishment died, hinted at his rudeness and insensitivity.

Ellenborough was regarded at the time as a superb High Court Judge, the very best for a generation, a man who wielded the heavy sword of justice with a steady hand. His knowledge of the Common Law was second to none, and far superior to that of his predecessor, Kenyon. His knowledge of the legal process, of the treatment and use of witnesses, and of historical precedent was unsurpassed. He spoke forcibly, mastered his facts, knew the details, and stoutly defended the system as it stood. He followed the law of the land, whatever the consequences. He could not be bought or bribed, and he treated people in front of him without fear of favour.

Starting with the prosecution, most of the criticisms are true. He was not alone in his vices. His colleague Vicary Gibbs was known as 'vinegar' – but he was the worst and was singled out constantly by critics of the system. The Chief Justice's behaviour sprung from two roots: a natural disdain of the establishment elite for everybody else and his desire to get his own way in court. He was also intent on moving proceedings quickly. If attorneys were not ready he would strike out the case and move on to the next one, threatening to charge them for the time wasted. If not fined, they would still be afraid of his rebuke.

The other motivation was his hatred of intellectual pretentiousness, perhaps a reaction to his own comparative failure as an academic. As a classics scholar, he would also know that sarcasm came from the ancient Greek *sarkazein*, meaning to tear flesh; it was not clever satire, moderate mocking, or understated contempt. It was meant to hurt or break the confidence of witnesses and law officers.

Newspaper reports of trials were summaries and rarely reported Ellenborough's cutting remarks, so most of his peevishness has been lost to history. But the anecdotes about his behaviour are legion. They were recounted by the Georgians because he was the most sarcastic of all judges, and by the Victorians because they regarded him as an amusing and colourful remnant of a bygone age. Not all are true; many come in different versions, and some are from only one source, but they sound very plausible.

One example of simple prejudice and witness discrimination comes from the story of a Quaker who appeared before Ellenborough as a witness at the Guildhall. He had no wide-brimmed hat or dittos and was dressed as a 'normal' citizen. The judge asked him if he really meant to impose on the court by appearing here in the disguise of a 'reasonable being'. The witness wanted to affirm rather than take an oath on the Bible, a concession that only existed to the Society of Friends at the time, so court proceedings were halted as the court official was unsure how to proceed. The general view of the Society of Friends was not favourable at the time, and they were often referred to as 'some of the persons called Quakers', as if they inhabited a different world. He may well have known about the Quakers' opposition to income tax in an 1816 petition, which referred to his house of parliament as the 'Upper House', as they refused to use the word 'lords' to describe a human institution. Quakers also irked him because they were constantly demanding reform of the Bloody Code, and yet, as people who acknowledged the existence of a supreme being, he could not accuse them of the usual moral shortcomings.[1]

Ellenborough, like many self-regarding people, deemed his own time to be especially precious. He knew more about the law than nearly anybody, so stating the obvious in court would rile him. One story involves a court official saying something blindingly true in this case: 'An estate in fee simple was the highest estate known to the law of England.'

Ellenborough stopped him with an ironic 'Stay, Stay!' and pretended to write it down in an exaggeratedly grateful manner, raising his busy eyebrows in mock surprise. 'Thank you, sir; the court is most grateful for the information.' This was not, in modern parlance, punching down, because the victim was Preston, a well-known and experienced Chancery lawyer; and it is part of the defence of Ellenborough that he was rude to everybody equally.

Another anecdote comes to us in two versions. Early in his career, he is said to have told a hesitant court judge who kept repeating the phrase 'I rule', that in his opinion he could not rule an exercise book. This sounds apocryphal; it would not be a good move for an early-career lawyer, even one with powerful connections. This appears in another version, when he was a much more established judge and publicly humiliated the Chief Justice of the Isle of Ely. When told it was his judgement being referred to, Ellenborough replied, 'give me the decisions of a Chief Justice of the land not somebody who is not fit to rule a copy book'. Some sources suggest that the petty magistrate in question was a distant relative on his mother's side, which sounds unlikely given his reverence for his family, especially on his mother's side, but it is not out of the question, given his quick temper.

Ellenborough hated long-winded speeches. When Randle Jackson started what promised to be a long and tedious speech with the non-legal phrase, 'In the book of nature it is written', Ellenborough interrupted him and asked for the page reference. His hatred of pomposity merged with his dislike of oratory and flowery language and of lawyers who had obviously and self-consciously inserted impressive phrases into an argument that he knew could influence a jury.

There was sympathy for nobody, great or small, and when one fresh-faced barrister hesitatingly referred to his 'unfortunate client' and then said the same thing twice more, Ellenborough leant forward and said, in a soft cooing voice that was all the more derisive because it was so gentle, 'you may go on, sir; so far, the court is with you.'[2]

It was an act; Ellenborough was playing the part of himself while forbidding others to act in their turn. He was often less rude to the legal officials than to the witnesses; indeed, he had promised to be nicer than

Lord Kenyon when he took up the post, but that was more of a rebuke of Kenyon's hatred of him and favouritism for Erskine. His supporters argued that Ellenborough had no favourites – 'he was impartial in his rebuffs and sarcasms'. He abolished favouritism by making anyone in court a potential victim of his tongue.

When Henry Hunt was up before him, claiming that he had been falsely accused of stirring up the people with his eloquence, Ellenborough told him that he had been much maligned – the implication being that he had overestimated himself; this was funny because Hunt was very, very egotistical. Some put-downs were cruder. Another anecdote records the story of Lord Ellenborough's cruel put-down: 'Why you are an industrious fellow you must have taken pains with yourself … No man was ever naturally so stupid.'

Ellenborough did not hesitate to doubt people's intelligence; this included prosecution, defence and witnesses, which could be construed as an unfortunate affectation for a judge. To the surgeon in the witness box who said 'I employ myself as a surgeon', Lord Ellenborough retorted, 'but does anyone else employ you as a surgeon?'

Some of the comments may have elicited genuine laughter once he raised his eyebrows to show that he was 'only joking' and therefore laughter was permitted. Most judges of his rank did it, but it would have provoked calculated rather than spontaneous laughter from people with a vested interest in humouring him. This was not humour – or irony, as his Victorian admirers tried to label it. It was designed to encourage the subjection of those who were afraid of him and glad that they were not the victims. To be fair, the level of sycophancy applied to all powerful judges, such as his friend Lord Eldon, but the relief was acute in Ellenborough's case because on some occasions he did wish to harm. It is hardly surprising that Ellenborough, a man who could cope with any level of unpopularity, reacted so alarmingly to Charles Mathews mimicking his voice: people were meant to be afraid or deferential when he opened his mouth.

From this lazy vice came a certain silver lining. He seemed to be fearless with his condemnations, and it usually did not matter who the person was. Ellenborough was unimpressed by rank or social status per se, and abhorred snobbery and pretentiousness. He admired and respected the law and applied it without fear or favour. One of the many cases that came before the Chief Justice was that of a particularly entitled joyrider. Major John Carrington Smith was travelling recklessly in his gig and assaulted driver William Newman with his whip for getting too close to him in the opposite direction. Newman was merely the groom; when the owner of the carriage, Thomas Jones, stepped out and challenged the major, Smith stood upright on his chaise, waving a whip around, calling him a scoundrel and a rascal. How dare they get in his way – did they not know that he was a major in the army? He pompously announced that he was 'on duty', and that was another reason not to obstruct his important progress.

He had picked the wrong person to intimidate. Thomas Jones was also the sixth Viscount Ranelagh and a major of the 66th (Berkshire) Regiment of Foot. He had served in that rank with the regiment in the early 1800s, when Carrington's ambition would have been to be a captain. Jones was not afraid of a physical confrontation and had in the past assaulted his own gardener, but he was not going to allow a stroppy stranger to do similar damage to his groom. Carrington Smith had said, 'Do you take me for a Cockney ride out on a Sunday? When this was repeated at the trial, Ellenborough assured him that he would not have been confused with such a person, as they behaved with decorum and propriety and did not attack his majesty's subjects. Carrington Smith was fined five pounds for assaulting William Newman and imprisoned for three months for attempting to humiliate Lord Ranelagh. There was no doubt that inconveniencing the aristocracy was more heinous than an unprovoked physical attack, but it is also clear that Ellenborough wanted to defend honest people of all classes and possibly had a prejudice against boy racers.[3]

In another case in 1809, Ellenborough essentially suggested that members of the Hertfordshire gentry and aristocracy were not telling the truth. It was a case of trespass. This was a civil, not a criminal matter, and so transgressors have to be sued, just like today. The Earl of Essex was taking his brother to court for leading the Berkeley Hunt onto his land and destroying his property. The defendant used the argument that they were trying to exterminate a noxious animal and should still be allowed to do so despite destroying herbage and fences; in reality, of course, they had assumed the right to go over anybody's land on the basis that hunting would be impossible if there were no-go areas. Despite the fact that this collection of bankers, clergymen and landowners had taken some trouble to congregate to hunt the fox, they still insisted that it was pest control. Ellenborough put the jury straight:

> Can it possibly be supposed that … gentlemen hunt for the mere purpose of killing vermin and not for their diversion? … Can any man of common sense hesitate in saying that the principal motive and inducement were not the killing of vermin but the enjoyment of the sport and diversion of the chase.[4]

The defendants were fined a token shilling, but the argument that fox-hunters were doing the nation a favour was killed stone dead.

Ellenborough was a 'highly constitutional judge', according to one newspaper. Another obituary suggested that any government wishing to become authoritarian would have found him to be a formidable enemy. The United Kingdom was freer than anywhere in Europe, with a government constrained by rules and processes, and Ellenborough followed them to the letter.

Ellenborough could not be bought or bribed. This is clearly a compliment, limited only by the observation that bribery was uncommon in the English judicial system and the cynical coda that the judges were far, far too rich to need bribes and that it would be much more cost-effective to offer money to the jurors. The pockets of the British state and its associated church were deeper than those of any criminal. Ellenborough was called a flatterer to those above him and a dogmatist to those beneath, and there is some truth in that. Ellenborough treated the rich and powerful without fear or favour, but this was easy because only a few families were higher than him. For his king and his family, he was prepared to break with his principles without much concern. In his mind, there was no greater principle than the protection of the state. He favoured the Crown, but he identified the prerogatives of the Crown with the general good.

Chapter Twenty-One

In Parliament

Ellenborough was a politician; officially for fifteen months during the Ministry of All the Talents, and unofficially from his appointment to the post of Attorney General. His promotions after 1801 meant a short stint in the House of Commons and a longer one in the House of Lords, neither of which were particularly successful.

His first attempt to become a politician pre-dated his rapid rise. The Warren Hastings impeachment postponed his attempt to become an MP in the 1790 general election. He would have been one of the many London lawyers in parliament. He was to be the MP for Westbury, not because he had any pressing interest in Wiltshire matters, but because he was to be put there by Willoughby Bertie, 4th Earl of Abingdon. There were sixty-nine land leases which entitled the owner to vote in the borough, and the noble lord owned all but four of them. This was not the age of one man one vote.

When Edward became too busy with the defence of Hastings, the seat was passed on to his brother, Ewan Law. Newspapers found this unremarkable, and those who reported it, such as the *Oxford Journal*, framed it as the small administrative adjustment that it was.[1]

Ewan Law and Samuel Estwick I were elected in the June 1790 general election. There was a delay in his taking his seat, caused by his name being spelled wrongly ('Evan' rather than 'Ewan') in the election return. Ewan passed on the news to their other brother John Law:

> I was to have filled the gap made by Edward's promotion but in the return the letter V was used instead of W in my Christian name. It therefore stands over till a person present at

> the election can appear and give such evidence as may induce the House to amend the return.[2]

There were rules, but not the ones we would expect today, and it was not uncommon for election results to be contested. When it was clear that Edward did not want the seat, Ewan stood down and the vacancy was filled by Samuel Estwick II, forming a father-and-son team.

In any case, the real power lay in the House of Lords, with the proviso that any government needed a majority in the Commons. Law would have been there as a mouthpiece of the government and the aristocrat who owned the seat. A few years later, the radical journalist William Hone, of whom more later, had calculated that 487 of the 658 MPs were directly controlled by the peers and other wealthy persons.[3]

Law's parliamentary career began on 25 February 1801 – a Wednesday (elections set on Thursdays were not the norm until 1931, and are still not legally required), when he was elected for the constituency of Newtown, Isle of Wight. Two establishment families held the property rights that entitled them to vote and controlled the majority of the thirty-nine votes available. The constituency had been formed in 1584, and there had been two elections in that time – 1727 and 1768, and on both occasions it was because the ruling local families fell out and could not agree how to divide the two seats. It was never to be contested again: as a rotten borough with forty voters, few of whom had the right to vote with their conscience, it was abolished in the Great Reform Act of 1832.

In exchange for a payment of £500 to the Treasury, Law was presented to the voters as the only candidate. This was a bargain; there was no need for hustings, expensive bribery or the hire of thugs. He was now one of the six MPs for the Isle of Wight; Cornwall had forty-two, London a mere four and the industrial towns of Manchester, Leeds, Bradford and others had none. Another advantage was that there was absolutely no need to visit the constituency. For members of the Georgian House of Commons, the constituency was more or less irrelevant. There would be absolutely no reason to go there, and there were no pressing needs to help constituents, as essentially there were none. The only person you needed to placate was the owner of the seat, and he probably lived on the other side of St James's Square.

This point was rather proved by Law's predecessor, Sir Richard Worsley, who had combined his position at Newtown with being His

Majesty's ambassador in Venice. This had been a straight trade-off – the seat was at the disposal of the Prime Minister precisely because Pitt had given him the diplomatic post; constituencies not only represented personal property in parliament, they were property in themselves. Worsley had recommenced his political career in 1790 after an eight-year break caused by his involvement in a famous adultery case where he had encouraged his wife's lover by helping him peer at her bathing naked in a bath house by giving him a piggyback up to the spy hole.

The new Attorney General was sworn in on 2 March. Law became a supporter of his dear friend Henry Addington's government. While in the Commons, he spoke and voted completely for the administration that had bought him. Nobody would have expected any different, and it would have been more shocking if he had done anything else. His career in the Commons, and even more so in the Lords, was not particularly stellar. It was never easy for major lawyers, who had other places to be when parliament was still sitting and would often be embarrassed about comments they had made before entering politics, but this was not why Ellenborough had difficulties. It was not even because of his views. With the exception of the abolition of slavery, Ellenborough took the most reactionary position possible on all issues; but this was not the reason for his unpopularity either.

The problem was the context. Unlike his work at the Old Bailey, the Guildhall or Assize, he did not have the final word. Parliament was a debating chamber, and the Chief Justice's view, no matter how well considered, was still an opinion. He found this irritating, and could not constrain his bad temper and inconsiderate tone with others.

His first appearance in the Commons proved this point. It was the first parliament of the new iteration of the state which incorporated the whole of Ireland. When the parliament in Dublin was closed, one hundred Irish representatives were added to the House of Commons, and his first speech was about the new Union with Ireland. There were always two ways of pacifying this reluctant partner in the United Kingdom: giving the Catholic population equal rights, or using force to suppress opposition. Law favoured the latter. On the subject of Catholic emancipation, speaking in the Lords in 1805, he regarded the term itself as improper: 'Their emancipation from civil and religious restraint as affecting themselves, and the rights to be enjoyed by them individually, is entire and complete.'

Ellenborough believed that Roman Catholics already had power over their own worship and own property and enjoyed, mostly, the same rights as other citizens of His Majesty. They needed to liberate themselves from their real enemy: 'The only remaining emancipation which they are capable of receiving must be acquired by an act of their own, be redeeming themselves from the foreign bondage and thraldom under which they and their ancestors have long unworthily groaned.'[4]

Catholics were the slavishly obedient sons and daughters of a foreign power and a baseless religion, and therefore could have no rights which gave them political influence in Britain. This was a respectable position, but his delivery on his first day in the Commons was terrible. The newspapers reported that he supported stronger action 'vehemently', a word that carried more implied criticism than it does today. He insisted that courts martial be made no harder to arrange; if the change was passed 'he should move to alter the title of the bill, and instead of an act to suppress, describe it as an act to facilitate and encourage insurrection and rebellion.'

His later speeches on Irish coercion were too extreme for a man in his position and he remained insensible to the fact. Lord Grey called his speech 'unduly warm', suggested it was noise and vehemence instead of argument, and hinted that better should be expected of the government law officer. The truth was that he was terrible at debating with politicians. He had used the same language at the Hastings impeachment, where his unpopularity with politicians started, and he continued to use it during his own parliamentary career.

He also regularly accused MPs and noble lords of not having done their homework and being ill informed, and on occasions he sounded like a condescending schoolteacher: 'If you would like some amusement in the holidays,' or that he wanted to 'cut the knot rather than waste time untying it.'

On his second day in the Commons he clashed with his fellow members again, accusing them of not reading the legislation properly, making arguments based on ignorance, and not understanding the law. He implied he was innocent of all three faults, and behaved accordingly.

He took his tone and attitude into the Lords, which exacerbated the problem because manners and behaviour were generally better, and it was believed that a newcomer like Ellenborough had no right to be rude and every reason to be deferential. He was regarded as a parvenu. In the courts, hard work, ability and connections counted, but the only thing that mattered in the Lords was heritage. Ellenborough was regarded as far too confident for a man whose peerage had started in 1802. His son turned out equally as rude, and was seen as much of a parvenu as his father by his enemies.

As a speaker he was forceful rather than elegant or particularly interesting, and this was not always what the audience wanted. He failed to deliver the necessary level of exaggerated politeness needed for the House of Peers. He could not brook restraint or tolerate contradiction, and showed this in the constant use of words such as foolish, puerile and unworthy, dull, impudent and even stupid. He was ready to tell any noble lord that they did not understand the law that was being debated, and sometimes went as far as suggesting that they knew it, but were misrepresenting it. He reminded them of his superiority by appearing in his black silk robes and judicial wig. When his mentor and ally Lord Sidmouth became Home Secretary in 1812 he had yet another connection to the top of the establishment, and his 'ebullitions of temper' increased.

Due to other commitments, his visits to the Lords were limited, so he tended to ration his speeches to areas where he claimed pre-eminent knowledge and experience – including proposed new laws, debt, national security and Ireland: the last two were often the same thing. He became particularly irked when existing laws were discussed; this was definitely his domain, and he would deal with contradiction with even less grace that usual. He particularly hated his time being wasted – on occasion, leaving a Lords' debate prematurely because of the pace of progress, he was heard to say that he was responsible to God Almighty for the use of his time. Lord Darnley was a victim of his impatience and lack of empathy when the noble lord yawned in the middle of a long rambling speech about the poor condition of Ireland – Ellenborough was heard to interpose that there was 'at least some sense in that part'.[5]

In his court, officials were too scared to be unprepared. In the Lords that writ did not run. One temper tantrum in 1805 was an extreme example of many. Somebody had not done their job: 'He considered it altogether indecent, that one noble lord should be compelled to look over the shoulder of another, in order to glean a little information from the papers.'

There were two problems here: first, that the papers were not quite ready, and second that some people were reading them now. Some of the paperwork was, literally, hot of the press. The word 'indecent' would have caused shudders in the House, but Ellenborough kept on digging:

> My lords, when I look at the papers just now printed and so reeking from the press that I cannot open them without endangering my health. When I look at a folio volume of 140 pages presented this day by the noble earl, and which we have not had a moment's time allowed us even to look into.[6]

When this happened in his court, he would strike out cases or threaten the guilty officials with some time in the cells, but in the House of Peers he could only get irritated. There was a petulant halt to his oratory: 'I pause, in order that some answer may be given to this proposal.'

Answer came there none, so he passive-aggressively agreed to act on insecure information. The debate commenced, and the learned judge told the House that the facts were wrong. No one knew more about the sovereignty of the Isle of Man than he, at least nobody here, was the insinuation. He knew best, and once again, he probably did. The Duke of Atholl, who was claiming compensation, was a mendicant; a greedy man not content with a fair settlement, who was going to claim as much as the government would allow him, and Ellenborough came quite close to comparing him to a vulture. It was a 'gross job', when 'job' was an insult that suggested a swindle had taken place. Ellenborough went on to add another injury by suggesting that the present parliament, about to be prorogued, had achieved nothing, and to give the duke money from the public purse was to move its performance from the neutral to the negative.

> Let us not, then, at the conclusion of this session during which unfortunately so little has been done for the honour or advantage of the country have the burthen on our minds of having agreed to such a bill as this. Let us not at a moment when all classes of the people are ground down with taxes add to their burthens by voting a boon to mendicant importunity.[7]

His opening caveat of 'I make no charge against any one', did not work. Lord Mulgrave bemoaned the standard of one particular debate; he described an unnamed lord of being boisterous and rude, and at that point

Ellenborough leapt up and gave the game away by hoping that this slur was not a reference to him, and was told politely that it was. He was also told that some of the expressions he had used were fitter for demagogues in Palace Yard.

The Whigs regarded him as a turncoat, and he regarded them as either hopelessly or malevolently naive. Lord Stanhope was a particular bête noir. Charles Stanhope was a Whiggish radical aristocrat, still supporting France in 1792. In 1795 he tried to get parliamentary support for a motion to keep out of the internal events of France and received no support at all, thus being responsible for the expression 'minority of one'. He also supported the rights of prisoners. He was a supporter of British radicals while Ellenborough was busy prosecuting them for seditious libel. He was 'Citizen Stanhope' – not an ironic insult, but a title he gave himself. This was much in character – he supported Fox's Libel act and the rights of juries in general.

Outside of the House Stanhope was an accomplished scientist; there is no reason to believe that Ellenborough had any respect for his character or his opinions about legal reform. In 1808 Stanhope opposed new powers for the Attorney General to demand bail from those held in court, on the basis that it would put too much power into the hands of a political appointee and hit the poor hardest. Ellenborough supported the law, and suggested, with insufficient diplomacy, that the noble lord did not know what he was talking about.

Ellenborough did not understand nuance. When Stanhope compared Ellenborough's intemperate language with some infamous judges from history who held the same position as Ellenborough, he was indignant: 'he had been grossly calumniated by an individual of that house having compared him to those monsters, who in former reigns had disgraced the bench of justice, such as Scroggs (and) Jeffries. But he should treat the calumny and the calumniator with contempt.'[8]

Scroggs was an intemperate anti-Catholic justice in the time of Charles II, and Jeffries was a more famous bigoted and severe judge. The fairness of the comparison is not the point, and a sympathetic observer might be able to see Ellenborough's point, but it was blasted out in an angry Cumbrian drawl alongside words like 'contempt'. This was the worst language of Billingsgate said some – mostly people who had never been there. His tone, now lost to history, was not appreciated either.

Stanhope made this stinging reply before deciding that it was all beneath his dignity:

> I meant no such comparison and if the noble and learned Lord from intimate acquaintance has found a resemblance this must be one of his singularities but his rash precipitancy in misapplying what fell from me convinces me that it might be dangerous to delegate the power created by the Bill even to the noble and learned Lord.[9]

There was another major falling out in 1811. Many more 'liberal' peers were concerned about the increased number of criminal libel cases that relied on *ex-officio* informations as the sole basis of the charge. This legal power allowed the Crown itself to open prosecutions for criminal libel on essential its own say-so, and such trials were processed by Ellenborough's own court of King's Bench. Lord Holland made this point: there had been thirty-eight such informations in the last three years before 1811, but only two in the three year period before that. These had been used to quell political dissent, but Ellenborough defended the practice, and did so vigorously. His words were described as dogmatism which disgusted one listener, who said he spoke 'with the coarse violence of a demagogue'.

A cartoon of 1811 shows Holland as trying to rescue the wounded body of the maiden Truth from attacks by the establishment. The Attorney General, Vicary Gibbs, attacks her with a bloodstained axe; Ellenborough, big and bulky, wields a sword to lacerate the truth; other establishment figures, Perceval, Lord Liverpool and Lord Eldon, give support. Lord Liverpool digs a grave to bury liberty.

The next flashpoint was in 1813 when the subject of the Delicate Investigation returned to the Lords to haunt the noble and learned lord. Ellenborough was – politely – accused of simply following the prince's wishes to blacken the reputation of Princess Caroline. The satirists had brought the subject up again in the print entitled: 'The delicate investigation or secrets of ----, Time Three o'Clock in the Morning!!!' The Prince Regent and his main allies are shown eating, drinking and dead drunk. The room is palatial and opulent, and the candles burnt down in their exquisite candlesticks to denote that the dissipation had gone on deep into the night. The prince, fat, full and too drunk to stand, is helped by his own acknowledged mistress Lady Hertford. The Douglases are there, as is Lord Eldon and Ellenborough. Eldon is stuffing a bird into his pocket to eat later, and Ellenborough has his mind on more food: 'Well of all investigations, none is in my mind so pleasing as that of a savoury eel pie.'

Ellenborough's role in the Delicate Investigation was public knowledge and the comments in the Lords were fair, but Ellenborough was not having it. The rumours spread by the princess's friends were warmly and vehemently refuted by the noble Lord – they were 'as false as hell', a much stronger word than now – and he once again refuted terms and description that were not ascribed to him. It was a malignant lie, a nefarious calumny, and one of the worst symptoms of the modern times in which we live, he bawled. He never really got the point of parliament.

Chapter Twenty-Two

The Peak of Unpopularity

By 1814, Ellenborough was a decade into his job. He was feared and loathed by the criminal classes. This was not so much a problem as part of his job description. Ellenborough despised the common man and woman on the street, and that hatred was heartily reciprocated, although he could tolerate those who knew their place and wished to stay there deferentially.

Sometimes the insults were obvious: he was 'Hellenborough', a neologism so apt and obvious that it is a surprise that it was not more used. His best friend Sidmouth became 'Sadmouth', but was usually called 'The Doctor'. The King's Bench prison in Southwark was known as 'Ellenborough Lodge' by the vulgar multitude, and the iron spikes on the 40ft-high wall which prevent escape, the *chevaux-de-frieze*, was known as 'Ellenborough's teeth'. The passageway in front of it was, inevitably, Ellenborough Walk. Many of these were statements of incumbency rather than personal slights. It was common to name the prison after the current Lord Chief Justice, so they became Abbott's teeth after 1818, but the name Ellenborough was still used in one newspaper as late as 1850, clearly with the assumption that it would be understood.

In the Georgian era, snuff was taken by all classes, with the poor buying the cheapest and nastiest varieties. In 1814, the *Critical Review* told its readers that tobacconists were selling a strong nasty smelling snuff normally called *Blackguard,* as *Ellenborough.* They both got up your nose in an unpleasant way, and it was the poor to whom the most damage was done. 'Blackguard' may sound too limp and lame to be a viable insult, but it was fighting talk at the time. On more than one occasion at the Old Bailey, defendants claimed that word in mitigation when they used violence.

The *Critical Review* was an upmarket literary publication read by the elite, mostly a liberal audience interested in reform, so they would have welcomed, but perhaps not have known, the news of what the plebs called Ellenborough. The *Review* went on to say that they were unwilling to make a comment on one of his legal publications: 'it is not safe to review a Reviewer who is a Lord Chief Justice with a bad temper'. Both the radical literati and the plebs hated him because he was such a powerful and effective judge. It is hard to say when his unpopularity reached a peak, but 1814 would be a good date – despite more outrages to come – as he rode roughshod over a national hero, destroying his reputation and finally cementing his reputation as an ultra-reactionary judge in an age of reactionary judges.

Ellenborough's most infamous trial was not about libel, sedition or treason, but the more modern sounding crime of manipulating the prices at the stock exchange. Britain was the only country in the world that had such an institution, and although from our modern point of view it was very limited, as it traded only in government debt and East India Company shares, it performed a vital function of financing the war against France. The war was won on a very extensive line of credit, organised by British financial institutions. Those citizens who had excess cash would invest in government consuls, or a slightly more complex product called omnium, and earn 3 or 4 per cent interest a year. Large swathes of the middle classes had their savings in consuls: Mrs Bennet in Austen's *Pride and Prejudice* had £5,000 in government stocks and the ruling classes used them even more extensively. Ellenborough's will was to contain £10,000 worth of stocks, and he stipulated different destinations for them based on how much their value had increased. It has been estimated that a quarter of a million people held government bonds, a four-fold increase in Ellenborough's lifetime. This was a substantial proportion of the respectable population who had a vested interest in the stability of the state.[1]

People earned an income by speculation as well as drawing interest. Omniums were particularly prone to risk taking. They could be purchased in instalments, with the investor paying around 15 per cent of the purchase price. This widened participation but increased the risk of making calamitous loses. Both consuls and omniums would rise in value with the news of military victories, and they had no fixed redemption date (the last was repaid in 2015).

So, the news of the death or definitive defeat of Napoleon would be very valuable to whoever got it first, and the establishment knew this. Financial Institutions and newspapers had agents on the south coast waiting for news they could exploit, but the government were normally able to keep a monopoly of news distribution. Through a series of effective measures it controlled the news from the south coast and East Kent. News of Nelson's victory at Trafalgar in 1805 was controlled by the government and reached the right people first through a series of post-chaises with a frequent change of horses.

Criminals had already worked out that it was much easier to be first with a lie than to be second to hear the truth. Today we worry that social media means that lies can be spread easily, but when there were few sources of news, then a plausible lie, especially one that people wanted desperately to be true, could be exploited for many hours. This was done successfully by a confidence trickster called Charles Random de Berenger on 21 February 1814. Like all confidence tricksters, he invested in himself and ostentatiously obeyed the rules (most of the time) to disguise his trickery. He appeared portentously at a Dover public house and announced that the war was over. He had invested in a disguise as Colonel Du Bourg, followed the correct government procedure by passing his lie to the authorities in Deal first, but chose a foggy day when the visual signalling system could not be used. (The signalling system could send a message successfully in two minutes and have it acknowledged in another two, and remained in use until 1847 when the electric telegraph killed it off.)

The fake Colonel Du Bourg spread the news himself as he travelled to London, throwing coins to make sure a crowd appeared – ensuring they were French coins so the crowd believed him. British gold coins were rare enough as the war had been financed by a blizzard of paper money, but gold Napoleons would have been a clincher to anybody who was still doubtful. The war was over: Napoleon was defeated and torn to pieces by Colonel Sacken's cossacks and the Bourbon monarchy was restored. When the news reached London, the price of consuls rose. His haste diminished as he arrived at Shooter's Hill; the fake news had to coincide with the opening of the Stock Exchange at 9 am.

At noon a group of soldiers in the uniforms of French officers drove over London bridge declaring victory. Meanwhile everybody bought government bonds – except eight people, who sold them. The next day, the hoax was discovered by a stock exchange investigation but these eight had already secured their profits. One of the select was Thomas Cochrane. He sold his complete holding, amounting to £139,000 of omnium shares, with a profit of £6,000 (some sources suggest less, about half this amount) on his purchase price, and he was friendly or familiar with three of the other accused. His uncle, Andrew Cochrane Johnstone, who was certainly dishonest, had sold half a million pounds' worth. Cochrane's stockbroker, Richard Butt, had sold nearly £400,000 worth, and worst of all, Cochrane was on business terms with De Berenger, who was the fake colonel with the fake news.

These men, alongside the pretend Bourbons on London Bridge, were tried before Ellenborough at the King's Bench in the Guildhall on 8 June 1814. None of the men had any reason to rejoice as the Lord Chief Justice shuffled and grunted to his place, as he had a reputation for wheedling the truth from people who were unwilling to reveal it, and most of these men would be easy prey because they were guilty. Thomas Cochrane was the only one of the defendants that the Lord Chief Justice would have recognised. To the masses, he was a famous naval commander who was regarded as the second Nelson by those who read about his exploits in the newspapers. The French gave him the nickname *le loup de mer* – the sea wolf.[2]

To those who actually knew him in the Admiralty and government, he was an over proud, slightly grasping prima donna, whose self worth could often be suffocating. Ellenborough was not impressed by national heroes, even those in possession of the Order of the Bath – consider his brusque interrogations of Nelson at the Despard trail in 1803 – but this was worse. Cochrane was a radical politician and Member of Parliament as well. He was a friend of William Cobbett and Henry Hunt, both of whom Ellenborough had already sent to prison for their politics. Ellenborough also noted that the defence consisted of William Best, James Park (who he knew well), but also Henry Brougham from the Hunt libel case.

It was even worse than that: Cochrane's full title was Lord Thomas Cochrane, the tenth Earl of Dundonald, and he held radical views on parliamentary reform and establishment privilege. This was incomprehensible to Ellenborough – that a member of the establishment should betray his class was morally repugnant to him. His seditious speeches made him sound like the radical Henry Hunt, a man who was not a lord but was still a substantial owner of 3,000 acres of land in Somerset and Wiltshire. How could such men challenge a system that was working well, and particularly working well for them? His reaction would vacillate between disbelief and disgust.

Ellenborough was not Cochrane's worst enemy however, that was Cochrane himself. He allowed himself to be tried with the other main defendants, perhaps in deference to his uncle's reputation, but probably because he believed that he could not possibly be found guilty. He did not attend the trial for the same reason. He was haughty, disdainful and argumentative, like the Chief Justice himself, but also very naive. His impetuousness made him a brilliant naval commander but a poor defendant against an establishment that held all the cards. Brougham thought he would have saved his skin if he had turned evidence on his uncle, but to turn evidence you would have to be admit guilt first. Cochrane's guilt or innocence has never been satisfactorily ascertained, but that hardly matters. The masses and radical politicians thought him innocent, but those with power had had enough of him and were happy to see him go down.

Both the trial and Ellenborough's summing up were criticised. The prosecution finished their case just after 10 pm: it had been a long thirteen-hour day and it was assumed that Ellenborough would adjourn until 10 am the next day. This was only half true; Ellenborough did start in the morning, but insisted that the defence started at 10.10 pm, ignoring many objections, including one from James Park, his former colleague from the Northern Circuit. They finished at 3 am, only to be told to start again seven hours later.

Ellenborough's reason for keeping the defence up all night was that there were three important witnesses who were busy the next morning and would not be able to attend. This rather showed his priorities. In Ellenborough's partial defence, he would often run a trial into the early morning in order to avoiding reconvening the next morning. To the point that it would be hard for the jury to stay awake – that was a problem for the prosecution as well.

The morning session was mostly about Cochrane. He knew De Berenger, having been introduced to him by his dubious uncle, but the defence tried to suggest that this did not mean he was equally guilty. Unfortunately for Cochrane, De Berenger had paid him a visit on the day of the hoax, and the prosecution had alleged that De Berenger had entered his house in the red uniform of a staff officer and changed in Cochrane's house, thus proving that Cochrane had known about the disguise and helped him change into something less damning.

Cochrane was convinced that it was a stitch-up, and that Ellenborough hated him. That was at least half true. Cochrane tended to over-state his case by claiming an establishment-wide conspiracy to do him down. There probably wasn't one, but there was a general wariness about Cochrane's self-importance, and a resentment that he should think himself important enough to be an establishment target.

Ellenborough's summing up was controversial. He had been dismissive and sarcastic with both sides when they failed to meet his high standards, but this was par for the course. It was the judge's concluding remarks that usually affected justice, and in this case his were breathtakingly one-sided. The whole debate was about colours of clothes. Ellenborough made his view obvious in the summing up. He regarded one piece of circumstantial evidence as utterly conclusive: 'The red uniform and grey trench coat, allegedly seen and disposed of by Cochrane, matched the one of the man knocking on pub doors in Dover on that foggy morning.'[3]

All defendants were found guilty. A week later, Cochrane was sentenced to a fine of £1,000, a year in prison, and to be pilloried outside the Royal Exchange, which was in Cochrane's own constituency. Those who wanted to believe that Ellenborough was more interested in punishing a political enemy than administering justice did not find it difficult.

Cochrane was dispatched to the King's Bench prison. He rented some comfortable high-floored rooms and enjoyed entertaining his friends and family like any other rich inmate, but his mood soured more or less immediately when he was removed from the Navy Lists, stripped of the Order of the Bath, and expelled from the Commons. Despite having many enemies in the navy Cochrane blamed Ellenborough personally, and when he was released to argue his case against expulsion, the speech was so libellous and sweary that it was expunged from the official record.

Many other of Ellenborough's enemies took the opportunity to join the Cochrane crusade. Sir Francis Burdett organised Cochrane's successful re-election to his Westminster seat and said that he would stand with Cochrane in the pillory. Cobbett rallied the opposition in one of the best-selling editions of his newspaper; Sheridan made way for Cochrane, and Brougham supported Cochrane's candidature reluctantly, with an eye to his own career. The radicals were united against him.

Once again, Cochrane proved his own worst enemy. He escaped from prison with four months left of his sentence and tried to enter the Commons but was rearrested and placed in a much worse cell in Ellenborough's prison, where he nearly died. When he was able to enter the Commons, he made a speech in March 1815 accusing Ellenborough of 'partiality, misrepresentation, injustice and oppression', which attracted the support of no MPs.

Cochrane's attempted persecution of Ellenborough coincided with the war coming to an end in reality, not merely in the imagination of the stock exchange fraudsters. Life in Britain was going to change, but not even the most pessimistic observer would have predicted how much worse things would become. The price of bread had increased during the war due to poor harvests and natural changes in climate that were not understood at the time, and this had caused much unrest. Ellenborough knew that the price of food – bread for the most part – was vital, literally, and like everybody else in the country, he kept an eye on the weather not out of idle curiosity, but because of the social consequences of scarcity. Most Georgian riots were about bread prices. A few years later, he wrote about this to Sidmouth:

> My dear Lord
> The expectations I sanguinely formed of the fine weather for our harvest when I wrote to you from Calais were sadly disappointed by a succession of heavy showers during the three following days. Since that time, if your weather is the same as that which we had here, your harvest may have recovered from the mischiefs that threatened its destruction. I feel an intense interest in this subject, as I think the peace of the country and exemption from calamities of the worst sort almost depend on the abundance and cheapness of corn.[4]

Harvests mattered to all, but the establishment also had to worry about agricultural profits. The landowning classes had done very well out of the war, with farming imports being restricted and prices high, allowing individuals to invest in agricultural improvement and make vast profits for themselves. When the war and the French blockade ended in 1815, landowners were threatened by a flood of cheap imports that undermined both their prosperity and the wages of the agricultural workers who relied on them.

The government acted to protect landowners and Ellenborough cooperated with this, voting in favour of the banning of corn imports until the price reached eighty shillings a bushel. The result was to keep profits and bread prices much higher than they would have been. Adam Smith's views on free markets were forgotten, and the London poor, with little other recourse to food, were furious. They had endured twenty years of war and deprivation; having won the war, they were not going to be allowed to eat cheaply in peacetime.

The hungry poor parked themselves outside the Palace of Westminster during the debate in March 1815. They stopped the carriages of the rich and influential and demanded to know their stance on the bill, and they abused and assaulted those who gave the wrong answer. Inside the besieged building there was no discussion about whether the poor should eat cheaply; there was only a debate about whether the trigger price should be eighty or seventy-four shillings before imports were allowed. The price had never been as high as either of these in peacetime, and now eighty shillings was effectively the new minimum. The aristocratic landowners in the Lords may have looked back wistfully to 1813, when it approached 120 shillings. In January 1815, it had been sixty shillings; this new law was therefore a compromise in their minds anyway. This was a victory for the wider ruling class over the government as well. Lord Liverpool, the Prime Minister, was well aware of having bread prices at a constant wartime level and suggested a sliding scale that would allow imports at a lower figure than eighty shillings, but this was blocked by the Commons.

In response, the crowd in Palace Yard turned into a hooting mob. It attacked the members of parliament, and when dispersed by the military, it headed for the houses of the half dozen people they blamed and hated the most. 'To Mr. Robinson's' 'To Lord Eldon's!' 'To Lord Darnley's!' and 'To Lord Ellenborough's!' was the cry, according to one source.

Robinson was the Chancellor of the Exchequer; his house was trashed, and his paintings were cut up and thrown onto the street. He had recently moved from Charles Street, and they did not find him there; he was easily found at his new house on Burlington Street. It was a small world. The Chancellor, Lord Eldon, had his house in Bedford Square completely demolished by the mob smashing in the windows, breaking down the iron railing, and hammering the panels of the door in the area, and at the main entrance, setting up a loud cries of 'No Corn Bill'. Eldon was lucky that soldiers were routinely stationed behind his house; he collected them, ordered a fixed bayonet charge, and caught two of the ringleaders himself. This was not bad going for a 64-year-old who, like most of the establishment, was not afraid of the mob, especially with the state's military forces behind him.

The military was vital to keeping order in emergencies. Both rioters and potential victims were in agreement that a regular paid police force was a Continental tyranny not to be borne by the free-born Englishman, but the establishment was solaced by the fact that only they had an army and the legal monopoly on violence. They had a majority of votes for their new corn law, but had an equally essential majority of bayonets. Since the French Revolution, barracks had been built all over the country, particularly in key parts of London. Whether the establishment was afraid or not, they could brazen it out well enough.

Ellenborough played no leading part in the increase in food prices for the poor; he had no particular part in the Corn Bill – except voting for it, but he was a leading judge whose unpopularity had peaked after the Cochrane Trial, and the mob remembered him. It was his turn for a visitation at St James's Square. The next part of the story does not ring especially true:

> Soon after they had commenced their assault upon the house, his Lordship, in the most intrepid manner, presented himself at the door, and inquired the cause of the outrages upon his dwelling? The reply was 'No Corn Bill, No Corn Bill', on which his Lordship addressed them in a few words, the purpose of which we have not heard, but the effect was that the mob instantly cheered the Noble Lord and departed.[5]

Ellenborough's words did not necessarily quieten the mob; they merely went somewhere else to do their damage, although they seemed to have attacked his ground floor before his soothing words. The facts are not fully clear, but it seems fair to say that all of the windows in his house were smashed. There would have been some attempt to burn his house down. What did he say? According to the newspapers, he addressed them about the 'dangerous impropriety of their conduct'.[6]

He was probably made braver by the arrival of the Life Guards, who cleared the whole street; his then 12-year-old son Henry Spencer Law (later Cambridge, Lincoln's Inn and then a barrister) would later join the regiment that saved him that day. The windows of Lord Castlereagh's house were repaired by the next morning. Ellenborough's took a while longer, but he went back to work immediately. The state that defeated Napoleon easily saw off hungry rioters. Campbell noted that 'the house of Lord Ellenborough was attacked and his person insulted, but he remained steadfast and refused to join in the recommendation to mercy'.

Chapter Twenty-Three

The Peak of Power

The last full year of the Chief Justice's life was one of economic and political turbulence. Ellenborough's harshness and zeal were always based on the belief that anarchy was just around the corner, and in 1817 he had more reason than usual to suspect it. He continued to work hand-in-glove with his friend and ally, Lord Sidmouth. His power and that of his establishment cronies seemed unassailable, but this was the year that events started to turn against him, although that would not have seemed the case at the time.

The political atmosphere was febrile. December 1816 had seen an attempted insurrection against the state, part comic and part deluded, but one that it suited the establishment to take seriously. The Spa Fields insurrection had grave objectives. The Society of Spencean Philanthropists, led by James Watson and Arthur Thistlewood, intended to storm the Tower of London and the Bank of England, declare a provisional government, and murder those members of the establishment to whom their philanthropy did not extend. Bags were carried to cut off heads, and poles were planned to put them on. They convinced themselves that this would spark a revolution among the desperate English and Irish workers in London. None of this happened. They were disorganised, poorly equipped and under supported; most of their temporary followers, roused by an earlier political meeting, contented themselves with looting gun shops, butchers and bakers. The guilty four were tracked down and arrested, to be tried by Ellenborough for high treason in 1817.

On January 1817, the Prince Regent's coach was attacked by a jeering and hissing mob as he left the state opening of parliament, which ran from January to late June most years. It was probably stones that smashed the windows, but the authorities preferred to believe it was bullets and deemed it an assassination attempt. One of the journalists who mocked the government for using two of the prince's slavish and sycophantic courtiers as definitive evidence of attempted murder was an obscure bookseller and journalist named William Hone.

Lord Sidmouth used the event as a pretext to suspend habeas corpus in cases of high treason, suspicion of high treason, or treasonable practices, the definition of which lay conveniently with the Crown law officers. Habeas corpus was the ancient right to challenge detention and insist on either a lawful trial or release from custody. For most of 1817, Sidmouth and his friend Ellenborough could lock people up with no reason, no trial and no explanation. It was not necessarily a tyrant's charter, as portrayed by many radicals at the time and some historians today, because it had an automatic sunset clause of the following year. It was not that much used, but it could intimidate people into silence. It was aimed at publishers like William Hone, and Ellenborough's old enemies Thomas Cochrane and Henry Hunt. On the morning of the attack on the regent's coach, they were raising yet another petition against corruption and sinecures and in favour of universal suffrage and annual elections; they both knew that the new powers would be used against them.

In May 1817, the Spenceans, Watson, Thistlewood, Thomas Preston and John Hooper were put on trial for their part in the Spa Fields Insurrection, a grand enough title that suited both their supporters and their deadly enemies. The government held all the cards: it could decide the charge, and as part of its campaign to silence dissent, the charge had to be high treason rather than aggravated riot. This would be a salutary warning to others and would justify any new political restrictions. The state prisoners were kept in the Tower of London before the trial and escorted in chains by a troop of lifeguards to and from court in order to confirm their treason before the trial even began.

The odds were stacked against them. Ellenborough would conduct the trial, which would be guided by laws made by Lord Sidmouth. It was a reactionary double act that would be hard to resist, and the only possible weakness was the attitude of the jury. The jury was to be composed of the best of the local population – or rigged in favour of the establishment, depending on opinion – as they had to be freeholders of the city paying £10 to be considered. Three potential jurors were removed on the first day because they did not qualify.

James Watson was first, and the others were to follow. Over 200 state witnesses were called, all attesting to the organisation of the events of 2 December. Had the charge been aggravated riot, then the trial would have been over in a day. This case was much more difficult for the prosecution than Ellenborough's trial of Despard. Despard planned to kill the king with cannon, but this mixture of looting, rioting and taunting the soldiers at the Tower was pathetic in comparison. The radical Francis Place said it could have been quelled by twenty constables, and the government would have privately agreed. Despite their spies knowing exactly what was going on, the government response was very emphatic. The state that defeated the armies of Napoleon was a match for the drunken, desperate, hungry and poor, but it suited them to suggest jeopardy.

Much was made of the events before the violence to suggest treasonous motives: the tricolours in the British revolutionary colours of red, white and green; the slogans on the banners; and Watson's inflammatory words at the hustings. The most incriminating evidence came from John Castle, who seemed to have been a major organiser and instigator of events. It was all going well until one of Ellenborough's radical enemies destroyed the case for prosecution.

Henry Hunt proved beyond doubt that Castle was both a spy and an agent provocateur, both reporting back to Sidmouth and suggesting illegal activity to the Spenceans rather than merely reporting it. Castle was a state agent and a moral disgrace, as Hunt argued. He was already used to turning King's evidence and had accepted pocket money, a new coat and travel expenses. At one point, Ellenborough objected to the phrase 'whorehouse bully', but it was about right. The defence did not accuse Castle of being a spy, or the state of organising espionage, as Ellenborough would have closed down any discussions of the state security apparatus.[1]

Ellenborough's summary to the jury was both comprehensive and one-sided. It went on for so many hours that he had to get a deputy to complete it. He did point out that terrible events might just have been a riot; he did concede that there was no active plot to murder the king, but what they had done was enough to convict them. Altering the law, the church, improving wages, or ending enclosure by the threat of armed force was still levying war against the king. He also suggested that Castle could be believed: the word of a brothel pimp, fraudster and former turncoat may be true in this case, and there was a need to be pragmatic – 'you must seek information through a channel that is not always pure'. This might be acceptable if the Vice Society were employing agents to purchase pornography, but not when the state uses it to execute its subjects.

The hand-picked jury was not impressed. Ellenborough told them to take their time, but he also reminded them that they would receive neither food nor fuel while deliberating. He suggested a cup of tea; one jury told him that it would be acceptable, others said not, as it would take ten minutes to organise. They all compromised on wine and water, with the judge joining the jury for refreshments. He must have been more than confident. They were away for ninety minutes – not because it was a difficult case, but because each juror spoke in turn. They were unanimous for a 'not guilty' verdict. When the word reached the court, there was applause and joy everywhere. Nobody, yet, would laugh in triumph inside Ellenborough's court when his power was successfully challenged. It was to happen in the next six months, and he would be powerless.

The next day, the other three Spenceans were released without charge and all four became unlikely heroes. It was more celebrated as a victory for liberty and a vindication of English liberty; the fact that it had saved some fantasists from the noose was soon forgotten by most. Wilberforce, like many of his classmates, lamented that these misfits could be turned into heroes by the state in a way that their own actions could never achieve. The lesson about spies appearing in court was not forgotten by the authorities.

Ellenborough had more success when he led the trial of the leaders of the June 1817 'Pentrich Insurrection'. This was, in the words of Lord Sidmouth, an attempt 'by force of arms to subvert and destroy the government and the Constitution'. It was led by Jeremiah Brandreth and forty or so framework knitters, stonemasons, labourers and miners from the Derbyshire village of Pentrich and surrounding areas. They were similar to the Spenceans in some regard; they believed that they could organise an armed revolt that would spark a revolution among desperate workers. Like the Spenceans, they were ready to use violence, and like the Spenceans, their poorly equipped rebellion ended in failure. The reason the rising was little more than a pathetic skirmish was that the state had a spy who both told the government the details, and helped Brandreth organise it. It was all over in a single day in June.

Ellenborough was one of the circuit judges who took part in the trial in Derby in October. Before the trial, there was a normal civic reception and service at All Saints Church with a sermon that had a point: Isaiah 5:20 – 'woe unto them who call evil good and good evil'. Like Watson, Thistlewood, Preston and Hooper, the prisoners were shipped in chains from prison, preceded by a cart of their pikes and sharpened agricultural implements.

However, this trial was going to be easier for Ellenborough and there would be no acquittals in this case. In this case also, the government had used agents provocateur to provoke these deluded men into action. The scandal of the spy, codenamed 'Oliver', had been exposed in June, and so there was enough time to arrange the events so that the story did not get out during the trial. One of the accused, Thomas Bacon, had full knowledge of Oliver and so the prosecution avoided calling him with the main ringleaders, and instead bundled him with eighteen others at the end who all pleaded guilty, asked for mercy and were not questioned. The jury of county gentleman was much more willing to take direction from the judge. Ellenborough sentenced Brandreth and two others to hanging and decapitation. There was no attempt at drawing and disembowelling, but the case did rather prove that the spy system could work well. Ellenborough probably gave no more regard to Brandreth, whose execution was botched and painful, but it was said that he cursed to the name of Watson to his dying day.

Another name that Ellenborough remembered in his last days was William Hone. In 1817, the reactionary duo of Sidmouth and Ellenborough picked on the obscure and impecunious bookseller William Hone. Hone had published three sets of parodies that satirised and condemned the greed and inefficiency of the Prince Regent and his ministers. His vehicle was a parody of the church liturgy.[2]

> PRINCE, ruler of the people, have mercy upon us, thy miserable subjects,
>
> O prince, ruler, &c.
>
> O House of Lords, hereditary legislators, have mercy upon us, pension-paying subjects,
>
> O House of Lords, &c.
>
> O House of Commons, proceeding from corrupt borough-mongers, have mercy upon us, your should-be constituents,

O House of Commons, &c

O gracious, noble, right honourable, and learned rulers of our land, three estates in one state, have mercy upon us, a poverty-stricken people,

Home also used a religious text to condemn a less than holy trinity:

For there is one Ministry of Old Bags another of Derry Down TRIANGLE and another of the Doctor.

But the Ministry of Old Bags of Derry Down Triangle and of the Doctor is all one, equal the profusion coeternal

Such as Old Bags is such is Derry Triangle and such is the Doctor.

Old Bags a Mountebank Derry Down Triangle a Mountebank the Doctor a Mountebank.

Old Bags incomprehensible Derry Down Triangle incomprehensible the Doctor incomprehensible.

Old Bags a Humbug Derry Down a Humbug and the Doctor a Humbug. And yet they are not three Humbugs but one Humbug

Old Bags was John Scott, now Lord Eldon, Lord Chancellor of England, who carried his Great Seal in a ceremonial case that explains his name. He was the county's leading judge of the Court of Chancery, with an influence similar to Ellenborough's but with a more political role. Derry Down Triangle was Lord Castlereagh. As Chief Secretary for Ireland (1798–1801), he was instrumental in the passage of the Act of Union and the suppression of the United Irishman, who had threatened his own brother the bishop in Dublin. The triangle was a torture device used on rebels. The Doctor was his friend Sidmouth. Hone called Sidmouth that because his father was a doctor and he could be shown in cartoons peddling quack remedies for the country's ailments. All three together were the holy trinity of oppression and greed. For the Chief Justice, this was an attack on the establishment made worse by the fact that Eldon had been his close colleague for decades, Sidmouth was his friend and mentor, and Castlereagh was family; Ellenborough's family made summer visits to Castlereagh's house in Kent, and his sister was married to Ellenborough's eldest son. It all came very close to home.

The squibs (cheap satirical pamphlets) had already sold at least 3,000 copies for as little as tuppence and had also been passed hand to hand after reading. Others were republishing them, as pirated copies. (Hone never made any money, as ever, from his work). Worried reports from magistrates suggested that they were being sung in plebeian public houses all over the country, and people were finding them hilarious. Their easy availability exacerbated the libel in the eyes of the authorities. Hone was by no means an atheist, and his wife Sarah was very pious. One of the agonies of his feud with Ellenborough was that he deeply resented being cast as a blasphemer. Hone did not regard these insubstantial parodies as hills to die on, and they were withdrawn on 22 February, quite quickly after publication.

Unhelpfully for Hone, the works were republished by Richard Carlile, who was a genuine atheist and enemy of the establishment. His own dedication was an invitation for the state to prosecute him: 'Printed and Published by R Carlile, at the Republican Office … and sold by those who are not afraid of incurring the displeasure of His Majesties Ministers, their spies or informers.'

Carlile's bluff was called and he spent four months in Ellenborough's prison, but the authorities decided to go for Hone as well. He continued to produce cheap political pamphlets and Sidmouth may have wanted to stop his voice by using the three tracts as a pretext. Hone was clearly struggling with both health and wealth by 1817; he had been a thorn in the side of the establishment for a while, and it was judged a good time to finish him off *pour encourager les autres*.

Sidmouth would also have calculated that a spell in prison would make it very difficult for Hone to run his newspaper, the *Reformist Register*, but Sidmouth probably did not know that Hone had no real sense for business anyway and that his greatest skill was theatrics, wit and playing to the gallery – or a court of law. Sidmouth and Ellenborough had made a mistake, but they did not know it yet. Hone had no money, relying on his radical friends and his harassed wife to make ends meet. Ellenborough would have noted that Hone was a friend of the Hunt Brothers and that his arch enemy Cochrane had helped raise £100 for Hone. The authorities hoped that this would encourage Hone to represent himself and aimed to keep him poor. They succeeded, but it was another mistake.

On 3 May 1817, Hone was detained on charges of blasphemy and sedition, although the warrant did not tell him this, just that Ellenborough had made the order. It was dated the previous Monday and called for his immediate arrest. The decision to wait until 5 pm on Saturday afternoon meant that bail would be very difficult to achieve. It wasn't impossible, as there was no such thing as the weekend at that time and this applied to the court, which was regularly in session on Saturday, but it was harder to find the relevant officials and easier to get away with Ellenborough's true intention of withholding bail. The final decision would be Ellenborough's in any case, and the bail would be so high that it would be unaffordable. Hone spent Sunday in a Wilson's lock-up house in Holborn, not knowing the charge and, in any case, not having access to legal advice. None of this was accidental.

Ellenborough had successfully used all of the weapons of the state to put Hone on the back foot, but there was to be more. Hone was a victim of *ex officio* information, which allowed court officers to issue accusations themselves rather than wait for an outside body to initiate a charge. Such informations could lead to somebody being plucked from the street to answer an accusation that they had not seen or knew nothing about. It's easy to see why Ellenborough always defended these legal instruments in his lawmaker's role in the House of Lords.

On 27 March, Sidmouth had advised magistrates that they could now detain hawkers and publishers of subversive pamphlets before any charges had been filed. Ellenborough had spoken in favour of these measures in the House of Lords on 12 May. It was easier to prosecute for distributing a pamphlet than to convince a jury that the content was seditious. Sidmouth's plan was to do both.

The first Hone heard of the charge was Monday morning, when he and Thomas Jonathan 'TJ' Wooler, another writer that the establishment wished to silence, were presented at the King's Bench. Wooler was on the establishment hit list. He had recently described the rich as a herd of locusts and said that England was a fine roast beef full of fat maggots. These were, not coincidentally, two of the three men that Sidmouth had accused of poisoning the minds of the plebeians with their lies and libel. The third, William Cobbett, suspended publication of his paper and went away to the USA. Cobbett suggested that Hone do the same, even offering to finance the move for his extensive family.

The *ex officio* information was read out in court. Hone, never having seen the details before, asked for a copy so he could decide how to proceed.

It was pointed out that he could not see it until he had put in a plea. It would have cost him £10 for a copy, an amount that the authorities thought he could not raise. Hone would not cooperate on principle, and Ellenborough told him that he could indeed postpone his plea. He could wait until the beginning of the next term but would spend the summer in gaol. Hone's arguments were cut short: 'the time of the court must not be occupied in vain discussions', said the man who would spend his own summer eating and drinking in Paris. There were other aggressions: Hone seemed to have problems passing water and was refused permission to sit. He was held in the King's Bench prison from May to December. He probably thought that would be his punishment – he wasn't the first dissenting voice to be put in prison without charge during this period. He weakened when confronted with this power, offering to burn all remaining copies of the three parodies and never do the like again. The reply to his surrender was a curt note, with one week's notice of his trial.

Chapter Twenty-Four

The Spell is Broken

> Lord Ellenborough – Where are the Sheriffs? I desired their attendance, and they shall attend!
>
> The Under-Sheriff – My Lord, I have sent for them, but they live a great distance from this, and they have not yet arrived.[1]

Hone believed, rightly, that the three days of trial in mid-December were designed to break him, send a message to others like him, and strengthen the government's power to muzzle the radical press in the future. On the morning of the first day, even a sympathetic observer would agree that the plan was working. There were to be three trials, all essentially on the same charge of libel, in different forms. If they were to succeed, then political satire would be condemned as blasphemy or sedition.

Hone was at a low ebb, ill, poor and exhausted from his treatment by Ellenborough and Sidmouth. He was a stressed, small and shabbily dressed dot in the magnificent emptiness of the Guildhall, the location that the state used when they wanted the maximum public audience for their expected triumph. Hone's *Reformist Register* had folded; he was still able to write, he just could not control his finances, a skill that was beyond him at the best of times. His radical friends had rallied around him, but this power was dwarfed by the state's intention to destroy him. Sidmouth had already called his parodies blasphemies. Attorney General Garrow had promised the House of Commons that he would be punished. T.J. Wooler put a black border around its newspaper. Leigh Hunt declared the trial by jury was over. The result was a foregone conclusion.

The first day was given to Sir Charles Abbott because Ellenborough was failing: he had stumbled back to his duties at Michaelmas term 1817 but relied on puisne judges, sometimes at short notice, and Abbott was his deputy at King's Bench. Hone was acquitted on the first set of charges on 17 December. Abbott had done badly; perhaps at this point Ellenborough remembered that T.J. Wooler had fended off Lord Abbott a few months earlier when the jury failed to convict him for sedition. Ellenborough's biographer said that on the first day Abbott 'was not thought to have held the defendant, who conducted his case with a boldness and ability worthy of a better cause, in sufficient subjection'.

Henry Crabb Robinson witnessed all three days and articulated the worries of many in the establishment. Why would Ellenborough succeed where Abbott had failed? Clearly, Hone was not a well man and would possibly find days two and three harder under Ellenborough, but what principles would change? The Chief Justice was not well either. Death had already put his seal upon him, opined Townsend – albeit retrospectively: 'he appeared in Court pale and hollow-visaged, but with a spirit unbroken, and more stern than when his strength was impaired'. Stern was not going to be enough; in the past, stern sufficed because he was healthy, feared, and intellectually acute. Hone was as ill and tired as Ellenborough, but he was clearly cheered by winning on day one with tactics that could be redeployed on day two. It was essentially the same charge, which commonsense suggested should have been withdrawn, but sense was not in charge.

There were warnings from those who were humble enough to heed them. It was hubris on Ellenborough's part to think he could do better, especially as he knew of, and warned against Hone's methods. On the first day of the trial, with Lord Justice Abbott in charge, spontaneous laughter had already halted court proceedings. A system that relies on fear cannot abide mockery. Abbott has received his fair share of the blame, but Attorney General Sir Samuel Shepherd has not, and his failure does as much to explain the failure of Ellenborough over the next two days. The whole government case, put forward by Shepherd, was a minefield. Hone's work may or may not have been seditious, but it *was* funny, and the poor deaf Shepherd had to read it out in a loud voice. When the government official was named Lick Spittle the court laughed, and later, when they were warned about it, they replaced the undermining laughter with fake coughing. The only consolation for the prosecution was that it was the audience that laughed, not the jury. They were a higher social class and would surely do their duty, and the giggles of the plebs rather proved the prosecution's point that Hone's so-called satires were poisonous. The jury took the same view. They knew who Hone was criticising, and it was not God Almighty. That is why he was acquitted.

Hone's plan on day two was to play the little man threatened by unreasonable force, and it suited his strategy that the replacement judge was viewed as even more reactionary than Abbott. Indeed, on day two with Ellenborough, Hone blamed Ellenborough's lack of humanity for his suffering over the last six months. With the Chief Justice himself in front of him, this became easier:

> 'I am glad to see you, my Lord Ellenborough,' shouted Hone: 'I know what you are come here for: I know what you want.' 'I am come to do justice,' retorted the noble and learned Lord: 'my only wish is to see justice done.' 'Is it not rather, my Lord,' said Hone, 'to send a poor bookseller to rot in a dungeon?'

As far as Hone was concerned, he was there to repel the assault on the freedom of the press, started by Sidmouth and now to be completed by Ellenborough. Crabb Robinson noticed Hone's increased confidence: on day one, he was bold; on day two, he was insolent.

Everything else was the same. Attorney General Shepherd used the same argument that had failed the day before and read out a new set of comic versions of the liturgy. The thousand people listening all laughed, and there was nothing Ellenborough could do about it: the sheriffs were not present. Hone's parodies – or any early ones which proved that parodies were not normally prosecuted – could be heard as evidence. At this point, Hone might have remembered the bitter comment of his radical ally, T.J. Wooler, when he was in front of Ellenborough: 'You appear before Law, you are tried by Law because the LAW of Libel is just what the judges say, when the jury will believe them.'

As noted in Chapter Sixteen, this wasn't true; juries had power they were not using, and for years Ellenborough chose to overlook Fox's 1792 Libel Act, which stated that juries could decide if something was libel and so had to hear the evidence. Instead, he relied on intimidation to get his own way and was planning on using his usual technique of *telling* the jury that the defendant was a libeller and therefore guilty.

It was Ellenborough's rival Erskine who pointed out the futility of employing a jury in libel trials if they could not be allowed to make this decision. Legally, the learned judge's views were mere opinions, and Hone told Ellenborough so. At that point, the court erupted, and the sheriffs (now arriving) unrealistically offered to arrest the next of the thousand people who laughed. Ellenborough had been known to fine and admonish court officials who were not ready when he was; now their impotence was obvious, as was his powerless rage. It was an 'I am Spartacus moment' – one person laughing is in trouble, but everybody doing so is the best defence.

As part of his rhetorical flourishes, Hone asked Ellenborough for his advice on how to proceed; he wouldn't give him any. Ellenborough was far too important: 'The Court has too much to do, to become the advisers of all persons who may consider themselves aggrieved … If we were to give you advice, then every subject in the realm might come here to know what he was to do.'

Hone told his jurors, 'you are my judges'.

The great Lord Ellenborough went back in time forty years, when he was no more than a special pleader. As the jury laughed at the humorous writing, having heard much worse on the street, they were not to be convinced that this slight man was trying to subvert the established religion but was clearly trying to attack the arbitrary power of the establishment, or those who drew large pensions and sinecures, or made laws without being elected. Men like Ellenborough.

Hone continued to read out, unpunished, parodies from history. Is laughter treason? surely not?

Ellenborough's voice was weak during the summing up. Even if he had been his normal stentorian self, the noise in the court would have made him inaudible.

He closed with the following words:

> I will deliver to you my solemn opinion as I am required by the Act of Parliament to do under the authority of that Act, and still more in obedience to conscience and my God, I pronounce it to be a most IMPIOUS PROFANE LIBEL. Hoping and believing that you are Christians, I do not doubt that your opinion is the same.

Ellenborough was wrong; he had the power to give the jury his opinion, but he was not obliged to, and they were not obliged to accept it, and they didn't. Hone had won again. Cheers ran around the chamber – jubilation that the establishment could not control. Hone went out with his friends to celebrate, though it would be a restrained affair, as the third day was still going ahead. The *Times* predicted a cancellation. This did not happen; Hone believed that the state was cynically taking advantage of his failing health.

Day three started with Hone's younger brother bringing a mountain of books to the court. These were Hone's collection of satires from the past that were based on religious texts but which were never prosecuted for libel. There was also a vast increase in the number of marshals, peace officers and sheriffs. The plan was to be more or less the same, but with more intimidation from the authorities.

Hone was bitter as well as ill. He laid down some new truths about the judge. He did not regulate the trial; he was merely an administrator. Ellenborough was biased, and could he refrain from making facial gestures to influence the jury? He would not want them to be beseeched into a guilty verdict.

Hone spoke for nearly eight hours. When it was suggested that a barrister could ask some pithy questions and shorten everyone's ordeal, he rejected this. Hone had supporters, and they would have financed a lawyer for him, but it would have hindered his cause:

> Will he be able to stand up against my Lord Ellenborough? Will he withstand the brow-beating of my Lord Ellenborough?' Ellenborough agreed tartly that no barrister would present such disgusting parodies and print them in the cause of the defence, or at least persist in such exhibitions, especially after the judge had expressed his decided disapprobation of them.[2]

Hone was right about the last point: no barrister would have dared to read out the religious parodies because this would annoy Ellenborough, and they might be in front of him again a week later.

When the subject of religious toleration was mentioned, Hone had a perfect example of a liberal bishop. He was about to read some of the unorthodox opinions of Edmund Law, Bishop of Carlisle. Henry Crabb Robinson, when he heard the exchange, recorded: 'Lord Ellenborough (in a broken voice): "Sir, for decency's sake, forbear." Hone withdrew it, and gained more advantage from this tasteful courtesy than the parody could have brought him, had it been ever so apposite.'

The jury let him down again. Hone was found not guilty by a jury clearly influenced by the events in the court, but also because the establishment had not been able to fully manipulate the composition of the jury. The 'packed' jury was a common trick whereby a jury was filled with members who the government could trust, rather than selected at random; so much so that the same jurymen appeared time and time again and took their fee (radicals called them guinea men) and left the court knowing that a repeat fee was dependent on the correct verdict. When Cobbett left the country in 1817, the inevitability of a packed jury at any libel trial was as great a fear as being locked up incommunicado.

Why was the jury picked rather than packed? This was the work of T.J. Wooler, who had fought against the packed jury system and ensured that this time, it was a truly random jury containing nobody who was making a living from supporting the government. Trial by jury had been saved by the jury – the only way it could have happened.

Chapter Twenty-Five

What Killed Lord Ellenborough?

Ellenborough died at his home in St James on 13 December 1818, just less than a year after the Hone trial. He was 69, a respectable lifespan in an era when three score years and ten was a hopeful aim rather than a solid expectation. As a zealous defender of the status quo who expended his whole life on maintaining the establishment, it could be said that he worked himself to death – but probably not. He worked intensively rather than extensively. Even though the most complex trials were over in a day or two, Ellenborough relied on his accumulated knowledge rather than regular graft, and the holidays were very long. The cause of his death was a mixture of the usual factors: age, his chronic illness, such as gout, a paralytic stroke or strokes in 1818, and his lifestyle – all in proportions that we cannot really calculate.

His enemies yearned for a different, more dramatic narrative, and it is one that is often cited as a fact in modern historical accounts. It goes like this: the humiliation of defeat in court had done him in; the Ellenborough tyranny was broken by Hone, and the man who was described as the 'Monarch of all he surveyed' was brought down to earth. It was Keats who announced, in a letter full of good news to his brothers George and Thomas that Ellenborough had been 'paid with his own coin'. The poet, who was a protege of Leigh Hunt, was pleased to see his friend vicariously revenged. Keats, like Hunt, was interested in theatre of all sorts and also called it 'amusing' – and that was the crux. Ellenborough's last performance on his own stage had been an abysmal failure. He was never to hold up his head in public again, said his biographer. Ellenborough had been neutralised by journalists, juries, free speech and the rule of law.[1]

This was a very comforting but simple view. Ellenborough was certainly shaken by the results of the Hone trial. His lifelong vigour and overconfidence had certainly been damaged, and at the end of the day (when he was spat at leaving the court), all he had left was bravado:

> Bishop Turner, who was present at the trial and accompanied the Chief Justice home in his carriage, related that all the way he laughed at the tumultuous mob who followed him, remarking that 'he was afraid of their saliva, not of their bite', and that passing Charing Cross, he pulled the check-string, and said, 'It just occurs to me that they sell the best red herrings at this shop of any in London; buy six.'

He announced his resignation to Sidmouth in a letter a few days after the trial. He finally admitted that he could not cope, making it clear that his incapacity was caused by the way he was feeling before the trial:

> The disgraceful events that have occurred in the Guildhall within the last three or four days have led me both on account of the public and myself to consider very seriously my own sufficiency particularly in point of bodily health and strength to discharge the official duties of my station in the manner in which at the present critical moment it is peculiarly necessary.[2]

He then requested permission to resign as soon as the government found it convenient. Sidmouth replied the same day from Richmond Park, accepting the resignation, rejecting the self-deprecations about his performance, but asking him to wait.

So, was it disease, or was it self-doubt that killed him? He certainly suffered from gout, and it could kill. It ran (metaphorically but not literally) through the whole of the Georgian Establishment. There seems to be a hereditary susceptibility to it within the family, but it tends to visit people who are wealthy enough to live off meat and fortified wines, and generally speaking, the fat of the land. The greatest celebrity gout sufferer of the age was the Prince Regent himself, and Ellenborough and his prince suffered at the same time. The lightest of bed sheets can feel like a lead weight on the toe for sufferers. It could both nail you to your chair and stop you from getting to it. It was a nightmare of immobility mixed with pain. Georgian illustrations show gout sufferers sleeping or sitting in chairs with their feet off the ground. In 1809, Ellenborough was so badly afflicted that he had to be helped to and from his seat at the King's Bench. His own brother, Ewan, suffered for most of the last two decades of his life as well. Like most of its victims, gout made life a painful misery – it was something you tended to die with rather than die from, but there were painful exceptions.

In 1816, he experienced a numbness in his left hand which he feared was a paralytic seizure (or stroke). When the hand became gouty a few days later, he was actually relieved – pain meant there was feeling, although it did start to affect him socially – 'I was a dead man at the clubs' – he reported. In a letter to Lord Sidmouth on 11 January 1816 he even indulged in some humorous observations about how his ambitious colleagues might be reacting to his indisposition. He had done the same when his predecessor Lloyd Kenyon had died in 1802. The first public references to Ellenborough's more general infirmity date from the Watson and the Spencean Philanthropists trial of 1817, where he was too tired to read his three hours of summing up; he had done most of it, leaving the mundane parts to a deputy, and this was noticed. It was at this point that his colleagues noticed a change in him, mostly when dealing with difficult legal processes. But his family was still optimistic: in August and September 1817, he rested in Paris, his first visit to France since 1785. He reported to his friend Sidmouth:

> I hope to reach England by the 20th of this month. I think that my tour has done me good but the symptoms of gout are still troublesome. I doubt much how I shall stand hard work at present. The nervous state in which I have been for some time past and the fatigues under which I have long laboured have affected my eyes very inconveniently The bracing weather which is now coming on may perhaps do me good. I shall visit Brussels and the glorious field of Waterloo in my way home.

Ellenborough had made his will in March 1817. People tend to push away from the intimidation of mortality, even those with the consolation of a deeply held religious conviction. Ellenborough kept on living and accumulating, perhaps with an eye on future generations, specifically his eldest son Edward. His will was revised in June and August 1818 to account for properties acquired in Shipley, Northumberland, and Oakley Green, Buckinghamshire, and a codicil was added in May about the distribution of assets after the death of his wife. Ellenborough was looking into the far future, one in which he would play no earthly part. There was no self-pity in his make-up, just like there was little pity for others: he was going to pay 'the debt due to nature' properly and die with a good Christian resignation.

After his death, one of his daughters released a pious prayer he wrote in France. It is a standard Christian reaction to the prospect of death: not very original but certainly showing a new side to Ellenborough. He is a sinful creature, and despite the treasures that he had most assuredly built up on earth, the only thing of real value was salvation granted by an omniscient creator. He thanks God for his many blessings, including the strength to help people, and hopes for an absence of bitterness:

> and grant, O Lord that no decay or diminution of any of these faculties and means of happiness may excite in my mind any dissatisfied or desponding thoughts or feelings, but that I may always place my firm trust and confidence in thy divine goodness and whether the blessings heretofore indulged to me shall be continued or cease, and whether thou shalt give them or take them away I may still in humble obedience to thy divine will submit myself in all things with patience and resignation to the dispensations of thy divine providence.

Sidmouth still hoped that he would recover, but he felt like the summer in Paris was only the beginning of his recovery. He mooted the idea of Ellenborough being absent from the new law term, something that would have required permission from the Prince Regent, but it never happened. To stop working when ill and quite old is an admission. Instead, he careered towards the Hone trials in December, already unwell and creating worry for his family and friends.

He did much less work in 1818. His biographer Campbell suggested that he became more irritable and unpredictable, interrupting when not necessary and merely sounding peevish. He wrote to a friend he could scarcely totter to his seat and could only take notes – '*manu lassissima et corpore imbecillo*' – 'with a weary hand and a feeble body'. Often, he was too weak to appear at all. He rallied at the end of term, hoping a rest would solve the problem. It was in September 1818 that he was finally able to discharge his duties. Ellenborough was particularly worried about his sight; he had consulted doctors who had not been able to diagnose anything specifically wrong with his optic nerve, but he contended that he was no longer able to take notes adequately. His handwriting was laboured and, afterwards, indecipherable. Whatever killed him, it started to affect his mental capacities as well. His colleagues noted this, and it became more obvious when he was performing his more intellectually difficult functions.

It was said that the ineffectual Sir Samuel Shepherd or the intractable Charles Abbott had been lined up as a replacement. Abbott got the post. Shepherd was deaf and was always shown with a golden ear trumpet in the cartoons; he was ruled out. It seems that a man who could not hear without help was unacceptable, while a man who refused to listen was fine. The Regent naively suggested that Ellenborough should be consulted, but his friend Lord Eldon pointed out that if so, they would not get the best candidate, just whoever came out best through the intrigue and gossip.

In July 1818, Ellenborough chose the Home Assize Circuit for himself – the least onerous – but was unable to go, retiring to Roehampton for the summer and then to the south coast. In late August 1818, some newspapers reported a chink of light: 'Lord Ellenborough fully recovered', said the *English Chronicle* on 20 August: 'Lord Ellenborough better', reported another.[3] In September 1818, he accompanied his wife to the south coast and wrote to Lord Sidmouth from there:

> My dear Lord
> The decay of many of my faculties, particularly my eyesight which I have painfully experienced since the beginning of the present year, strongly admonishes me of the duty which I owe to the public and myself on that account, and as I have now held the office of Chief Justice of the Court of King's Bench for more than sixteen years, viz from the 12th day of April 1802.

Perhaps he thought about the fate of his predecessors. Lord Kenyon had become visibly ill and incapable in court; Lord Mansfield had become weaker and less effective to the detriment of his great reputation; both men had moved to Bath to take the water, almost an admission of impending death for old, famous and worn-out men. Bath had been suggested to him as well, but it was felt the journey would be too much of a strain, so the message was clear. Instead, he wrote his letter from another of God's waiting rooms, Worthing. A sense of duty made him stay on; even his most bitter enemies would concede him that virtue. He also asked for his pension to be paid.

He then moved quickly onto Brighton, where the papers announced that the Ellenboroughs would stay for the whole winter and that Lord Ellenborough was once again improving and would benefit from the marine exercise. A week later, they had returned to London. Ellenborough seems to have resigned, gone back to Brighton, and then returned to London. Perhaps he knew that there would be no winter anywhere for him. Others kept up the pretence that he had some time left; the Prince Regent wrote an elegant and heartfelt letter of condolence and congratulations and wished him a happy retirement.

He was certainly still trying to do his job in October 1818. Farington reported that he spent the whole night in the House of Lords, and the next morning went straight to the King's Bench, having only time to drink a coffee and wash (hands and face in cold water would have counted). Sidmouth saw him at his home on 19 October. A successor had not been found despite frantic efforts, and Lady Ellenborough reported back to Sidmouth that he was depressed by their failure. By 29 October he was in such a weakened physical and mental state that it was noted with relief by Sidmouth that he was still able to organise the preparations for his own resignation.

Gossip at the end of October 1818 suggested that one leg was now useless and unresponsive due to palsy. He had apparently suffered this setback while riding in his carriage; he was trying to continue as normal. During November 1818 he was reported to be weak in body and mind and needed help to get into his carriage, and he had had a stroke in mid-November. He last appeared in public around 20 November 1818, when he and Lady Ellenborough went to Carlton House to offer their condolences to the Prince Regent on the death of his mother, Queen Charlotte. In November, his son Edward came back from Ireland after tending to his sick wife. On

28 November the *Morning Post* announced that the situation had moved from despair to fatal. The Bishop of Chester was now with his brother as well. On 8 December, it was reported that he could no longer speak or hold down food.

He had resigned as Lord Chief Justice on 6 November 1818, and died on Sunday 13 December, a retirement of thirty-five days. It happened at home with his family 'without pain, struggle, or a sigh', as Sidmouth reported to the Prince Regent the next morning. He was buried at his school, Charterhouse, on 22 December, in a fog so deep that the legal and political establishment assembled there could see nothing.

Chapter Twenty-Six

Legacy and Influence

At 4pm on the hot, dusty afternoon of 16 August 1819, Major Thomas Dyneley wrote a hastily scribbled report to Lord Sidmouth in London from the now-deserted open space of St Peter's Field in Manchester. A few hours earlier, a large crowd of men, women and their families had attended a peaceful demonstration calling for political reform and were trampled down and cut with sabres. At least eighteen were to die that day or later. Hundreds suffered from life-changing injuries and were often too poor or too scared to get treatment. Most of the injuries were caused by an amateur militia, the Manchester and Salford Yeomanry Cavalry, led by Dyneley. He wrote in triumph: 'The first action of the Battle of Manchester is over, and I am happy to say ended in the complete discomfiture of the Enemy.'

Dyneley was a constant letter writer during the Peninsular campaign of the Napoleonic wars, and obviously thought that this attack on civilians was somehow similar. He continued: 'Hunt made his appearance about 12½ in his carriage, accompanied by three males, a very good-looking female, bearing a very fine silk flag, about 3,000 rabble with a band of music, several, perhaps 6 colours, one Cap of liberty.'

Hunt was there, and was arrested; Mary Fildes was the woman who nearly lost her life when dragged off the hustings. There were nearer 60,000 in the crowd and the silk flags said things like 'Liberty or Death'; only one was available on that day, and Dyneley had helped provided it: 'The number that were rode over might have been very great. I don't know that any of them were killed. I saw several carried very badly wounded to the Hospital. I am sorry to say that one of the Manchester Cavalry was shot dead.'

His indifference to the innocent victims was clear, as was his supreme confidence that he had the backing of his bosses. The establishment survived the massacre of innocent protesters at St Peter's Field in 1819. New laws were enacted restricting the press, making libel subject to fourteen years of transportation, and suppressing large gatherings. A few ringleaders – including Ellenborough's old enemy Henry Hunt, and William Hone's supporter Richard Carlile – were imprisoned in the years after the Chief Justice's death. Without doubt, he would have approved.

It is perfectly possible to blame the dead Ellenborough for the lack of justice for the victims and the political repression afterwards. This was partly because his old friend Sidmouth was alive and well and the force behind the legislation, but mostly because the law that allowed them to escape their cruelty was the work of the former Chief Justice.

Riots were common during the life of Ellenborough and had been for the best part of a century. The main legal weapon against the out-of-control mob was the Riot Act of 1715. It had to be read out formally, exactly and audibly to a crowd by a legal or civil official to a group of twelve or more, make disobedience a felony, allow the mob to be dispersed by force, and indemnify any army or militia using force to do so.

The status of the Riot Act during the St Peter's Field massacre (which became known as Peterloo) is ambiguous. The authorities, naturally, claimed that it had been read; in any case, the statutory hour had not passed between the proclamation and the deadline to disperse. In 1801, the then Edward Law had been asked what, in his legal opinion, the military should do in a sudden emergency to quell riots and tumult. It was clear that it would be better to follow the instructions laid down by law, but in Law's legal opinion, it was acceptable for the military as they saw fit in very extreme situations.

This is not what happened at Peterloo, of course: there was no sudden tumult, unless you include the reckless decision to storm the hustings and forcibly push the crowd out of the way in order to arrest Hunt. The massacre was mostly the work not of trained soldiers, but of an amateur militia of local worthies who hated the working class. The newspapers and the government attempted successfully to create a false narrative about the day's events; they found Law's legal decision very useful. It was republished in 1819 for that purpose and was later an annexe in the Queen's Regulations.

There was also Lord Ellenborough's 1803 Act, which made cutting and maiming with intent to kill a capital offence. The Manchester Yeomanry Cavalry, infused with a fear and hatred of the protesters on that day, were never going to be accused of that, and so Major Dyneley could write his crowing, arrogant letter with confidence.

Dyneley probably gave this no heed on his wedding day in June 1827, when he married Hon. Mary Frederica Law, daughter of the Chief Justice. The now dowager Lady Ellenborough had at last found a suitable match for her daughter; her husband would have certainly approved of such a man.

So, Ellenborough's influence seemed to live on, as one would expect. He died rich, respected and lauded to the skies by the press and the people who mattered. Most radicals could obtain no joy from an individual's death, having a basic humanity and knowing that Ellenborough was just one link in a chain of oppression, but there was one major exception. The radical T.J. Wooler, who played his part in Ellenborough's final humiliation, had no reason to like the late Chief Justice and no reason to hold back when he died:

> And now Lord Ellenborough is only a heap of senseless clay. His titles are lost to his ear, his wealth can no longer minister to his appetite. Yes, my friend, this haughty, this imperious judge, this conceited minion of authority, is as helpless as the meanest of his victims. He will brow beat, he will insult no more. No more will he wrap himself in the vanity of his ermine, no more will the terrors of the law seem to centre in his frown.

This was Wooler's attack on a whole system; as he said, the former Chief Justice was a minion of a bigger and crueller network of authority, but it was also personal. At the 1817 trial, Ellenborough waved him away with a dismissive hand movement, which Wooler still remembered. The 'little black friend' is from the name of his newspaper, *Black Dwarf*:

> Little did thy poor little black friend imagine when this once arrogant man told him he had done with him FOR EVER that his puny labours would outlive the giant arm that raised in fancied potency to crush him to the ground. I have now done with him for ever. He is now silent: his authority is extinct: he passes to the tribunal of heaven, not as a judge but as a sinner.

Ellenborough would agree with this last sentiment but would expect a better reception in heaven than Wooler was hoping for:

> an *ex officio* information has been filed in the court of time against himself and he must abide the sentence that will be pronounced without the power of appeal. He has not however to fear the practice of his own court, nor the precedents he has established.

Wooler couldn't resist the usual play on words, presented as a reproach:

> He will have justice, whereas he dealt only in law. But that justice may not be more favourable to him than the law which he administered to others.

This feels like a very large bunch of sour grapes, but there was some truth in Wooler's wishful thinking. Ellenborough's influence was fading faster than he could have ever imagined.

Ellenborough finished his reign with a judgement so reactionary that it even made his peers think twice. In a nationally famous case in 1817, Abraham Thornton was acquitted of the rape and murder of Mary Ashford after they had left a dance in Sutton Coldfield together. She was found dead in a pit of water the following morning. Thornton was acquitted after a six-minute discussion by the jury. He had an alibi, in the proper legal meaning of the word, as witnesses had attested that they had seen him somewhere else at the crucial time.

Her brother William Ashford then made a desperate attempt for justice:

> William Ashford, Mary's younger brother, raised an appeal of murder, resulting in Thornton being brought to trial a second time. Here, the key incident of the case occurred: Thornton declared himself not guilty, casting his glove onto the floor and stating, 'I am ready to defend the same with my body.'

William Ashford did not pick the glove up. Thornton was a strong, muscular man and it would have been a one-sided contest. Trial by combat was more or less unknown, but it was still legal. If there was no obvious evidence of guilt, then the law as it stood would allow it. Ellenborough presided over the court designed to clear up the legal status of the situation. He was told that the law was last used in the mid-seventeenth century and was obsolete. Ellenborough disagreed when the legal argument was put forward by Ashford's counsel, Mr Clarke:

> The trial by battle is an obsolete practice which has long since been out of use and it would appear to me extraordinary indeed if the person who has murdered the sister should, as the law exists in these enlightened times, be allowed to prove his innocence by murdering the brother also or at least attempting to do so.
>
> [Lord Ellenborough] It is the law of England, Mr Clarke; we must not call it murder.

Ellenborough concluded that 'the general law of the land is in favour of the wager of battle, and it is our duty to pronounce the law as it is, not as we may wish it to be'. It was Ellenborough's ruling, but also his general philosophy. A centuries-old law could not be discarded in a day. There was no such thing as a dead letter. His deputy, Abbott, backed him up.

A trial by combat was arranged, and – sensibly – William Ashford did not turn up. This was a perfect example of how the law needed to change but had not done so. Henry Crabb Robinson noted that there was 'astonishment ... at beholding before our eyes a scene acted that we had read as one of the disgraceful institutions of our half-civilised ancestors'. Wager of Battle was abolished in February 1819 in rather a rush, passed by the House of Lords with all three readings in one night when another case was on the cards.

Ellenborough's world disappeared quite quickly after his death. He may not have necessarily believed in trial by ordeal, but he did believe that an ancient and unused law was still valid; this was not to be the new view. Disembowelling traitors, promised with some gravity at the Despard trial, was abolished in 1814, and the punishment became hanging and postmortem decapitation, as the establishment was not brave enough to be so cruel. The pillory was restricted to perjury. Most pillories outside London fell into disrepair. Peter James Bossy was the last victim, found guilty of perjury in 1830.

A mere four years after his friend's death, Sidmouth was replaced as Home Secretary by a new type of Tory, Robert Peel, who was able to take advantage of less social turmoil by improving policing and softening criminal punishments – the type of changes that, merely a decade earlier, Ellenborough had claimed would destroy society. Sidmouth lingered on in the Lords but could not stop change. Catholics were emancipated in 1829, and the Great Reform Act removed the worst aspects of the electoral system. Ellenborough would have been appalled. The seat that both he and his brother occupied in 1802 was completely abolished by the Whig government.

His enemies mostly entered the establishment. Henry Hunt and William Cobbett eventually became members of parliament. Lord Brougham, already a member, was part of a Whig government that restored his enemy Thomas Cochrane to his full rank in the navy.

The era of the libel trial for journalists was over. Ellenborough may well have known that himself, but after 1820 it was abandoned as a weapon against political dissent. The state was too weak to enforce the rules, and the random application of justice, which helped deter the common criminal, could not stop the determined publisher. Free speech was safe from the overbearing political judge. Perhaps it was because politics had changed and the turmoil of revolution and economic depression made them less necessary, but that was further proof that Britain had moved on.

The role of the judiciary had changed too. His behaviour in court would not be tolerated for much longer. His combination of judicial and legislative roles was never repeated, and his son Edward reported that later in life he regarded it as a mistake. Judges who were also politicians, like Ellenborough, became unacceptable.

The son understood that his father's world was coming to an end. In February 1830, as a member of the Cabinet of the Duke of Wellington, he railed against the new spirit of the age when it came to lawbreakers:

> He is disposed to diminish gradually the number of crimes for which the punishment of death is awarded. The Duke seemed reluctant and so did others. However, the Chancellor did not object. My father considered that where a man could not protect his own property the law ought to protect it for him by higher penalties.[3]

Ellenborough's philosophy of punishment was dead: 'However, now it seems a man must protect his own property, and punishments are to be proportioned more to the extent of the moral offence than to the necessity for preventing crime.'

Ellenborough would have prophesied that lesser punishments would lead to a crime wave and the need for more hangings, not fewer. In 1838, Lord John Russell pointed out that the number of executions had fallen from fifty by 1831 to eight in 1837, with a decrease in overall criminality. It had been ninety-six in the year of Ellenborough's death. Russell praised the knowledge and integrity of the late noble judge, but his implication was clear. A mere twenty years after his death, Ellenborough had been wrong.

* * *

A new Lord Chief Justice of England and Wales was appointed on 1 October, 2023. Their background was as would be expected: major public school, top-ranking Cambridge college, in this case Trinity, and a member of the Inner Temple. They were called to the bar in 1987, specialising in commercial law, and were made QC in 2003 at the age of 38.

This sounds very much like Ellenborough, which is a bit dispiriting for anybody who puts a premium on social mobility, but there is one crucial difference. The new Lady Chief Justice is Dame Sue Carr, now Baroness Carr of Walton-on-the-Hill, the first woman to hold the post after over a hundred men and 775 years of history. Her father is a businessman with interests in Arsenal Football Club, and his grandfather was a professional cricket player. As well as having a stellar legal career, she has also had three children – that seems to matter to the newspapers that reported it, so not everything changes. The other contender for the job was Dame Victoria Sharpe, who, reassuringly for some, had four children in five years and took no parental leave in order to help her career.

The question of what Ellenborough would think of all this is perhaps a silly one, as he died two hundred years ago and was deeply unsure about the way society was moving when he was alive. So, let's not ask it; just report that the king, on the advice of the Conservative government, chose a dedicated, talented and privileged member of society to the highest judicial appointment in the land, both in 1802 and 2023. The establishment continues and now includes females, but still manages to look more or less the same. With a judiciary still dominated by private schools and ancient universities, a grossly unfair electoral system, and great disparities of wealth, Ellenborough may well have been grumpily satisfied with the resilience of his ruling class.

The hereditary peerage gained by Ellenborough continues into the twenty-first century. The family live in Clipston, near Market Harborough. The ninth baron is Rupert Edward Henry Law. His father, Richard Law, eighth baron, was a Conservative-supporting member of the House of Lords until 1999, but was not one of the ninety-two hereditary peers who retained their voting rights when the House was reformed. His son Rupert was educated at Eton and Sandhurst and enjoyed a distinguished military career in the Coldstream Guards, serving in Northern Ireland and being promoted to the rank of major. He later worked in private banking and wealth management. His eldest son, Hon. James Rupert Thomas Law (born 1983), is the heir. James attended Eton, Newcastle University and Sandhurst and is a lawyer. He has a son, born in December 2020, who will be the eleventh Baron Ellenborough. His name is Edward Law.

References

Chapter One – The Curate's House at Buck Crag

1. Faith, Science, Joy, and Jane Austen blog.
2. Stockdale, *Annals of Cartmel*
3. Ibid
4. Corston, *Historic Sites of Lancashire*

Chapter Two – An Establishment Education

1. Townsend, *Life of Twelve Eminent Judges*
2. Turner, *The Old Boys: The Decline and Rise of the Public School*
3. Campbell, *The Lives of the Lord Chief Justices*
4. William Roper, *Chronicles of the Charter-house*
5. www.pet.cam.ac.uk
6. Byron Letters via https://ir.vanderbilt.edu/
7. Tableau de la Grande Bretagne via Wilson. B, *Decency and Disorder*
8. James Woodforde, *Dairy of a Country Parson*
9. Sydney, *England and the English in the Nineteenth century*
10. Campbell, *The Lives of the Lord Chief Justices*

Chapter Three – Law Chooses Law

1. www.middletemple.org.uk
2. *The Quarterly Review* (London) – Volume 41
3. *The Annual Biography and Obituary for the Year* (Volume 13)
4. *The Law Chronicle* Volume 3,1856-57, via google books

Chapter Four – National Breakthrough

1. Luxton, *UPROAR!: Satire, Scandal and Printmakers in Georgian London*
2. *Grand Pitched Battle* (via Wikipedia commons)
3. Brougham, *Historical Sketches of Statesmen who Flourished in the Time of George III*
4. Burke's writing and speeches via Project Gutenberg

Chapter Five – Anne Towry: Bloomsbury Beauty to Establishment Lady

1. English Historical Fiction Authors, *An Amiable Wife* (englishhistoryauthors.blogspot.com)
2. Farington, *Diaries*
3. Bigelow, *Bench and Bar*
4. *Universal Magazine of Knowledge*, 1812
5. *True Briton* 10 August
6. Mary Berry, *Diaries,*
7. Feltham, *The Picture of London for 1806*
8. thepeerage.com
9. *The Star* (London) 4 September
10. Lord Russell, *The Life and Times of Charles James Fox*

Chapter Six – Unpopular with Lord Kenyon

1. Hey, D, Biography of Lloyd Kenyon
2. Campbell, *The Lives of the Lord Chief Justices*
3. Hay, *The State and the Market in 1800*
4. www.britishmuseum.org

Chapter Seven – Rising Like an Aeronaut

1. *British public characters of 1798-9*, Volume 5.
2. Campbell, *The Lives of the Lord Chief Justices*
3. Pellow, *The Life and Correspondence of the Right Honourable Henry Addington*

4. *Hampshire Chronicle* 15 February 1802
5. 'AF' The Criminal Register, 1802
6. Pellow, *The Life and Correspondence of the Right Honourable Henry Addington*
7. *Sun (London)* 26 April 1802
8. *Carlisle Journal* 28 August 1802

Chapter Eight – Protecting Asses and Assets

1. www.capitalpunishmentuk.org
2. www.oxfordreference.com
3. House of Lords Debates, 1810
4. Cobbett, Parliamentary Debates
5. *Routledge, Chapters in the History of Popular Progress:*
6. www.media.nationalarchives.gov.uk, *The Real Little Dorrit*
7. Hansard debates 1806
8. dickensmuseum.com/blogs/charles-dickens-museum
9. media.national.archives.gov.uk

Chapter Nine – A Law unto Himself

1. Cassan, *Lives of the Bishops of Bath*
2. www.capitalpunishmentuk.org
3. about1816.wordpress.com, Abortion becomes a criminal offence

Chapter Ten – Against High Treason

1. www.exclassics.com *Trial of Ned Despard*
2. Gurney, *The Trial of Edward Marcus Despard, Esquire*
3. Walpole, *Life of Spencer Perceval*
4. Gurney, *The Trial of Edward Marcus Despard, Esquire*
5. Walton, *Madame Tussaud, her Life and Legacy*

Chapter Eleven – Against Vice

1. theprintshopwindow.wordpress.com
2. Ibid

3. Brown, *Fathers of the Victorians: The Age of Wilberforce*
4. *www.regencyhistory.net* Thomas Hope Art Collector
5. Norton, *A Sodomite Club in Warrington, 1806*
6. *Public Ledger and Daily Advertiser*, 6 July 1815
7. Norton, *A Sodomite Club in Warrington, 1806*

Chapter Twelve – The Broad Bottoms and an Indelicate Investigation

1. Walpole, *Life of Spencer Perceval*
2. British Museum satirical prints, *Two Heads are better than one*
3. Ibid *More Pigs than Teats*
4. Blake, *The History of Slavery and the Slave Trade*
5. Aspinall, *The Correspondence of George, Prince of Wales*
6. Perceval, *An inquiry, or delicate investigation into the conduct of the Princess of Wales*
7. *Bell's Weekly Messenger*, 10 April 1808

Chapter Thirteen – Humanitarian?

1. Private Papers of William Wilberforce
2. www.supremecourt.uk/cases/docs/uksc-2021-0062-judgment.pdf
3. *Westminster Journal and Old British Spy*, 27 May 1809
4. *Cumberland Pacquet, and Ware's Whitehaven Advertiser*, 17 May 1791
5. www.jtrails.org.uk/trails/richmond-and-south-west-london/history?page=8
6. www.holytrinityroehampton.org
7. Bissessarsingh,A *Torture Most Foul, Trinidad Guardian*
8. *Gazette,* December 1808
9. *Oracle and the Daily Advertiser*, 5 April 1805
10. *London Courier and Evening Gazette*, 1 June 1802
11. archive.org/details/lifeofedwardjenn02barouoft

Chapter Fourteen – Influence and Money

1. Arnould, *Life of Thomas, first Lord Denman, formerly Lord Chief Justice of England*

2. Walpole, *Life of Spencer Perceval*
3. historyofparliamentonline
4. *Examiner* via google books
5. *The Times*, 6 July 1818
6. Annual Register 1813

Chapter Fifteen – Ellenborough Against the Libellers

1. Houghton, *A People's history 1793-1844 from the newspapers*
2. *Belfast Commercial Chronicle* 14 March 1812
3. 1812.now,blogspot.com
4. Brougham, *The life and times of Henry George Brougham*
5. Moore, *Correspondence Between A Lady And Gentleman, Upon The Advantage Of (What Is Called) 'Having Law On One's Side* via publicdomainpoetry.com

Chapter Sixteen – The Rusty Machinery of Oppression

1. Shelley, Letter to Lord Ellenborough
2. via romantic-circles.org/reviews-blog/examiner
3. Hunt, *Biography of Leigh Hunt*
4. Dickens, *A Tale of Two Cities*
5. Cobbett's Political Register, 4 June 1804
6. Curzon, www.madamegilflurt.com,

Chapter Seventeen – Against Adultery?

1. Parr, *The trial of Ralph Benson, Esq for Crim. Con.* (via google books)
2. Johnson's *Sunday Monitor*, 5 August 1810

Chapter Eighteen – The Public Ellenborough

1. Bigelow, L, *Bench and Bar*
2. Jackson, *Memoirs of Charles Mathews, Comedian*

Chapter Nineteen – The Private Ellenborough

1. Berry, *Diaries*
2. Berry, *Diaries*
3. Farington, *Diaries*
4. *Frasers Magazine* 1833 Volume 7
5. *Thorne,* The House of Commons By R.G. Thorne, 1986
6. Jeaffreson, *A book about lawyers*,
7. *Law magazine* 1833 Volume 9
8. Thomas Lawrence, *Letter Bag of Thomas Lawrence*
9. *Kent Guardian*, 27 November 1804.

Chapter Twenty – In the Courts

1. *Frasers Magazine* Jan 1833
2. Bigelow, *Bench and Bar*
3. Via Wilson. B, *Decency and Disorder*
4. May, *The Fox-Hunting Controversy, 1781–2004 Class and Cruelty*

Chapter Twenty-One – In Parliament

1. *Oxford Journal*, 16 June 1790
2. historyofparliamentonline
3. Routledge, *Chapters in the History of Popular Progress*
4. Hansard 1805
5. Townsend, *Life of Twelve Eminent Judges*
6. Hansard 1808
7. Cobbett, Political Register, Volume 8, 1805
8. Hansard,1808
9. *The Englishman*, Vol 1 1874 via google Books

Chapter Twenty-Two – The Peak of Unpopularity

1. Bates, *1815 Regency Britain in the year of Waterloo*
2. regencyredingote.wordpress.com

3. Cochrane, *The Case of Thomas, Lord Cochrane: Before Lord Ellenborough, 1814*
4. Pellow, *The Life and Correspondence of the Right Honourable Henry Addington*
5. *Chester Chronicle* of 17 March 1815 http://ludditebicentenary.blogspot.com/
6. *Instructor and Select Weekly Advertiser*, 8 March 1815

Chapter Twenty-Three – The Peak of Power

1. Fairburn, *Edition of the Whole Proceedings on the Trial of James Watson*
2. Kent, *Regency Radical: Selected Writings of William Hone*

Chapter Twenty-Four – The Spell is Broken

1. Tegg, *The Three Trials of William Hone, Second Trial*
2. Milne, ' I rise, in my own defence': Character, the courtroom and radical address in British writing, 1792-1824' (via etheses.whiterose.ac.uk)

Chapter Twenty-Five – What Killed Lord Ellenborough?

1. Campbell, The *Lives of the Lord Chief Justices*
2. Pellow *The Life and Correspondence of the Right Honourable Henry Addington*
3. *Imperial Weekly Gazette*, 29 August 1818

Bibliography

Atlay, J, *The Trial of Lord Cochrane Before Lord Ellenborough* (1897 Smith via Gb)

Brougham, *Historical Sketches of Statesmen who Flourished in the Time of George III* (Griffin, 1861)

Brougham, H, *The Life and Times of Henry Lord Brougham Blackwood* (via google books, 1871)

Brown,F, *Fathers of the Victorians* Cambridge 1961

Bigelow, L.J, *Bench and Bar,* (Harper 1871)

Bury, J, *History of the Freedom of Thought* (Digicat 2022)

Bywaters, E.G.L, *Gout in the Time and Person of George IV* (via ard.bmj.com)

Cambell, John, *The Lives of the Lord Chancellors* (google books 1848)

Chanter, J, *Sketches of the Literary History of Barnstaple* (via googlebooks)

Cobbett, *Parliamentary debates* (via google books)

Cocks, H, *Safeguarding Civility: Sodomy, Class and Moral Reform in Early Nineteenth-Century England past and Present* (OUP via The Muse Project)

Cordingly, D, *Cochrane The Dauntless,* (Bloomsbury 2008)

Crago, N, *Lord Ellenborough as Criminal Legislator* (Western Australian Law Review via JSTOR)

Edelman, T, *The Jews of Georgian England* (Ann Arbor 1999)

Erskine-May, T, *Constitutional History of England* (Longman 1898)

Fennelly, T, 'Ned Despard, the Irishman Hanged in London for High Treason' (*History Ireland*, Vol 30)

Godwin, J, *The Theosophical Enlightenment* (University of New York 1994)

Grego, J, *The Works of James Gilray* (Chatto and Windus1873)

Gurney, J, *The Trial of Edward Marcus Despard, Esquire: For High Treason* (via google books)

Hackwood F, *William Hone, His Life and Times Fisher Unwin* 1912 (via google books)

Harling, P, *The Laws of Libel and the Limits of Repression 1790–1832* (JSTOR)

Hay, D, *The State and the Market in 1800: Lord Kenyon and Mr Waddington* (via JSTOR)

Henry, Frances, *Love, Sex, and the Noose: The Emotions of Sodomy in 18th-Century England*, Electronic Thesis and Dissertation Repository, 2019

Hey, D, *Biography of Lord Kenyon* (OUP 2004)

Houghton, R, *A People's History 1793–1844 from the newspapers* (via houghton.hk)

Howell, T, *State Trials, 1783 to the present time*, Volume 21 (via google books)

Hunt, Henry, *Memoirs of Henry Hunt* (via Project Gutenberg)

Jay, Mike, *Riot, Revolt, Revolution: The Despards,* (London Review of Books July 2019)

Jeaffreson, J, *A Book about Lawyers* (Hurst and Blackett 1867)

Law, Edward, Baron Ellenborough, *Political diary 1828–1830* (Bentley 1881)

Layard, G, *Sir Thomas Lawrence's Letter bag* (Allan 1906 vis google books)

Living Age, Volume 208 (via google books1896)

Lloyd, H.E., *Memoirs of the Life and Reign of George III* (via google books, 1830)

Luxton, A, *UPROAR!: Satire, Scandal and Printmakers in Georgian London* (Icon, 2023)

Milne, F, *Character, the courtroom and the radical address in British writing 1792–1824* (etheses.whiterose.ac.uk)

Morris, C, *The Life of William Wilberforce* (via google books, 1857)

Pellow, G, *The Life and Correspondence of the Right Honourable Henry Addington* 1847

Rictor Norton (Ed.), 'A Sodomite Club in Warrington, 1806', *Homosexuality in Nineteenth-Century England: A Sourcebook*, (May 2008 via google books)

Robinson, H, *Diary, Reminiscences, and Correspondence of Henry Crabb Robinson* (Macmillian 1869)

Stockdale, J, (Editor) *Annual Register* (1813)

Tegg, W, *The Three Trials of William Hone,* (1876 via google books)

Thompson, E, *The Making of the English Working Class*, (Penguin 1968)

Townsend, William C, *The Lives of Twelve Eminent Judges*, (Longman 1846)

Various, *Fraser's Magazine* 1833
Wentworth, J, *A Complete set of Pleading*, (Robinson 1798)
Whytle, G, 'Lord Ellenborough's Law of Humanity', *Irish Jurist* Vol 60 (via JSTOR 2018)
Wilson, B *Decency and Disorder* Faber and Faber (2007)
Woodforde, J, *Diary of a Country Parson* (Canterbury Press, 1999)

Websites

thecharterhouse.org (2019 Sutton Lecture)
blogs.nottingham.ac.uk/ (1806 sodomy trials)
englishhistoryauthors.blogspot.com
hansard.parliament.uk
historyofparliamentonline
theprintshopwindow.wordpress.com
topazcrossbooks.com (Jane Austen)
www. lawgazette.co.uk
www.capitalpunishmentuk.org
www.digitalcollections.manchester.ac.uk (Peterloo)
www.digitalcollections.manchester.ac.uk/ (Society of The Bears)
www.madamegilflurt.com
www.middletemple.org.uk (Society of the Bears)
www.pet.cam.ac.uk (Peterhouse)
www.public-domain-poetry.com
www.regencyredingote.wordress.
www.regencyresearcher.com
www.thepeerage.com (family of Ellenborough)

Index